5.95

W9-AXJ-865

68.23373 (10.31.68)

# THE REMNANTS OF POWER

# THE REMNANTS OF POWER

The Tragic Last Years of
Adlai Stevenson

*by Richard J. Walton*

COWARD-McCANN, Inc.
NEW YORK

WINGATE COLLEGE LIBRARY
WINGATE, N. C.

Copyright © 1968 by Richard J. Walton

*All rights reserved. This book, or parts thereof, may not be reproduced in any form without permission in writing from the Publisher. Published on the same day in the Dominion of Canada by Longmans Canada Limited, Toronto.*

*Library of Congress Catalog Card Number: 68–23373*

PRINTED IN THE UNITED STATES OF AMERICA

*To Margaret, whose idea this book was and without whose support it would not have been possible*

40516

# *Preface*

Mᴏsᴛ of the books written about Adlai E. Stevenson have concentrated on the years in which he sought the Presidency and in so doing raised the level of political debate. Yet the only high national office he ever held was that of United States Permanent Representative to the United Nations. Thus, any final assessment of Stevenson as public servant and man must weigh carefully his four and a half years service at the UN. This is what I have attempted to do.

One cannot be so arrogant as to suggest that this will be the definitive picture because Stevenson was a complex man. But if these complexities make it more difficult to render his portrait, they also make him, in my view, the most interesting political figure of his time, certainly more so than the two men who followed him as leader of the Democratic party, John F. Kennedy and Lyndon B. Johnson. They are, of course, enormously interesting and because they became President, historically much more significant. But their insatiable thirst for and implacable pursuit of power outweighed their other qualities and made them curiously alike—although, God knows, there were vast differences, not only in style but in capacity—and makes them, for this writer, at least, less intriguing. For the pursuit of power, despite its indisputable influence on events, is a dreary commonplace of history. What makes Stevenson so fascinating are his self-contradictions. To be sure, he sought great power and was eager, perhaps pathetically eager, to grasp what lesser power was avail-

7

able to him; yet this appetite for power, important as it was, did not dominate him as it did Kennedy and Johnson. For it was always modified by his deep understanding, so richly reflected in his humor, that man, and he as a man, was basically an absurd, posturing creature. Kennedy, despite his sometimes self-deprecating wit, and Johnson, despite his folksy humor, saw themselves as heroes, great men of history, not merely as men strutting, stylishly or not, across the stage. It was Stevenson's Hamlet quality—a glib but perhaps inevitable characterization—that makes him so significant. Certainly he sought power and certainly his failure to achieve it left its mark, but he did not regard human beings, as Kennedy and Johnson sometimes did, primarily as aides or obstacles to personal success. He saw them always as human beings, and therefore worthy of consideration and respect. It was this humanity, this concern for man, that caused his agony over decisions that led to the unjust characterization of him as indecisive. And it was this humanity, despite whatever flaws he may have had, that made Adlai Stevenson unique among great political figures.

Although they cannot be held responsible for what I did with the indispensable information they so graciously provided, I must thank Secretary General U Thant, Secretary of State Dean Rusk, and Chief S. O. Adebo, Ambassador Achkar Marof, Joan Baez, George Ball, Ambassador Jonathan Bingham, Kay Boyle, Ambassador Lord Caradon, Francis Carpenter, Clayton Fritchey, Paul Goodman, Donald Grant, David Guyer, Nat Hentoff, Wally Irwin, Dwight Macdonald, Mary McGrory, David McReynolds, Ambassador Richard Pedersen, Ambassador Francis T. P. Plimpton, Robert Schiffer, Arthur Schlesinger, Eric Sevareid, Harvey Swados, Ambassador Marietta Tree, James Wechsler, Ambassador Charles Yost, and many of my former colleagues of the United Nations Press Corp.

For invaluable help in research, I must also thank A. G. Mezerik, whose International Review Service publications are essential to any student of the United Nations, and Robert M. Blaisdell, director, and Inez Hess of the library of Western Connecticut State College. And I am particularly grateful to my editor, Ellis Amburn, and his associate, Mrs. Patricia Brehaut Soliman.

# Contents

*Illustrations follow page 80.*

# THE REMNANTS OF POWER

## ❧ I ❧

# *The Beginning*

WHEN Adlai Ewing Stevenson fell dead on a London street
on July 14, 1965, there was regret not only in America
but all over the world—the feeling that a good and decent man
was gone at a time when he could not be spared, a man who, although a politician, had transcended the grasping game of politics
and become a spokesman for human aspiration. Even the mighty
who had opposed him saluted his great service for peace and justice, hailing him in death and defeat as they would never have in
victory, for it is fashionable in America to honor those who
possess ideals but not the power to translate them into measures
that would limit privilege or profit. There were also those who
honored his decency even if they did not share his politics, and
there were thousands more, perhaps millions, who saw Adlai
Stevenson as a rare spirit whose vision was unequaled by any other
political figure of his time. It was for these that President Johnson
spoke—although I am not sure he was one of them—when he said
that Stevenson, like his great hero Lincoln, had died vindicated,
high in the esteem of his fellow man. But there were others, many
of them those who had once valued Stevenson above all politicians, who had a different view of Adlai Stevenson at the end.
Their view, hurtful and cruel, some would say, was expressed by
Barbara Garson in the parodied Hamlet soliloquy of her brutally
satiric play, *MacBird!*

WINGATE COLLEGE LIBRARY
WINGATE, N. C.

"To see, or not to see? That is the question.
Whether 'tis wiser as a statesman to ignore
The gross deception of outrageous liars,
Or to speak out against a reign of evil
And by so doing, end there for all time
The chance and hope to work within for change,
To work within the framework, there's the rub.
For who would bear the whips and scorns from boors,
The oppressor's wrongs, the proud man's contumely,
The insolence of office and the spurns
My patient merit of this braggart takes—
But for the fear of something worse than death.
In speaking out one loses influence.
The chance for change by pleas and prayers is done.
The chance to modify the devil's deeds
As a critic from within is still my hope.
To quit the club! Be outside looking in!
This outsideness, this unfamiliar land
From which few travelers ever get back in—
It puzzles mind, it paralyzes will,
And makes us rather bear those ills we have
Than fly to others that we know not of.
Security makes cowards of us all.
I fear to break; I'll work within for change." [1]

Cruel indeed, yet there are those who argue that this is a just description of Adlai Stevenson in his final months. Which picture is valid, Barbara Garson's or President Johnson's or perhaps another? In the following pages we will attempt to find out.

Many books have recorded the gallant failures of Stevenson's political campaigns. This one begins in the twilight of his political hopes. Although most perhaps would dispute it, I believe there is little doubt that Stevenson could have had the nomination for a third time in 1960 if he had wanted it badly enough. He wanted it very badly indeed, but not wholeheartedly enough to fight for it. I am convinced that he could have beaten Kennedy in a couple of primaries, certainly in the vital California primary, and it was only Kennedy's air of invincibility that gave him the nomination. Stevenson could have shattered that air. And Stevenson would certainly have done no worse against Richard Nixon than Kennedy, who very nearly lost. Although Stevenson no longer had all the shine and freshness of his first try, he was still in his way a formidable campaigner. In a sense, Nixon against Stevenson would have been a contest of losers, but if Nixon was a loser because of his faults, Stevenson was a loser because of his virtues. In that campaign, as the man of principle and vision, he would have shone in contrast to the expedient Nixon, whereas Kennedy to many was only a scrubbed Ivy League version of Nixon. But Stevenson did not want it badly enough. He thought perhaps that having had the nomination twice, it would be unseemly of him to seek it, a fastidiousness seldom found in a politician and perhaps in a politician a serious flaw. But he clearly hoped that lightning would strike thrice and did nothing irrevocable to discourage it.

So Kennedy got the nomination, and the assumption outside his circle of intimates was that Stevenson would be named Secretary of State—that indeed, any other choice was unthinkable. There's no doubt Stevenson could have had the job if he had leaped aboard the Kennedy bandwagon as it rushed toward San Francisco. But Stevenson had pledged his neutrality, and despite the incredible pressure put on him by the Kennedy machine, he kept his pledge to the other candidates even though he desperately wanted the job, perhaps even more than the Presidency. The men around Kennedy, however, and maybe Kennedy himself never forgave Stevenson for that act of sacrilege, for having had the presumption to stand, even so briefly, in the path of the anointed.

Stevenson was clearly the best-equipped man in the Democratic party to serve as Secretary of State, and his appointment would have been welcomed the world over. His claim by qualification was buttressed by his performance during the 1960 campaign. Although in such a close election one can assert that it was this or that which made the difference, there is no doubt that Kennedy would have lost and lost badly if Stevenson had not rallied his disaffected supporters. As the Kennedy campaign leadership discovered to its horror, great numbers of liberal Democrats, supporters of Adlai Stevenson, saw little difference between Kennedy and Nixon. They found not only apathy to Kennedy's nomination but outright hostility. Only Stevenson could do something about it and, despite whatever resentment he might have felt at having had the nomination snatched from him by the ambitious young Kennedy, he plunged into the campaign, crisscrossing the country to concentrate on areas where his popularity was still undiminished. Soon it became clear that he was rallying his supporters to the Kennedy standard. He made eighty-four speeches, many times the number originally contemplated by him and Kennedy. Even if, for some at least, he was not able to convince that Kennedy was a legitimate successor, he was able to get them to the polls. Murray Kempton, who was later to express such regret at what had become of Stevenson, wrote fittingly, "Let us never forget that if a light still rises above this dreary land, it is because for so long and lonely a time this man held it up." [2]

In an election that close, it is impossible to say what tipped the balance: the Kennedy-Nixon debates, perhaps, or Johnson's strength in the South, or any of a dozen other factors. But it is clear that if Stevenson had not enlisted his followers by that exhausting campaign, Kennedy would not have won. Thus, whatever enmity the Kennedy clan felt against Stevenson for not submerging his own lingering ambitions in favor of Kennedy's, it should certainly have been dissipated by Stevenson's tireless— and absolutely essential—campaigning. But it was not, and this enmity was to plague Stevenson's relations with the White House even after Kennedy's death.

Nor was Stevenson's service to Kennedy confined to the campaign. In July, after the convention, Stevenson had suggested to Kennedy that he prepare for him a comprehensive report on foreign policy to be submitted shortly after the election. Because Stevenson became so deeply involved in the campaign, he asked George Ball, one of his earliest and most influential supporters in 1952, to help with the report. Ball, who later became Under Secretary of State and then resigned from the Johnson Administration, at least in part because of his disenchantment with Vietnam policy, prepared a long and comprehensive draft and discussed it with J. William Fulbright, Chester Bowles, David Bruce and Thomas Finletter. The weekend before the election, Ball took it out to Stevenson at Libertyville, his Illinois residence outside Chicago, and Stevenson put it into its final form. It was delivered to Kennedy at breakfast on November 14. Kennedy dipped into it immediately, read the section on priority recommendations and when he finished, looked up and said, "Very good. Terrific. This is excellent. Just what I needed." [3]

It was in this context that Kennedy considered who should be appointed Secretary of State. The nation, and Stevenson himself, expected that he would get the job. Indeed, Kennedy had said during the primary campaign that he "assumed" any Democrat would name Stevenson to the post. But, to the nation's great loss, Stevenson was to be disappointed. According to Arthur Schlesinger, "when the President-elect returned from Palm Beach in late November, he told Stevenson that he had taken too many public positions on prickly issues and would in consequence be too 'controversial' for Congress; given the margin of the election, Kennedy said that he needed most of all a Secretary of State who could get along on Capitol Hill. In addition, Kennedy privately questioned Stevenson's capacity for decision and no doubt did not want a Secretary of State with whom he feared he might not feel personally comfortable." [4] This sounds less than straightforward, as if Kennedy knew he had to have a reason and this was the best one he was able to come up with.

Although there might have been some element of the truth in this explanation, it seems something more is needed to explain Kennedy's decision. Many have suggested that it was in fact motivated by revenge, that despite Stevenson's qualifications and his subsequent service to Kennedy, he was punishing Stevenson for not having given the Kennedy bandwagon the push that would have removed any lingering doubt about the inevitability of Kennedy's nomination. This might have been a subconscious factor—and certainly Kennedy's intimates never forgave Stevenson—but it seems unlikely that Kennedy was the kind to cut off his nose to spite his face. Also Kennedy no doubt got counsel from the Acheson group that Stevenson was too soft. But it seems to me that although all of these factors might have had some influence, the basic reason was Kennedy's determination to be his own Secretary of State. He realized that Stevenson was better known the world over than he, that there were many Stevenson partisans already in the State Department, that many more would be given positions of influence in the Kennedy Administration and that Stevenson might get such a grip on the State Department that it would not be responsive to Kennedy's will. This, of course, was a possibility, although there was little likelihood of Stevenson becoming another, although, God knows, different, John Foster Dulles. For one thing, Stevenson had too great an appreciation of the constitutional role of the President as determiner of foreign policy. Furthermore, his was not the overpowering, messianic ego of Dulles. And despite his independence of mind, he was, as we shall see, very much a team player.

Whatever the reason—and the reason is unimportant compared to the result—Kennedy made a mistake of grave and historic proportion, perhaps because the man so famous for his confidence lacked confidence in his ability to control one of his subordinates. It is inconceivable that if Stevenson had been his chief foreign policy adviser, Kennedy would have made the unspeakable decision to unleash the Central Intelligence Agency and the Pentagon on what was supposed to be, but fortunately for America was not, the defenseless Cuba. If there had been no Bay of Pigs, there would have been no fearsome approach to the nuclear brink the following year. And if Stevenson had been Secretary of State, it is doubtful that Kennedy would have ventured so far out onto the limb in Vietnam that Johnson was later to saw off. Nor, assuming Stevenson remained as Secretary after Kennedy's death, would there have been the aggression against the Dominican Republic.

But whatever the reason, Kennedy did not want Stevenson to be Secretary of State. He asked him instead to serve as Ambassador to the United Nations, maintaining that as the Democrat with the greatest prestige in international affairs, he could make his greatest contribution there. Stevenson took this latest in a series of bitter disappointments like the gentleman he was, but refused to accept Kennedy's offer until he knew who the Secretary of State was to be. Kennedy himself had not yet decided but assured Stevenson that he needn't worry on that score; he had Kennedy's promise that whatever arrangement they made about the UN job would be respected. But no, Stevenson would not take the post until he knew Kennedy's choice as Secretary; he had heard reports that it would be McGeorge Bundy, and he didn't feel there could be the necessary rapport with a man who had twice voted against him. (This lack of rapport did exist when Bundy became Kennedy's top White House adviser on foreign matters.) Stevenson was convinced that Bundy was hostile to him personally and to the UN generally. How valid was Stevenson's belief is hard to know. Some Kennedy intimates have said that Bundy was often sympathetic to Stevenson's suggestions that the United States work through the UN. On the other hand, Bundy was a hard-liner, one of the group that had little use for Stevenson's "idealistic" approach to the problems of the "real" world.

Anyway, Stevenson would not immediately accept, and he kept Kennedy waiting for more than a week. Schlesinger writes, "Kennedy was nettled at this reaction and strengthened in his belief in Stevenson's indecisiveness." [5] However, it can be argued that Stevenson was being very decisive in refusing to commit himself until he was sure of his position. This was a difficult time for both men—for Kennedy because it would be a major political embarrassment if Stevenson refused to serve in the Administration, and for Stevenson because his instinct to serve the new President was counterbalanced by the gravest reservations about the job.

During this period Stevenson discussed the situation with a number of close friends. One night, for instance, he was at George Ball's house, talking it over until one or two in the morning. Ball said, "Anybody in his right mind, and Adlai was in his right mind, knew he was taking on something frustrating. It has all the trappings, but to a large extent it doesn't play much of a role." [6] This is an ironic observation in view of the fact that Ball himself was later, after Arthur Goldberg's resignation, to become American Ambassador to the UN. Both recognized the dilemma that was eventually so to torment Stevenson: "When a big man takes the job, it locks him in. He can't speak his mind and he can't quit." But Ball feels, as do most of Stevenson's friends, that he had no choice but to accept the post. "He had no place to go. He would have been unhappy in private life with a Democratic Administration in power."

Yet if the decision to accept was perhaps inevitable, Stevenson did not rush to it. At the time he told a friend, "I just don't know. I know everyone wants me to jump up and down with delight and say this is the thing I want to do more than anything else in the world, but I just don't know. I don't want to be a lawyer arguing a case whether he believes in it or not. I'm not interested in explaining or defending a policy; I want to be involved in the making of that policy." It was almost as if he had a premonition of what was to come.

Needless to say, pressure on Kennedy was intensifying to announce his appointment as Secretary of State, the most important in the new Administration. And perhaps, even if he hadn't picked his Secretary, Kennedy had decided to end all the speculation centered on Stevenson. On December 8, 1960, Kennedy and Stevenson appeared on the front stoop of the President-elect's home in Georgetown, and Kennedy informed newsmen who kept a constant vigil there that he had asked Stevenson to be the UN Ambassador. It was assumed, of course, that Stevenson's presence signified acceptance. But Stevenson surprised the newsmen: "I appreciate Senator Kennedy's confidence, and I share his view about the difficulty and the importance of this assignment. The United Nations is the very center of our foreign policy, and its effectiveness is indispensable to the peace and security of the world.

"While I have not sought this assignment, I want to be helpful. I have some matters both of organization of the work and of ways and means of strengthening it that I want to discuss with [Kennedy] further. This I hope to do in the very near future."

A reporter asked, "Governor, are we to understand you have not accepted it?"

"I have not accepted it, pending a further talk," Stevenson answered.

This was surely an extraordinary occasion: a forceful President-elect announcing that he had asked a man to serve in a Cabinet-level post only to have the man say publicly, in effect, "I will serve only if my conditions are met." But at least he had removed Stevenson from the speculation as to who was to get the State Department job. Now Kennedy could concentrate on finding a Secretary. He considered a number of men—J. William Fulbright, Chester Bowles, David Bruce—but he finally settled on Dean Rusk, presumably because he had such a firm grasp on the technical aspects of the job, an important qualification to a

President who wanted to be his own Secretary of State. It was to prove an appointment with fateful and melancholy consequences. Kennedy no doubt thought he was getting a liberal. He was—but that peculiar kind of liberal, unhappily not uncommon in postwar America, who combined a broad and generous spirit at home with an implacable determination to wage the cold war abroad. But that was in the future. What concerns us now was that Rusk entirely shared Kennedy's desire to get Stevenson for the UN job, and in Rusk's presence Kennedy telephoned Stevenson and pressed him very hard. Shortly thereafter, Stevenson accepted. His conditions had been met, but as he himself realized, no matter what the agreement, no matter that Kennedy and Rusk acted in good faith, his role was destined to be marginal. He would essentially be the lawyer pleading a case. And it would not be long before he was pleading a most difficult case, one so sickening to him that he almost resigned within months of taking office.

If Stevenson did not want the job, he was nonetheless well prepared for it. Although it was not well known, Stevenson had played an absolutely key role in the founding of the United Nations. In San Francisco in the spring of 1945 the new Secretary of State, Edward R. Stettinius, headed a high-powered delegation that included such prominent figures as John Foster Dulles and Harold Stassen, Tom Connally and Arthur Vandenberg, the top Democrat and Republican on the Senate Foreign Relations Committee, and a host of diplomatic and legal experts. It was a delegation well qualified to represent the United States in writing the United Nations Charter, but for some reason, perhaps because there were so many strong-willed men in it, the delegation's press relations were a disaster, so bad that editorials were being written about it. Arthur Krock, then the New York *Times'* Washington correspondent and the most influential newspaperman of the period, suggested that Adlai Stevenson be sent for. He knew of Stevenson's first-rate work in a number of government agencies during the early days of the New Deal and during the war. Stevenson quickly straightened things out, demonstrating then his great skill at working with newsmen, indeed his great sympathy for their work of informing the public.

However important that job was, it was merely preparation for a much bigger one. In July 1945, after the Senate ratified the UN Charter, Stevenson resigned from the State Department and went home to Illinois. But he wasn't to remain there long. While on vacation in Michigan—his first since 1940—he received separate phone calls from Stettinius and the man who had succeeded him as Secretary of State, James Byrnes. They asked him to serve as deputy to Stettinius, who would be the chief American delegate to the Executive Committee of the Preparatory Commission of the United Nations. This work would be of the utmost importance. Although a charter for the UN had been adopted in San Francisco, the London conference would determine the actual structure of the new organization. Stevenson accepted, but this time he had resolved not to be separated from his family. His wife Ellen followed him to London with the two older boys (Adlai III and Borden), while the third son, John Fell, stayed at school in Lake Forest. Soon after Stevenson arrived in London in early September, Stettinius fell sick and flew back to the United States for gallstone surgery. It was decided to leave Stevenson in charge, and during weeks of patient, resourceful negotiating (he had many polite clashes with Andrei Gromyko, head of the Soviet delegation), he was largely instrumental in determining the shape of the UN. When the Executive Committee finished its work after weeks of day-and-night sessions, Stevenson, together with Gladwyn Jebb of Britain, worked out the agenda and election procedure for the full Preparatory Commission. Later, after the commission had decided to headquarter the UN in the United States, Stevenson, in an interview with C. L. Sulzberger of the New York *Times,* demonstrated his unique perception. Even before the cold war had begun, Stevenson warned that members of the UN "must never permit the organization to be divided into two camps, as the issue of slavery divided the Federal Union before the Civil War." Of course, unity was not to be, although when Stevenson became a national figure seven years later, with the cold war already hardened into the dominant fact of the postwar world, he was an eloquent advocate of taking steps to establish it.

Stevenson was senior adviser to the American delegation for the first session of the UN General Assembly in London in January 1946, and furthered his reputation. "Nor was this recognition confined to his own compatriots: delegates from all the fifty-one [charter member] nations, many of whom after the long weary weeks had become his fast friends, regarded him as the key figure in the total proceedings—intelligent, trustworthy, utterly dedicated to the cause of international organization." [7] Thus, when at a joint news conference on December 15, 1960, Dean Rusk said that Stevenson probably knew more about the United Nations than any other American, he was not merely being gracious to the man who had so desperately wanted the job Rusk got.

Indeed, there is probably no political figure in postwar years who has received so much public flattery as Adlai Stevenson. This was so at the UN as elsewhere. On February 1, 1961, when he appeared for the first time on the Security Council, that body gave him a spontaneous outburst of tribute. This was not inappropriate, for Stevenson was by far the most important person who had ever sat on the Security Council as his nation's permanent representative. And it is probably true that no political figure had ever traveled as widely and knew personally so many of the world's leaders. Stevenson replied fittingly by speaking of his and the United States' hopes for the United Nations. But what concerns us here is his opening sentence: "I have sometimes said that flattery is all right, Mr. President, if you don't inhale." Although Stevenson knew the dangers of inhaling, he inhaled—and deeply. He was entirely aware that he was a unique figure in American life. He enjoyed this status and the admiration, even adulation, that went with it. He regarded himself as superior to the men who had succeeded in reaching the White House where he had not. There is little question that he was superior to Eisenhower, and after 1952 he prepared himself to serve in the Presidency, whereas Kennedy and Johnson prepared themselves to get the Presidency. And he believed himself clearly better equipped to serve as a chief adviser on foreign policy than any of the hardnosed "realists" around Kennedy and Johnson, whose realistic advice was to lead to one foreign policy disaster after another. He certainly was on firm ground here. Also, he was not a little vain of his skill as a public speaker, and he was entirely aware that he alone of the Kennedy and Johnson Cabinets had a significant political following. Stevenson liked to think of himself as an intellectual and took considerable pride in being the politician most welcome in faculty clubs and lecture halls, although toward the end he must have realized that while still welcome, indeed sought after, by the presidents and trustees of universities, he had lost his hold on their faculties and students.

But if Stevenson had his full share of vanity, it never developed into arrogance, something that can hardly be said of Kennedy or Johnson. Perhaps it was his appreciation of the absurd that saved him. Whatever it was, he could not always take himself too seriously. This was demonstrated in many ways. One must start with his humor, his irrepressible urge to make fun of everything, especially himself. Many writers are of the opinion that his humor helped to defeat him, for Americans like their leaders solemn. It would be nice to be able to dispute this, to argue that Americans like serious men to be funny, but unhappily it is probably true that the electorate prefers solemn asses; it certainly has elected enough of them. Still, even if Stevenson had been able to repress his humor, he could not have defeated Eisenhower, so it was our gain that he did not try.

Sadly, the United Nations does not seem to engender much humor, perhaps because it is the repository of man's political failures, the place where disasters end up when no one else will take them in. What humor exists is usually of the "inside" variety, meaningful only to members of the club. That is not to say that Stevenson was not funny during those years; he often was uproariously so, but these occasions were seldom recorded: ad lib remarks before he began the prepared text of a speech, amusing incidents recalled to warm up an audience and, of course, his wisecracks and stories when with friends. One of his favorite anecdotes on such public occasions was about the middle-aged clubwoman who came up to him after a speech and said with a flutter in her voice: "Oh, Mr. Stevenson, your speech was superfluous."

"Thank you, madam. I've been thinking of having it published posthumously."

"Oh, won't that be nice. The sooner the better."

Many of his stories, of course, were based on his failure to get to the White House. In November of 1961, when Dr. Dana M. Greeley was elected president of the Unitarian Universalist

Association (Stevenson's funeral would be held in the tiny Unitarian Church in Bloomington), Stevenson wrote him this note: "Congratulations on your election as president. I know from hearsay how satisfying that can be."

Stevenson always delighted in the absurd, and this story was told me by Wally Irwin, one of his early speech writers at the UN. He recalls it from a luncheon at the delegates' dining room. It was a fairly formidable gathering of diplomats, and Stevenson was, as usual, because of his impossible appointments schedule, a few minutes late. He came rushing into the dining room with that curious waddle of his, excused himself, sat down and immediately pulled out a clipping he had found somewhere that morning. With that merry smile of his, he read:

> "I get up in the morning and brush off my wits,
> Then I open the paper and read the obits.
> If my name is not there, I know I'm not dead.
> So I eat a good breakfast and go back to bed."

Then, too, even as Ambassador he remained careless about his appearance; he was still the Stevenson of the hole in the shoe, with his suits old and rumpled and his thinning hair frequently in need of a trim. And if he was careless of his appearance, he didn't much care about appearances, either. In this he would prove far different from his successor. A good example is the matter of offices. When Stevenson began traveling to Washington on UN affairs, he worked in an office in the Bureau of International Organization Affairs. A big office was occupied by the Assistant Secretary of State for IO (as they say at State, which is what they call the Department of State; often it is called simply The Department, as if there were no other). Then a couple of deputy assistant secretaries had smaller offices, and Stevenson's was approximately the same size. In this small, second-rate office Stevenson worked away without saying a word. Perhaps he didn't even notice. But when Goldberg later got the job, he took one look at the office, demanded—and got—a suite with a big office and a separate reception room.

Although this reluctance to throw his weight around was a rare and happy quality in a man in high position, it was occasionally to be something of a handicap. Whereas Goldberg didn't hesitate putting through a call to the President, indeed seemed to enjoy it, Stevenson was just as happy to talk to Schlesinger or someone else on the White House staff. He didn't want to be a nuisance and disturb the President unless it were essential. Also he hesitated to use his political leverage. He was a reasonable man who believed that the argument itself and the man who advanced it were what should count, not the amount of bureaucratic pushing and shoving. In this he would be proved wrong. In government, as in any bureaucracy, it is seldom the idea that counts, almost always the force with which it is pushed. This hesitancy, although Stevenson no doubt thought of it simply as good manners, was to limit his influence. But as we shall see later, this was only one of the factors involved.

All during 1960 Fidel Castro's government had been accusing the United States of various aggressive acts against Cuba. The issue first came before the UN on July 18, when the Security Council met to hear a complaint from Cuban Foreign Minister Raul Roa, who had charged that a "grave situation" existed, "with manifest danger to international peace and security, as a consequence of the repeated threats, harassments, intrigues, reprisals and aggressive acts" by the United States. Cuba accused the United States of harboring Cuban war criminals, aiding counterrevolutionary forces, violating Cuban airspace and carrying on a campaign of economic strangulation.[8]

In response, the United States put before the council a memorandum it had submitted to the Inter-American Peace Committee of the Organization of American States (OAS) that accused Cuba of carrying out a campaign against the United States of distortions, half-truths and outright falsehoods. On July 19 the council—then, as always, dominated by the United States—decided that since the situation was being considered by the OAS, it would defer any further discussion until after their report had been received. Since the OAS has always been an instrument of the United States, this obviously buried the Cuban complaint.

Then on the last day of 1960, Cuba again asked for an urgent meeting of the Security Council, charging that the United States intended to commit direct military aggression against Cuba "within a few hours." [9] It said it had evidence of such a plot. Cuba was, of course, essentially correct, except for the timing of the invasion. On January 3, 1961, little more than two weeks before Kennedy was to take office, the Eisenhower Administration broke off diplomatic relations with Cuba, an act that should have been left for the new Administration. Then, on January 4 and 5, the Security Council again discussed the question and heard Cuban Foreign Minister Roa accuse the United States of setting up exile training camps in Guatemala, Honduras and Florida in preparation for an invasion of Cuba. Again the United States denied the charges, and again the Security Council took no action.

Also on January 5, Cuba blamed the rupture in diplomatic relations on the "Administration of President Eisenhower, which first brought about the deterioration of these relations." This was evidently a signal that Havana hoped for improved relations after the Kennedy Administration took power on January 20.

But the signal was ignored. At a press conference just five days after his inauguration, President Kennedy said, "We have no plans at present to resume diplomatic relations with Cuba." This alone would not have disturbed Castro, since no Cuban could expect an abrupt about-face by the new Administration, but Kennedy went on to say that the United States could not have "happy relations" with countries where revolutions "are seized by external forces and directed . . . toward imposing" an alien ideology. This statement was made even though there was absolutely no evidence then—nor has there been any since—that the Soviet Union dictated Cuban policy. Indeed, there are many examples indicating the opposite. Furthermore, the Kennedy statement made it clear that his Administration, like the Eisenhower Administration, did not recognize the right of Cuba to have a government of its own choosing.

Then on January 30 in his State of the Union Message, Kennedy told Congress, "Communist domination in this hemisphere can never be negotiated. . . . We are pledged to work with our sister republics to free the Americas of all such foreign domination and all tyranny . . . ." And it soon became clear how Kennedy intended to "work with our sister republics."

By this time Adlai Stevenson was settled in at the United Nations, and on February 23, in a letter to the president of the General Assembly, Cuba wrote, "the slender hopes" it had for "a change of outlook and methods" on the part of the new American Administration "are already beginning to evaporate." Cuba accused Kennedy of "devising" and "carrying out a new plan of aggression against Cuba" in collaboration with "puppet governments" in Latin America.

All during this period, reports were circulating that the United States was indeed preparing an invasion force of exiles at a training camp near the Guatemalan mountain town of Retalhuleu. The story first appeared in the *Hispanic American Report,* where Ronald Hilton, then director of Stanford University's Institute of Hispanic American and Luso-Brazilian Studies, wrote that it was common knowledge in Guatemala that the CIA was training exiles for the invasion of Cuba. The *Nation* was informed of the story and, after checking with Dr. Hilton, wrote an editorial on November 19, 1960, that said, "Fidel Castro may have a sounder basis for his expressed fears of a U.S. financed 'Guatemala-type' invasion than most of us realize." The editorial concluded:

"We ourselves, of course, pretend to no first-hand knowledge of the facts . . . . If Washington is ignorant of the existence of the base, or, knowing it exists, is nevertheless innocent of any involvement in it, then surely the appropriate authorities will want to scotch all invidious rumors . . . . On the other hand, if the reports as heard by Dr. Hilton are true, then public pressure should be brought to bear upon the Administration to abandon this dangerous and hare-brained project.

"There is a second reason why we believe the reports merit publication; they can, and should, be checked immediately by all U.S. news media with correspondents in Guatemala."

The *Nation* distributed seventy-five copies of proofs of the editorial, together with a news release based on it, to major news outlets, including the foreign press, in New York and followed many of them up with phone calls. Of the nation's daily newspapers, only the York, Pennsylvania, *Gazette and Daily* ran an immediate story based on the *Nation* editorial. The New York

*Times* carried nothing until nine days later, when it quoted Guatemalan President Miguel Ydigoras Fuentes as branding the reports as a "lot of lies." No other information. For months the American press, which prides itself on being the best in the world and beyond being influenced, ignored the stories or just nibbled at the edges. Even the New York *Times* on April 7—just ten days before the invasion—doctored a report by the able Tad Szulc, eliminating references to the CIA and to the imminence of the invasion. The whole dreary story of the failure of the self-professed "sentinels of democracy" to do their job is told in frightening detail by Victor Bernstein and Jesse Gordon in the fall 1967 issue of the Columbia University *Forum*.

But despite the delinquency of the American press as a whole, reports continued to circulate, particularly at the United Nations. There is no indication of how much Stevenson knew about all this until April 8, when he was briefed but not consulted by Arthur Schlesinger and Tracy Barnes of the CIA. Schlesinger reports in his *A Thousand Days* that Kennedy was worried about the UN aspects of the invasion (but not seriously enough to ask Stevenson's opinion) and decreed that Stevenson should be fully informed "and that nothing said at the UN should be less than the truth, even if it could not be the full truth. 'The integrity and credibility of Adlai Stevenson,' he had remarked to me on April 7, 'constitute one of our great national assets. I don't want anything done which might jeopardize that.' " [10]

Schlesinger goes on to describe the briefing given Stevenson:

"In preparation for the [UN] debate, Tracy Barnes and I had a long talk with Stevenson on April 8. But our briefing, which was probably unduly vague, left Stevenson with the impression that no action would take place during the discussion of the Cuban item. Afterward, when Harlan Cleveland, the Assistant Secretary of International Organization Affairs, Clayton Fritchey of the United States Mission to the UN, and I lunched with Stevenson at the Century, he made clear that he wholly disapproved of the plan, regretted that he had been given no opportunity to comment on it and believed it would cause infinite trouble. But if it was national policy, he was prepared to make out the best possible case."

Another report about this briefing goes into greater detail:

"The project, he was told, had been inherited from the Eisenhower Administration. But it had been carefully reviewed by key people of the new administration, including Secretary of Defense McNamara, Secretary Rusk and (of course) the President, who now gave it final approval. Its major premise was that the Castro regime had no popular support and was so incompetent, Castro himself being an hysterical fanatic, that it could not effectively react to a well-prepared surprise attack. The attack itself was to be carried out by exiled Cubans and only Cubans; they would fly the air cover, they would comprise the landing parties; and they understood that, once landed, they were on their own, literally and figuratively. There would be no direct U.S. military involvement. Absolutely none. But then none would be necessary: the landing was bound to trigger a popular uprising and an armed force defection whereby the Communist-dominated Castro regime would be swiftly toppled, and at virtually no risk or cost to the U.S. So argued the CIA and the Joint Chiefs of Staff, principal advocates of the project." [11]

Another account of a Stevenson briefing comes from Francis T. P. Plimpton, his deputy at the U.S. Mission. According to Plimpton, what the CIA told them "bore no resemblance to what happened." They were advised that the exile force was financed by Cuban emigrés, and they got the impression—as Plimpton put it with wry bitterness—"that in the dark of night a few canoes were going to Cuba and that the men would gather in the Sierra Madre." [12]

No matter what the exact terms of the briefings, it is clear that Stevenson was appalled. He knew that in a few days he would be facing the Cubans in the UN General Assembly with a wholly incredible story. He knew that no one could possibly believe that a Cuban exile invasion could materialize in Cuba without substantial outside help—and outside help in that degree could come only from the United States. Moreover, he thought the invasion morally wrong, one that would cause enormous long-term damage to the United States. But he felt it was his obligation to do the best he could at the UN to minimize the diplomatic damage he felt sure was on the way.

Perhaps Stevenson felt better when, on April 12, President Kennedy at a press conference declared flatly, "There will not be, under any conditions, any intervention in Cuba by United States armed forces, and this government will do everything it possibly can . . . to make sure that there are no Americans involved in any actions inside Cuba." This statement, if not a downright lie, was so close to it as not to make any difference. But if Stevenson's spirits were raised by Kennedy's statement, they were soon to be plunged to the depths.

The UN General Assembly's Main Political Committee had been scheduled to discuss the Cuban charges on the following Monday, but when on Saturday eight B-26's, relics of the Second World War, bombed three important Cuban airfields, Foreign Minister Roa was able to get the meeting urgently rescheduled for that afternoon. These were American planes, with American-trained pilots, flying out of an airfield in dictator-controlled Nicaragua as arranged by the United States. In a passionate speech to the assembly committee, on which all member nations are represented, Roa charged that the United States had planned and financed the air raids as a "prologue" to a "large-scale invasion of Cuba." Roa told the committee that seven Cubans had died in the attacks and that the Cuban government had in its possession fragments of the bombs used.

When Stevenson took the floor to reply, it was after hours of frantic telephone calls back and forth between Washington and New York, as he attempted to organize his defense. Assistant Secretary Cleveland called the State Department Bureau of Inter-American Affairs, which called the CIA. The CIA informed him that the pilots of the B-26's were genuine Cuban defectors. Cleveland, in turn, passed the word to Stevenson. So Stevenson, speaking solemnly and with his unique skill, told the UN that the pilots and planes were not American but Cuban and had taken off from Cuban airfields. He presented photographs demonstrating that the planes bore Cuban markings, not realizing that the pictures were CIA fakes. And he repeated Kennedy's assertion that U.S. forces would not intervene in Cuba, that the differences were among Cubans themselves.

The assembly was far from convinced, and the Russians angrily denounced American "aggression," pointing out that although the United States had said Americans would not participate in an invasion, it had not promised to prevent "hostile" actions from being organized on its soil. And in a fateful foreshadowing of the Cuban missile crisis, Russia pledged "assistance" to Cuba.

Almost immediately the cover story began to crack. Charles W. Yost, Stevenson's superb deputy, had had an intuition that the photos might be faked; as a former ambassador abroad, he was familiar with the CIA and its clumsy tricks. Not being directly involved and having nothing more than a hunch to go on, however, he kept silent. But at last, newsmen began to ask tough questions, and it became apparent that Stevenson had put his integrity on the line for a lie, and a fragile one at that.

Shaken and distraught, Stevenson had little time to brood over what he had done. On Monday worse was to come. Early that morning 1,400 Cuban exiles, brave and dedicated even if foolish, were sent by the Americans to sure capture and death at the then obscure but now historic Bay of Pigs. An outraged Roa told the UN that Cuba had been invaded "by a force of mercenaries organized, financed, and armed by the government of the United States." Stevenson could only reply feebly that the United States was not involved, that there were "no Americans involved in any actions inside Cuba." So Stevenson lied on Saturday—although he had not known he was lying—and on Monday he lied again; and this time he knew it.

As all his close colleagues confirm, Stevenson was in anguish. He felt betrayed by the Administration. He felt that his integrity had been violated, his credibility compromised forever. In less than three months, his worst fears had been realized. Not only had he been required to lie, but he had not even been consulted before the United States had committed itself to a folly that would require him to stand before the world and tell transparent lies. He had to resign, but how could he and compound the embarrassment of the government he had sworn to defend?

But there was even more to his distress than that. Kenneth S. Davis put it well in his book:

"No small part of his suffering at that moment was the seeming confirmation of his darkest suspicions of Kennedy as man and as President. All men make mistakes, of course. But there was in Stevenson's view a kind of mistake that truly honorable and intelligent men *never* make. Of this kind was the Cuban adventure—or so it seemed at the moment. How could any man of moral sensitivity, with power to control the event, have permitted so criminal a violence to proceed in so soiled and tattered a cloak of lies? How could any man of honor, possessed of normal human sympathies, so ruthlessly use a man of Stevenson's stature, at the expense of Stevenson's honor, merely to lend plausibility to these lies? And how could any mature man possessing common sense have believed that egregious stupidities thus compounded could achieve even a strictly limited, purely pragmatic end?" [13]

But Davis, having gone that far, relents on both Stevenson and Kennedy. To be sure, things always seem worse at the moment. And Stevenson did find out that neither Kennedy nor Rusk had had any intention of deceiving him so that he could, in turn, be more convincing in deceiving the UN. It is true, too, that Kennedy and Rusk were determined to keep Stevenson better informed in the future, and that to an extent this promise was kept. And it is also true that Kennedy took all the blame himself. Further, it engendered a kind of sympathy for Kennedy that Stevenson had previously lacked. He had always been somewhat resentful of Kennedy's unremitting good fortune. Now he saw that even Jack Kennedy could suffer a hard knock but had the resilience to bounce back. Also, Stevenson's colleagues at the UN sympathized with his public humiliation and admired the way he took it. After all, the same thing could happen to them any day. Kennedy, too, was grateful for the way Stevenson soldiered on. And it is true, but only in a sense, that "with remarkable rapidity," as Davis wrote, "the catastrophe shrank in most minds to the proportions of an episode—an unfortunate episode but one whose effects were by no means all bad."

All the above may well be so, but the fact remains that Stevenson's indictment of Kennedy was essentially just. Perhaps because

the Kennedy myth has become so fixed in American culture, the
Bay of Pigs is usually brushed off as just a boyish mistake of no
consequence, one that contributed to the education of the President. After all, it is pointed out, Kennedy did manfully take full
responsibility for it, didn't he? Of course he did, and well he might
because he *was* responsible. The worldwide shock and disgust were
merited. Kennedy was supposed to be the bright young liberal,
surrounded by liberal intellectuals, who would rescue America
from the dreary, self-righteous, moralistic days of the Eisenhower
Administration. Here was a new President who was, above all,
supposed to be intelligent embarking on an adventure so absurd
that it would have been dismissed as fantasy by a Boy Scout patrol
leader. To some, it did not matter that the invasion was immoral
—immorality is hardly a stranger to the leaders of mighty nations.
But stupidity, that was inexcusable. Of course, the ultimate objection to the Bay of Pigs is not its stupidity, although that alone
would have been sufficient indictment, but its immorality. True,
Kennedy did accept the blame and blamed himself bitterly, but
one never felt that it was because the invasion was wrong but
because it hadn't worked. "But there was in Stevenson's view a
kind of mistake that truly honorable and intelligent men *never*
make."

The United States always expects the rest of the world to share
its view of things. Yet in any country having a parliamentary
system, the government that planned and executed such an adventure would surely have fallen. In 1956 the United States joined
Russia in stopping Britain, France and Israel from bringing to a
successful conclusion their attack on Egypt. Surely the American
adventure was no more noble than that. And also in 1956 the
United States trumpeted to the skies—rightfully so—horror at
Russia's criminal actions in crushing the Hungarian revolution.
And for years afterward, we used this bloody deed as an indictment
against them at the UN and elsewhere. Yet the United States, and
even historians, who should be able to look beyond the present,
feel that the Bay of Pigs should be forgiven and even forgotten
simply because the United States admitted it had made a mistake.
And it was a pretty grudging admission, for Kennedy told the
American Society of Newspaper Editors on April 20, when it

was clear that the invasion was a fiasco, "We do not intend to abandon" Cuba.

Arthur Schlesinger joined Davis in trying to find a silver lining:

"The impact of the failure shook up the national security machinery. It taught every adviser something about the President, the other advisers, himself and his own department. It was a horribly expensive lesson; but it was well-learned. In later months the President's father would tell him that in its perverse way, the Bay of Pigs was not a misfortune but a benefit. I doubt whether the President ever fully believed this; the thought of the men of the Brigade suffering in Cuban prisons prevented easy consolation. But no one can doubt that failure in Cuba in 1961 contributed to success in Cuba in 1962." [14]

It was loyal of Schlesinger to write that, and indeed there are those who believe it, but it seems to me that he had it backward. Rather it was that failure in Cuba in 1961 made all but inevitable the frightening journey to the brink in 1962, that Kennedy must share fully with Khrushchev the responsibility for those dread days. How much was actually learned from that "horribly expensive lesson" is debatable. Kennedy continued to use the same advisers—in any other field they would have been fired summarily for gross incompetence—and Vietnam and the Dominican Republic would result. And there was one more far-reaching effect. Our lies during the crisis, added to those about Guatemala, the U-2 flights and subsequent falsehoods about Vietnam and the Dominican Republic, have caused the rest of the world, and many Americans, too, to wonder if they can any longer have faith in America's word. This was certainly demonstrated when the Navy spy ship *Pueblo* was captured by North Korea in January 1968.

So then there is essential justice in Stevenson's assessment of Kennedy after the Bay of Pigs, and any attempt to view him as a "great" President must overcome this almost insuperable obstacle. And if that is overcome, there is still Vietnam. But the immediate question is, should Stevenson, feeling the way he did, have stayed on the job? He certainly would have had every justification for resigning, but it is understandable that he did not. The President was young and so was his Administration, and Stevenson quite probably thought both that there was still time for it to embark on a reasonable path toward peace and that he could help by remaining at his post. Nonetheless, he should have resigned. For "there was in Stevenson's view a kind of mistake that truly honorable and intelligent men *never* make."

One final note about the Bay of Pigs. Those who believe that the Russians run the United Nations should examine closely what happened then. Although the invasion was discussed by the General Assembly, and although the United States did not have a leg to stand on legally or morally, the UN General Assembly took no action whatsoever against the United States. Not even the mildest wrist-slapping resolution was passed. Despite international outrage, U.S. domination of the UN remained unchallenged.

A few weeks later, on June 4, Adlai Stevenson began an eighteen-day tour of Latin America. Partly he was sent by Kennedy to demonstrate the President's faith in him, but primarily it was an attempt to repair the grave damage done by the Bay of Pigs. He talked with as many people as he could, at as many levels, and when he returned, he made a comprehensive report to the President. He told Kennedy something that the United States did not understand then and still does not: that many Latin Americans see the Cuban revolution not as the establishment of a Soviet beachhead in the hemisphere, but as a legitimate expression of the aspirations of the downtrodden. And he told the President that if Communism were not to be attractive to the Latins, effective action would have to be taken to attack economic and social problems that were threatening political stability in many nations. These recommendations no doubt contributed to Kennedy's developing concept of the Alliance for Progress.

But while the Bay of Pigs was in some minds shrinking to the proportions of an unfortunate episode, it is clear that it was in fact the ugly prelude to the dread days of October 1962, when the world teetered on the brink of nuclear war. The conclusion is inescapable that, had it not been for Kennedy's folly in the spring of 1961, there would have been no Cuban missile crisis in the fall of 1962. The frightening events to come were foreshadowed by a letter from Premier Khrushchev to President Kennedy on April 18, 1961, while the exile brigade was still fighting for its life on

Cuban shores. Not only did Khrushchev charge that the United States "trained, equipped and armed" the invaders, but he appealed to Kennedy to stop the invasion, warning that it "may touch off a chain reaction in every part of the world." And he pledged "all necessary assistance" to Cuba. It would be a year and a half before an astonished Administration would find out what that assistance was.

There can be little doubt that Castro felt a desperate need for help as the United States continued to tighten the economic and political noose around Cuba, and there is every reason to believe that his fears of another invasion were genuine. For if the United States had launched one invasion and, following its failure, embarked on an economic and political blockade that approached wartime severity, one can hardly blame the Cubans for expecting another attack. What the United States was doing, of course, was demonstrating anew its profound misunderstanding of the revolutionary fervor of the peoples of the developing nations, their determination to get—by force if necessary—a better life. And America was also demonstrating its basic intolerance of other systems of government. Although it has always proclaimed a belief in diversity, for some reason America has been obsessed by a fear of Communism so virulent that it is afraid to coexist with it. The United States, of course, did not dare to try to stamp out Communism in the Soviet Union and neighboring states, but it was determined to try wherever it thought it could get away with it— whether in Cuba next door, or in Vietnam halfway around the world. Exactly what this fear is based on is hard to say, perhaps a lack of faith in American institutions. For if the American way is as superior as most of our countrymen insist, then surely it need not go in fear of competition from an inferior foe.

But whatever the reason, the United States continued to intensify its hostile campaign against Cuba with the support of most, but by no means all, of the American people. And so the prophecy became self-fulfilling. The more the United States proclaimed that Cuba was a Communist camp, the more it took steps that could have no other result but to drive Cuba into Russian arms. Nonetheless, although Castro became beholden to the Russians, perhaps even economically dependent on them, Cuba, contrary to what successive American Administrations have said, has never become a satellite, as events have proven time and again.

Tension between the two countries continued to mount throughout the rest of 1961, and still further in 1962. By late August 1962 it was evident from aerial photographs that the Soviet Union had established surface-to-air missile sites in Cuba. Intelligence reports said that about 5,000 Soviet technicians were already in the country, with more men and sophisticated electronic equipment on the way by ship. Some people in the CIA, notably John McCone, its new director, had a hunch that the SAM missiles were being installed as antiaircraft protection for "offensive" longer-range missiles. As the world was to see, semantics were to play a large part in the missile crisis. The Soviet Union and Cuba were to describe the missiles as "defensive," whereas the United States characterized them as "offensive." In modern strategic terms, however, these two words have ceased to have much real meaning, whereas to politicians and propagandists they have assumed enormous significance. One wonders if perhaps the world were not a saner and far safer place when euphemisms were scorned and the War Department was the War Department, not the Department of Defense. What it comes down to is that our missiles aimed at the vitals of the Soviet Union and China are "defensive," whereas Russian, and eventually Chinese, missiles aimed at us are "offensive"—with, of course, just the opposite designation obtaining in Moscow and Peking.

At any rate, the Administration did not believe that Khrushchev would be reckless enough to introduce into Cuba, just ninety miles from the United States, "offensive" missiles capable of carrying nuclear warheads. Of course, it had not been reckless for the United States to establish "defensive" missile bases in Turkey, which has a common border with the Soviet Union, or indeed to ring the Soviet Union and China with missile bases. But just to make sure, Kennedy issued a stern warning on September 4 that although there was "no evidence" of "significant offensive capability" in Cuban hands, "were it to be otherwise, the gravest issues would arise."

A week later, obviously in response to the President's statement, Khrushchev asserted that the "armaments and military equipment sent to Cuba are designed exclusively for defensive purposes," adding, "There is no need for the Soviet Union to shift its weapons for the repulsion of aggression, for a retaliatory blow, to any other country, for instance Cuba. Our nuclear weapons are so powerful in their explosive force and the Soviet Union has such powerful rockets to carry these nuclear warheads that there is no need to search for sites for them beyond the boundaries of the Soviet Union."

Kennedy responded to this statement by telling reporters at a September 13 press conference that the Soviet shipments were not a serious threat, but he pointedly warned the Soviet Union and Cuba that if the island were to "become an offensive military base of significant capacity for the Soviet Union, then this country will do whatever must be done to protect its own security and that of its allies." And he backed up this warning by asking Congress for stand-by authority to call up the reserves. He also doubled the number of U-2 flights over Cuba.

At first, photographs taken during these flights revealed a continuing buildup of Soviet material but nothing of an offensive character. However, on October 14, a flight over western Cuba returned with photographic evidence of a launching pad, a number of associated buildings and even one missile lying on the ground at the site near San Cristobal. That night McGeorge Bundy got the news at the White House. He asked that supporting evidence be assembled, and the next morning at breakfast he presented the evidence to Kennedy. Kennedy examined it and then announced that the missiles would have to go. He directed Bundy to have more photographs taken, closer to the ground, and to call a meeting of top officials. The following day, October 16, Stevenson was at the White House to attend a luncheon for the Crown Prince of Libya. After lunch, Kennedy summoned Stevenson to the President's second-floor study and told him what had been learned. Keeping his promise after the Bay of Pigs catastrophe, he asked Stevenson to join the top-level discussion, so Stevenson postponed his return to New York. Kennedy reportedly said that the United States would have to act swiftly, and he "supposed" that an air strike would be necessary "to wipe them out" before the missile launching pads became fully operational.

Stevenson was alarmed, not only by the evidence but by Kennedy's apparent determination to take precipitate action. Stevenson said he thought there should be no air strike until the United States had exhausted every peaceful means of removing the threat. And throughout the tense, often heated discussions that continued during the next ten days in what has come to be called the ExCom of the National Security Council, he persisted in this stance. It was this persistence, this determination that the United States should seek a peaceful solution, that later caused him to be unadmiringly dubbed the original "dove."

Stevenson had to return to New York on Wednesday, and the ExCom continued its agonized debate. When he got back to Washington on Friday (everyone in the Administration was attempting to carry on his duties much as usual in order not to tip off the press and thus the Russians), he found to his vast relief that the air strike proposal had lost favor, substantially because Robert Kennedy had opposed it with such passion. " 'A sudden air strike at dawn Sunday without warning,' said the Attorney General in rather impassioned tones, would be 'a Pearl Harbor in reverse, and it would blacken the name of the United States in the pages of history' as a great power who attacked a small neighbor!" [15] In addition, a sneak air attack on Cuba might have made the Russians feel they had no alternative but to retaliate, perhaps even with nuclear weapons. So the group turned to the idea of a naval blockade, with which Stevenson agreed completely, because it gave Khrushchev time to take considered action. Equally important, it made backing down less difficult for him. Here again, semantics played a part. It was decided to call the blockade a "quarantine." That had a nice ring to it, as though it were merely a medical necessity instead of the act of war it was. For called by any other name, a blockade is still by international law an act of war, as the Russians would lose no time in emphatically pointing out to the Security Council.

Stevenson suggested that Kennedy postpone his television disclosure of the Soviet missiles and the announcement of the blockade until Monday night and that he say the "quarantine" *would* be imposed, not that it had already been imposed. This would allow the United States time to inform the Organization of American States of its plans and get prior approval. The OAS would, of course, have approved the blockade, even after the fact, as it

did three years later after the American invasion of the Dominican Republic, but it would be better public relations and would
strengthen Stevenson's hand at the UN if he could announce prior
OAS approval. Kennedy agreed with these suggestions and also
with another of Stevenson's proposals: that simultaneously with
Kennedy's speech, the United States request an emergency meeting of the UN Security Council and submit a resolution calling
for the removal of the Soviet missiles. This would forestall the
Soviet Union and open the debate with America having the initiative rather than the Soviet Union.

On Monday night, October 22, 1962, at 7 P.M., President Kennedy, speaking on television and radio from his study in the White
House, made one of the gravest announcements ever made by
an American President. He told a stunned nation that the Soviet
Union, despite its statements to the contrary, was building "offensive missile sites" in Cuba for medium and intermediate-range
ballistics missiles capable of striking most major cities in the Western Hemisphere. He declared that "this urgent transformation of
Cuba into an important strategic base ... constitutes an explicit
threat to the peace and security of all the Americas" and "cannot
be accepted by this country." In "defense of our own security and
that of the entire Western Hemisphere," President Kennedy announced the following steps:

1. A naval and air "quarantine" on shipment of all "offensive"
military equipment to Cuba and a turning back of all ships carrying such cargo to Cuba;

2. Increased aerial surveillance of Cuba;

3. Adoption of a policy that "any nuclear missile launched
from Cuba against any nation in the Western Hemisphere" would
be deemed "an attack by the Soviet Union on the United States,
requiring a full retaliatory response upon the Soviet Union";

4. Reinforcement of the American naval base at Guantanamo;

5. A call for an immediate meeting of the Organization of
American States;

6. A call for an emergency meeting of the UN Security
Council;

7. A plea to Chairman Khrushchev "to halt and eliminate this
clandestine, reckless and provocative threat to world peace."

At 7:30 P.M. Stevenson sent a formal request for an emergency meeting of the Security Council to its president, who that month was, ironically, Ambassador Valerian Zorin of the Soviet Union. Attached to the request was a draft resolution calling for the immediate dismantling of Soviet missiles and the immediate removal, under UN observation, of the missiles and Soviet IL-28 bombers, for an end to the "quarantine" once the "offensive" weapons had been removed, and for negotiations between the United States and Russia "on measures to remove the existing threat."

Back in Washington, Arthur Schlesinger, who had known nothing of the crisis even though he was in the White House daily—so superbly had the secret been kept—was told about it by Stevenson, who asked him to help with the speech he would deliver on Tuesday.[16] Schlesinger spent all day Sunday until well after midnight working on the speech at the State Department with Assistant Secretary Harlan Cleveland and two of his top aides, Joseph Sisco and Thomas Wilson. On Monday at 10 A.M., Kennedy called Schlesinger and instructed him to go to New York to assist Stevenson; the President later met with Schlesinger to go over the UN speech with Rusk, Robert Kennedy and others. The President suggested a number of omissions, including a passage threatening an air strike if the missiles were not removed. He wanted to leave that to Russia's imagination. As Schlesinger was leaving, Robert Kennedy drew him aside. "We're counting on you to watch things in New York. . . . We will have to make a deal in the end, but we must stand absolutely firm now. Concessions must come at the end of the negotiation, not the beginning." In this he was clearly reflecting the fear felt by many around the President that Stevenson would be too soft to make America's case effectively. They were terribly wrong, as they so often were about Stevenson. He made the case with superb effectiveness; if anything, he was too tough.

Thus, after Kennedy's Monday night speech the scene shifted to the United Nations. It is impossible to convey the sense of dread that pervaded the corridors, the lounges, the Security Council chamber, the entire place. Representatives of the smaller nations were scurrying to and fro, desperately trying to think of something to forestall the disaster that seemed imminent. But they were learning, as they had never learned before, that when the giants are locked in struggle, there is nothing, absolutely nothing, the pygmies can do. They were scared stiff—and they were far from alone—that the world was going to blow up over a struggle in which they had absolutely no interest. There is an African proverb that says, "When the elephants fight, the grass is trampled." They were mortally afraid that the cold war, which they had struggled so hard to keep out of, was nonetheless going to engulf them. But if the small nations themselves were unable to do anything, the UN was far from powerless.

The United States, as the member that had first requested the Security Council meeting (the Soviet Union and Cuba did later), spoke first. In my "Voice of America" broadcast booth a few feet above and to the side of the huge horseshoe table at which the delegates sat, I had a ringside seat. With his customary eloquence, Stevenson put forward the American position. But when he entered the chamber, the OAS was still meeting in Washington; it had not yet authorized the American blockade. This was important, for OAS action was necessary to establish what the United States considered the legal justification for the blockade. As soon as the OAS had acted, Harlan Cleveland was notified, and he called Joseph Sisco at the UN. Watching the Security Council meeting on television, as was much of the nation, Cleveland saw Sisco leave the chamber to take the call. Moments later, Sisco reentered the chamber and slipped a piece of paper in front of Stevenson. Lost in his address, Stevenson didn't seem to notice it. Kennedy, also watching the session, called Cleveland to ask if Stevenson had been notified. Cleveland said he had, but that he wasn't sure if Stevenson had been aware of it. At that moment Stevenson reached for the slip of paper and Kennedy said, "I guess he has it now." Without breaking his unique cadence, Stevenson announced to the council that the OAS had just unanimously adopted a resolution empowering OAS member states "to take all measures individually and collectively, including the use of armed force, which they may deem necessary." Soon afterward, Stevenson concluded: "Since the end of the Second World War, there has been no threat to the vision of peace so profound, no challenge to the world of the [UN] Charter so fateful. The hopes of mankind are concentrated in this room. . . . Let [this day] be remembered, not as the day when the world came to the edge of nuclear war, but as the day when men resolved to let nothing thereafter stop them in their quest for peace."

Kennedy turned from the television set and dictated a telegram: "Dear Adlai: I watched your speech this afternoon with great satisfaction. It has given our case a great start. . . . The United States is fortunate to have your advocacy. You have my warm and personal thanks."

Even though he had achieved the goal Stevenson had sought, Kennedy was never able to overcome a certain envy of Stevenson's unequaled skill at delivering speeches. Although he was superb in the informal give-and-take of a press conference, Kennedy must have realized that in formal speeches he had a tendency toward stridency and choppiness. He envied not so much Stevenson's eloquence of language, but the cadence and dignity with which he spoke.

Stevenson's gift for speechmaking became something of a legend and for good reason, for he was far and away the finest political speaker since Roosevelt. But as is the way with legends, the Stevenson legend tended to run away from the facts. For years the belief persisted that Stevenson wrote all his own speeches. This belief continued long after even the most casual observer should have noticed that even if he had wanted to, Stevenson simply did not have the time to do so. Perhaps it was a hangover from the first campaign, when Stevenson kept reporters waiting past their deadlines as he worked over a speech to be delivered at his next whistle-stop. Or perhaps it was a hunger to believe that great men, or at least one great man, still expressed his own beliefs in his own words. But the blunt fact is that Stevenson, the great speechmaker, was no longer the great speech writer. He wrote virtually none of his own speeches; indeed, there are those who would say that in the last years he didn't write a single one of his own long, formal addresses. Yet not infrequently, the New York *Times,* which certainly knew better, would observe in an admiring editorial that Stevenson had made a point "with his accustomed felicity of language." This must have caused many a weary shake of the head by the anonymous speech writer at the U.S. Mission or at the State Department who had labored for days through draft after draft to write a speech that would sound like Adlai Stevenson.

This was why Kennedy didn't envy Stevenson's eloquence; he knew that it, like his own, was the product either of a single ghost-writer or of a committee of faceless, though often famous, speech writers. What he did admire was Stevenson's ability to deliver a speech, which after all, no one could do for him.

But of course, Stevenson did not have the floor alone. The Soviet Union challenged the right of the United States to "attack vessels of other states on the high seas" and to "dictate to Cuba what policy it must pursue . . . and what weapons it may possess." Russia said its assistance to Cuba was "exclusively designed to improve Cuba's defensive capacity." And Ambassador Zorin introduced a draft resolution condemning "the actions of the Government of the United States . . . aimed at violating the United Nations Charter and at increasing the threat of war." Cuba called the "quarantine" an "act of war unilaterally committed" by the United States as the culmination of a series of aggressive acts against Cuba.

Although both the United States and the Soviet Union expressed a willingness to confer on the situation, when the Tuesday meeting was adjourned, there was no perceptible lessening of the tension. Neither side at the UN had indicated any readiness to back away from the nuclear confrontation. Tuesday night and Wednesday morning dragged on. Soviet ships had not turned back, and there was no indication from Moscow that they would. But on Wednesday, at the urging of the smaller nations, U Thant entered the situation with a suggestion that has not been given due credit for its significance in ending the crisis. That day, October 24, Thant notified the Security Council that he had sent identical messages to Kennedy and Khrushchev, urging the parties "to get together" and to facilitate this by suspending arms shipments as well as the quarantine measures for a period of two to three weeks.

After Thant's announcement, Russian Ambassador Zorin adjourned the meeting so that both countries could consider the Secretary General's proposal. No sooner had he banged the gavel than Zorin turned to Thant, who was in his customary seat at the council president's right, and said, "Mr. Secretary General, this is a very bad proposal. It equates the aggressors and those aggressed against." The Russian position was, of course, exactly that of the United States: the other was the aggressor. In his deceptively bland manner, Thant merely replied, "Mr. Zorin, why not come to see me tomorrow?" He set the time at 2:45, after a luncheon date, but a few minutes before he had to preside at a brief ceremony at which the flag of Tanganyika, a newly admitted member, would be raised in front of the UN buildings.

The Washington view, as shared by the U.S. Mission, was the same as the Soviet Union's, except for switching the names: an acceptance of the Thant proposal would mean that the American response was equated with the Russian aggression. Nonetheless, Stevenson and John McCloy, who had been added to the American delegation at the UN to give it the traditional crisis-time bipartisan flavor, both argued that the United States should not slam the door on further diplomatic moves.

At this point, with tension still rising, Averell Harriman entered the case. Although there was no American in history who had had more experience in dealing with the Russians at the highest level, inexplicably Harriman had not been consulted by anyone in the State Department or at the White House. Evidently because his current assignment did not concern Soviet-American affairs, it simply hadn't occurred to anyone to ask his advice, a preoccupation with the table of organization that frequently plagues the government. Fortunately, however, he refused to wait any longer and called Schlesinger at the U.S. Mission.[17] Harriman said it was his conviction that Khrushchev was looking for a way to get off the hook and that if the United States didn't allow him to, he might push the crisis, already at an almost unbearable stage, beyond the point of no return. Schlesinger was utterly convinced by Harriman's warning and passed it along to Kennedy, who called Harriman the next morning, Thursday.

That day an extraordinary scene took place in U Thant's office, one that has never, to the best of my knowledge, been made public. As scheduled, Ambassador Zorin appeared on the thirty-eighth floor at 2:45, accompanied by Ambassador Platon Morozov, the able and experienced diplomat who had served a succession of Soviet representatives as number two man. Zorin immediately began criticizing Thant, telling him bluntly that he should have condemned the American action on the high seas instead of making a suggestion that equated the aggressors with the victim of aggression.

Thant, calm as usual, pointed out to Zorin that he might have spoken differently, depending on his instructions, if he were still the representative of Burma. But he was now the Secretary General and had to try to find some way out of this dangerous deadlock. Zorin, however, counterattacked angrily, and Thant finally lost his temper—a rare occurrence indeed. He snapped at Zorin, "Please, Mr. Zorin, why don't you condemn me publicly at the Security Council this afternoon?"

Zorin drew back a bit. "No, no, that wouldn't be good."

Still furious, Thant noted that it was one minute to three and that he had to leave for the flag-raising ceremony. So Zorin, Morozov and their interpreter left.

A few seconds later Thant, too, left his office and saw the three Russians huddled together with a fourth at the thirty-eighth-floor elevators, reading something with long faces. Thant passed them without a word and went outside the General Assembly entrance for the flag-raising. After the ceremony, Thant went to the great assembly hall to sit on the podium next to the president, as he did whenever he could find the time. At about 3:20 his secretary came to him with a note, saying that Zorin had an important message for him in the Secretary General's little office behind the podium. There Thant found Morozov, who explained that Zorin was getting ready for the Security Council meeting on Cuba that was to start soon. Morozov asked Thant if he had received a message from Premier Khrushchev. Thant said he had not, and Morozov looked puzzled, although Thant could not understand why. But the reason became clear. Morozov was holding in his hand a copy of the message sent from Khrushchev to Thant, the original of which Thant had yet to receive. What Thant had seen when the four Russians were clustered together at the elevators near his office was a horrified Zorin reading a copy of the Khrushchev reply brought to the UN Secretariat building by a Russian Mission staff member. As Zorin and Morozov read the message, they naturally thought that during the entire time Zorin had been reviling Thant for his proposal, the Secretary General knew of Khrushchev's acceptance, as embarrassing a situation as a diplomat could imagine. Shortly thereafter Zorin was replaced, although whether or not this incident had anything to do with it is known only by the Kremlin.

Morozov handed Thant the copy. The answer was, of course, entirely different in tone and substance from Zorin's bitter attack on Thant of a few minutes before. "I have received your appeal and carefully studied the proposals it contains. I welcome your initiatives. I understand your concern about the situation obtaining in the Caribbean, since the Soviet government also considers this situation as highly dangerous and requiring an immediate interference by the United Nations." And then Khrushchev made the statement that meant that the immediate danger was over: "I am informing you that I agree with your proposal, which meets the interests of peace." He had accepted Thant's proposal that the Soviet ships not try to break the American blockade.

A short time later, Zorin told one of Thant's aides that it takes a long time to get instructions from Moscow, that his situation was not like that of the U.S. Mission, which has only to pick up the phone to Washington. The aide, of course, told Thant, and Thant asked him to pass the message back to Zorin that in the future, if he didn't have instructions, he should keep quiet or at least identify his remarks as personal opinion. For Thant was angered by more than Zorin's personal attack on him. He had feared that Zorin was acting on instructions and that his criticism meant that the Soviet Union had rejected Thant's appeal and was going to run the blockade, making almost inevitable an armed clash between the two greatest nuclear powers.

Thant also received that day a reply from Kennedy that, although it did not accept his proposal, kept the diplomatic doors open.

"I deeply appreciate the spirit which prompted your message of yesterday.

"As we made clear in the Security Council, the existing threat was created by the secret introduction of offensive weapons into Cuba, and the answer lies in the removal of such weapons.

"In your message and your statement to the Security Council, you have made certain suggestions and have invited preliminary talks to determine whether satisfactory arrangements can be assured.

"Ambassador Stevenson is ready to discuss promptly these arrangements with you.

"I can assure you of our desire to reach a satisfactory and peaceful solution of this matter."

Armed with these two replies, Thant sent further messages off to Khrushchev and Kennedy. To Khrushchev Thant wrote in part:

"I would like to bring to Your Excellency's attention my grave concern that Soviet ships already on their way to Cuba might challenge the quarantine imposed by the United States and produce a confrontation at sea between Soviet ships and United States vessels, which could lead to an aggravation of the situation. What concerns me most is that such a confrontation and consequent aggravation of the situation would destroy any possibility of the discussions I have suggested as a prelude to negotiations on a peaceful settlement. In the circumstances I earnestly hope that Your Excellency may find it possible to instruct the Soviet ships already on their way to Cuba to stay away from the interception area for a limited time only, in order to permit discussions of the modalities of a possible agreement which could settle the problem peacefully in line with the Charter of the United Nations.

"I am confident that if such instructions could be issued by Your Excellency, the United States authorities will take action to ensure that a direct confrontation between their ships and Soviet ships is avoided during the same period in order to minimize the risk of any untoward incident taking place.

"If I could be informed of the action taken by Your Excellency on the basis of this appeal, I could inform President Kennedy that I have assurances from your side of your cooperation in avoiding all risk of an untoward incident."

That same day, Thursday, October 25, Thant sent a message to Kennedy, recapping what he had cabled to Khrushchev and making this appeal:

"In continuation of my message of yesterday and my speech before the Security Council, I would now like to appeal to Your Excellency that instructions be issued to United States vessels in the Caribbean to do everything possible to avoid a direct confrontation with Soviet ships in the next few days in order to minimize the risk of any untoward incident. If I could be informed of the action taken by Your Government on the basis of this appeal, I could inform Chairman Khrushchev that I have assurances from your side of your cooperation in avoiding all risk of an untoward incident. I would express the further hope that such cooperation could be the prelude to a quick agreement in principle on the basis of which the quarantine measures themselves could be called off as soon as possible."

Because of the faster communications between New York and Washington, Thant got Kennedy's reply the same day and Khrushchev's the next. Kennedy replied in part:

"If the Soviet Government accepts and abides by your request 'that Soviet ships already on their way to Cuba . . . stay away from the interception area' for the limited time required for preliminary discussion, you may be assured that this government will accept and abide by your request that our vessels in the Caribbean 'do everything possible to avoid direct confrontation with Soviet ships in the next few days to minimize the risk of any untoward incident.' I must inform you, however, that this is a matter of great urgency in view of the fact that certain Soviet ships are still proceeding toward Cuba and the interception area.

"I share your hope that Chairman Khrushchev will also heed your appeal and that we can then proceed urgently to meet the requirements that these offensive missile systems in Cuba be withdrawn, in order to end their threat to peace. I must point out to you that present work on these systems is still continuing."

The next day, Friday, October 26, Thant received Khrushchev's reply, which said in part:

"We therefore accept your proposal and have ordered the masters of Soviet vessels bound for Cuba but not yet within

the area of the American warships' piratical activities to stay
out of the interception area, as you recommend.

"But we have given this order in the hope that the other
side will understand that such a situation, in which we keep
vessels immobilized on the high seas, must be a purely tem-
porary one; the period cannot under any circumstances be of
long duration."

With that, the worst was over. The Soviet Union had specifically
agreed not to challenge the American blockade.

I have cited the messages to and from the UN in some detail
because American writers on this period have tended, perhaps
naturally, to downplay the significance of U Thant's intervention
and to concentrate on the messages between Kennedy and Khrushchev. These latter were, of course, of great importance.

Although in retrospect it seems that the worst was over by
Thursday, it didn't seem so at the time. And on Thursday, when
Stevenson made his most famous speech, perhaps the most widely
quoted speech ever made at the UN, Khrushchev's decision not
to challenge the American blockade was not yet generally known.
That night, work on what Schlesinger terms the "nuclear missile"
launching pads was still under way in Cuba. However, although
there seems little doubt that the Soviet missiles were capable of
carrying nuclear missiles—or, as the military like to say, had a
"nuclear capability"—I do not remember having heard, then at
the UN or later, any direct charge that Soviet nuclear warheads
were actually in Cuba. Stevenson returned to the attack and dismissed the Soviet charge that the United States was responsible
for the crisis. "This is the first time I have ever heard it said that
the crime is not the burglary, but the discovery of the burglary."
And he defended the blockade by saying, "Were we to do nothing
until the knife was sharpened? Were we to stand idly by until it
was at our throats?"

Zorin made what Schlesinger called a "cocky and evasive reply."
It was evasive because Zorin still did not know what his government had decided to do. He knew that Khrushchev was not going
to try to force the immediate blockade, at least not for the time
being, but that was all. However, he attempted a counterattack,
claiming that the United States lacked evidence of offensive missiles

being in Cuba and that world opinion was against the American action. Stevenson listened attentively, as he always did in the council, scribbling an occasional note.

When Zorin finished, Stevenson gestured that he wished to speak. Zorin, the council president, recognized him. He leaned forward, positioned the microphone on the desk in front of him, and began, speaking extemporaneously from notes, one of the most extraordinary scenes in the history of the United Nations. Stevenson, famous and sometimes even derided for always speaking temperately, lost his temper. Exhausted by ten days of extreme tension and little sleep, bruised by his encounters with the hard-liners in Washington who called him soft, nettled by Zorin's sarcastic response (Russian diplomats at the UN almost always have a gift for sarcasm) and perhaps employing the lawyer's trick of appearing angry, Stevenson leaped to the attack:

"I want to say to you, Mr. Zorin, that I do not have your talent for obfuscation, for distortion, for confusing language and double-talk. And I must confess to you that I am glad I do not!

"But if I understood what you said, it was that my position had changed, that today I was defensive because we did not have the evidence to prove our assertions that your government had installed long-range missiles in Cuba.

"Well, let me say something to you, Mr. Ambassador— we do have the evidence. We have it, and it is clear, and it is incontrovertible. And let me say something else—those weapons must be taken out of Cuba.

"Next, if I understood you, you said—with a trespass on credibility that excels your best—that our position had changed since I spoke here the other day because of the pressure of world opinion and the majority of the United Nations. Well, let me say to you, sir—you are wrong again. We have had no pressure from anyone whatsoever. We came here to indicate our willingness to discuss U Thant's proposals, and that is the only change that has taken place.

"But let me also say to you, sir, that there *has* been a change. You, the Soviet Union *has* sent these weapons to Cuba. You, the Soviet Union *has* upset the balance of power in the world. You, the Soviet Union *has* created this new danger, not the United States.

"And you ask with a fine show of indignation why the President did not tell Mr. Gromyko on last Thursday about our evidence, at the very time that Mr. Gromyko was blandly denying to the President that the USSR was placing such weapons on sites in the new world.

"Well, I will tell you why—because we were assembling the evidence, and perhaps it would be instructive to the world to see how far a Soviet official would go in perfidy. Perhaps we wanted to know if this country faced another example of nuclear deceit like that one a year ago when, in stealth, the Soviet Union broke the nuclear test moratorium.

"And finally, the other day, Mr. Zorin, I remind you that you did not deny the existence of these weapons. Instead, we heard that they had suddenly become *defensive* weapons. But today again, if I heard you correctly, you now say, with another fine flood of rhetorical scorn, they do not exist, or that we haven't proved they exist.

"All right, sir, let me ask you one simple question: Do you, Ambassador Zorin, deny that the USSR has placed and is placing medium and intermediate-range missiles and sites in Cuba? Yes or no? Don't wait for the translation. Yes or no?"

Stevenson was referring to standard practice in the Security Council. While a delegate is speaking, his remarks are translated simultaneously into the other official UN languages. And then when the delegate finishes, his words are again translated into English and French to make sure there are no misunderstandings. However, Stevenson, knowing that Zorin had heard his remarks in simultaneous translation, asked him to reply immediately without waiting for the subsequent translation.

Zorin, quite properly, if somewhat lamely, declined to answer:

"I am not in an American court of law and therefore do not wish to answer a question put to me in the manner of a prosecuting counsel. You will receive the answer in due course in my capacity as representative of the Soviet Union."

But Stevenson plunged ahead before the hushed, crowded chamber that leaned forward to get every word of this unprece-dented confrontation.

> "You are in the courtroom of world opinion. You have denied they exist, and I want to know if I understand you correctly.
>
> "I am prepared to wait for my answer until hell freezes over, if that's your decision. And I am also prepared to present the evidence in this room—now."

Stevenson paused and Zorin, who was, we remember, council president took advantage of the pause to call on the next speaker on his list, the delegate of Chile. Quite understandably, Zorin wanted to get off the spot. He knew he was being watched on tele-vision all over the United States and heard on radio in many parts of the world. But the Chilean representative, supporting the United States, would not let Zorin off the hook. With the courtly, flowery language typical of the Latin delegates, he graciously waived his right to speak in favor of Stevenson. Stevenson again rushed to the attack. The UN had never seen anything like this before. And this was not the anti-Communist crusader Henry Cabot Lodge; this was the gentlemanly Adlai Stevenson. Like everyone else in the place, I leaned farther forward. Stevenson was just below me.

> "I have not finished my statement. I asked you a question. I have had no reply to the question, and I will now proceed, if I may, to finish my statement.
>
> "I doubt if anyone in this room, except possibly the repre-sentative of the Soviet Union, has any doubt about the facts. But in view of his statements and the statements of the Soviet Government until last Thursday, when Mr. Gromyko denied the existence or any intention of installing such weapons in Cuba, I am going to make a portion of the evidence avail-able right now. If you will indulge me for a moment, we will set up an easel here in the back of the room, where I hope it will be visible to everyone."

Aides bustled quietly into the chamber and set up a big easel on which a number of greatly enlarged photographs were displayed one after the other. However, they were brought into the council chamber with a readiness that Stevenson himself did not feel. His top aides had been after him to make such a dramatic presentation, but Stevenson was dead set against it, not having recovered from the traumatic shock of having once before presented to the UN photographs about Cuba that turned out to be CIA fakes. Furthermore, Pierre Salinger, Kennedy's press secretary, wanted them saved for a television broadcast by the President. The State Department was equally reluctant to have them used at the UN. But Francis T. P. Plimpton, Stevenson's deputy, was convinced that the UN was the most effective place for their revelation; he called Secretary Rusk, who was then at the White House, and got permission. It was a wise decision, for their impact was extraordinary. As Stevenson described the various photographs and explained when and where they had been taken, it was apparent he had carried the day. He had been entirely successful in shifting UN—and world—attention away from the Russian defense that the Soviet Union and Cuba were entirely within their rights, to the American contention that the two countries had caused a fearful danger to world peace. It was, in the mind of many Americans, even many who had never admired Stevenson, his finest hour. He had finally demonstrated that he was not "soft" on Communism by hitting it harder and more dramatically than it had ever been hit before.

But there were some of us who, while recognizing the effectiveness of Stevenson's presentation, felt he had gone a bit too far, that in his personal attack on Zorin he had departed from the diplomatic usage in which he himself placed such store and that, more important, he had backed Zorin and the Soviet Union into a corner, making it difficult for Russia to change its position. And although his mail proclaimed him to be the latest American hero, Stevenson himself had reservations about having played the prosecuting attorney. Perhaps the vehemence of his attack on Zorin explained the bitterness with which he was personally attacked by the Russians on one or two occasions in later months.

Yet, effective as Stevenson had been, the real decisions could be made only in Washington and in the Kremlin, far from the glare of publicity. As we saw, Khrushchev in his first reply to Thant had begun to reconsider his position. This became clearer with his second reply and, more importantly, with his private message to Kennedy. On Friday, a long message from Khrushchev to Kennedy came by cable. In brief, it said, with something approaching passion, that the two leaders must stop the drift toward nuclear war, and that if Kennedy would give assurances that the United States would not invade Cuba or allow anyone else to do so, something could be worked out. At the same time Zorin, who must have been fearfully embarrassed every time he faced U Thant, made a similar approach to the Secretary General. And the Cubans at the UN were saying that if their territorial integrity were assured by the United States, the missiles wouldn't be needed anymore. The crisis was clearly subsiding, although an anxious world did not yet realize it. Indeed, because of confusion over a second Khrushchev letter that seemed to supersede the reasonableness of the first, Washington thought for a moment that Russia was preparing for nuclear war and that the situation was worse than ever. However, somehow—evidently the Kremlin bureaucracy was as capable of incredible bloopers as Washington's—the sequence of the two letters had gotten reversed. Fortunately, Robert Kennedy had a simple solution, although at the time it seemed audacious. Why not reply to the reasonable letter and ignore the other? That the President did, telling Khrushchev that if Russia "would agree to remove these weapons systems from Cuba under appropriate United Nations supervision and undertake with suitable safeguards, to halt the further introduction of such weapons systems into Cuba . . . we, on our part, would agree—upon the establishment of adequate arrangements through the United Nations, to insure the carrying out and continuation of these commitments—(a) to remove promptly the quarantine measures now in effect and (b) to give assurances against an invasion of Cuba. I am confident that other nations of the Western Hemisphere would be prepared to do likewise."

Then, foreshadowing his American University speech of a few months later, in which he moved toward an accommodation with Russia, Kennedy wrote:

"The effect of such a settlement on easing world tensions would enable us to work toward a more general arrangement regarding 'other armaments,' as proposed in your second letter, which you made public. I would like to say again that the United States is very much interested in reducing tensions and halting the arms race; and if your letter signifies that you are prepared to discuss a detente affecting NATO and the Warsaw Pact, we are quite prepared to consider with our allies any useful proposals."

But it should be noted carefully here that it was not Kennedy who took the initiative toward the *detente* that began some months after the Cuban missile crisis and lasted until American escalation in Vietnam. Kennedy was responding to an initiative, as is clear from the context of his letter, made by Khrushchev in a Soviet note not made public.

Washington's anxiety over which letter truly represented the Soviet position lasted until Sunday morning, when Khrushchev's response to Kennedy's latest note arrived:

". . . the Soviet Government, in addition to earlier instructions on the discontinuance of further work on weapon construction sites, has given a new order to dismantle the arms you described as offensive, to crate and return them to the Soviet Union.

". . . The threat of invasion of Cuba and all other schemes for creating tension over Cuba are designed to strike the Cuban people with a sense of insecurity, to intimidate them, to prevent them from peacefully building their new life.

"Mr. President, I should like to say clearly once more that we could not remain indifferent to that and the Soviet Government decided to render assistance to Cuba with the means of defense against aggression, with means for the purposes of defense only. We have supplied the defense means which you describe as offensive means. We have supplied them to prevent an attack on Cuba, to prevent rash acts.

"I regard with respect and trust the statement you made in your message of October 27, 1962, that there would be no attack, no invasion of Cuba, neither on the part of the United States, nor on the part of other nations of the Western Hemisphere, as you stated in the same message. Then the motives which induced us to render assistance of such a kind to Cuba disappear."

Then Khrushchev repeated his willingness to have UN observation of the Russian removal of the missile equipment. With that the Cuban missile crisis was over, although it took some weeks for Stevenson at the UN to wrap up the loose ends. Despite a visit to Cuba by Thant, Castro refused to allow UN observer teams to enter the country, insisting it would be a violation of Cuba's sovereignty. However, by means of U-2 overflights and visual observation of Soviet vessels from nearby U.S. Navy ships, the United States was able to satisfy itself that the Soviet missile equipment and IL-28 bombers were removed from Cuba. And although the United States has remained hostile to Cuba—a hostility fully reciprocated—there has not been a hint of an invasion of that island by the United States directly or indirectly.

At that time and since, the withdrawal of the Soviet missiles has been widely regarded as an enormous triumph for Kennedy, a shining example of how the ungodly were defeated by the firm but measured application of American might. Once again the good (the United States) had overcome evil (the Soviet Union). However, when great powers are locked in a struggle, morality is seldom the attribute of just one side. Future historians, freed by the larger perspective of time from the national fervor of the moment, will not cast Khrushchev solely as the villainous Black Knight and Kennedy as the virtuous Knight in Shining Armor, but rather as two leaders of powerful antagonistic nations improvising policies that for a few fearsome days seemed to make inevitable what man has dreaded since that first atomic bomb exploded over Hiroshima in 1945. Both were victims of the inertial forces of the cold war. Both took unconscionable risks, and both were wrong. It was the ultimate game of "chicken," in which the USSR—whether out of fear or prudence—swerved aside first. And from all the accounts of those scary days, it seems perfectly clear that the Kennedy Administration had no real idea what it would have done had Khrushchev ignored the American ultimatum and Thant's appeal. Perhaps then America would have swerved aside or perhaps not, and if not, that might have been the end.

Now, at this writing, more than five years after those days when the worst seemed likely, perhaps some reassessment can be attempted. First, it seems incontrovertible that the Cuban missile crisis would never have arisen were it not for the Bay of Pigs.

Perhaps in time, historians will have access to Kremlin records or to the memoirs of high-ranking Russians of that time and know with certainty why the Soviet Union took the reckless gamble of putting long-range missiles in Cuba. True, it would be foolish to say that the Russians took this extraordinary step entirely out of a desire to aid the threatened Cubans. That would be as foolish as saying that the United States went to South Vietnam solely out of altruistic concern for the people of that unhappy half-country. Perhaps Khrushchev thought that the Bay of Pigs had completely tied America's hands as far as Cuba was concerned. Perhaps Russia thought that its missiles, so near the United States—just as American missiles were hard up against Russian frontiers—would help redress the nuclear balance. Perhaps it thought this would strengthen its hand in Latin America and profoundly embarrass the United States. Perhaps it thought this would give it a card of enormous value to play in the main game, NATO versus the Warsaw Pact. All these and still other considerations may be true, but one cannot exclude the very real possibility that at least one factor, even if not necessarily the controlling one, was a genuine desire to help beleaguered Cuba, which had entirely legitimate reasons to fear further American actions against it. To argue otherwise would be to say that our aid to Greece or Turkey or South Korea was based entirely on cold war considerations and not out of a genuine concern for those nations. However, even if, for the sake of argument, we agree that Russia's reason was entirely altruistic, it is hard to see what it hoped to gain. Although it could be argued that the United States and other anti-Castro governments would never attack a nuclear-armed Cuba, it is almost certain that any use of these missiles would have meant a full retaliatory attack on the Soviet Union itself, hardly what Russia was interested in promoting. In these circumstances, the Soviet Union would have learned what the U.S. had learned, that nuclear strength does not prevent conventional attacks anywhere but in areas absolutely critical to its national security. The Soviet Union should have realized that even if the United States were, directly or indirectly, to attack Cuba with conventional weapons, the Soviet Union would have been unable to use its Cuban missiles without beginning nuclear war.

Further, in reassessing the Cuban missile crisis, it must be recognized that there are those, not only abroad but in this country as well, who do not understand why the United States has the right to ring the Soviet Union and China with missiles bases, whereas they do not have the right to do likewise. Not to appreciate this would be to expect the rest of the world, increasingly skeptical of the United States, to accept the American belief that everyone knows the United States means no harm and can be trusted with nuclear weapons, whereas everyone knows that the Communists cannot be so trusted. Our virtue, in which many of us have a genuine belief, is not necessarily so obvious to others.

And despite the foolishness of the Russian act, we must recognize that Cuba as a sovereign nation had every right, moral and legal, to request such Soviet aid and that the Soviet Union had every right to offer it, just as we have had the legal and moral right to provide military aid to scores of countries when they have requested it. The question is not whether such aid is legal or moral but whether it is wise. Not to recognize this right is to insist on a double standard that favors the United States. We must further recognize that the American "quarantine" was but a blockade by another name and as such was an act of war to which the Soviet Union could have legitimately responded with the use of force. Although we can only be forever thankful that it did not, the Kennedy Administration was taking the enormous gamble that the Soviet Union would accept the fact that in the Caribbean the military odds were long indeed against them.

So what was at issue in the confrontation was not morality or legality, although we Americans always like to clothe the cold war in moral raiment, but, as has so often been the case in history, considerations of power. Indeed, if the issue were to be judged solely on moral and legal grounds, the United States could not await the judgment with confidence. The issue was simple. The Kennedy Administration decided that national interests were at stake and, like all governments, it adopted a moral stance. But what really concerned Kennedy was the balance of power, or perhaps Churchill's "balance of terror." The military balance would not have been changed all that much, for the United States' retaliatory capacity then, as now, was so great that there was little likelihood that the missiles in Cuba would ever have been used. Nonetheless, one can understand why any American Administration would be nervous about having such weapons so nearby, particularly under the possible control of what it regarded as an unstable dictator, Fidel Castro. Russia would certainly have attempted to remove the American missiles in Turkey if it had thought it could get away with it; the United States thought it could prevent the establishment of such missiles in Cuba if it acted promptly, and it was right.

The United States also feared, no doubt correctly, that its influence would wane rapidly and Castro's rise just as rapidly if Cuba could boast, as it eventually would, that it possessed missiles that could reach most of the Western Hemisphere. And domestic political considerations, particularly in an election year, made it unthinkable that any Administration would tolerate such missiles in Cuba. And there was also the fear, quite possibly justified, that if Khrushchev succeeded in so bold a ploy, he might become further emboldened to try something in Berlin, a constant preoccupation of successive American Administrations.

Thus, although it can be argued that logically it is no worse for the United States to live with missiles in Cuba than it is for Russia to live with missiles in Turkey, it was entirely unlikely, in view of American actions since the Second World War, that any Administration would tolerate Russian missiles there. Khrushchev should have known this, and to have acted the way he did, for whatever motive, was reckless and caused a real possibility of nuclear war, which was the last thing he or Kennedy wanted. But having said this, it also seems true that Kennedy could have achieved the removal of the missiles without taking the terrible risks he did, and this is no minor indictment. The naval blockade established the potential for an incident that could have triggered a series of events which, once having started, neither side could have stopped without an intolerable loss of face. And it must be recognized that the United States is as sensitive to loss of face as any oriental nation. Firm but judicious pressure carried on with diplomatic discretion could have achieved the same end, for the Soviet Union did not want a confrontation. Even if one insists that the Russians were the ungodly, they were fully aware that they had no compelling national interest at stake and, even more important, that they were at a tremendous disadvantage in the Caribbean, just as the United States, despite its legitimate outrage over the Russian brutality in Hungary in 1956, was at an impossible disadvantage and thus powerless to do anything to stop the cruel repression of the revolt.

But finally the Soviet Union did dismantle its missile bases; it did remove the missiles and bombers. This, of course, has been celebrated as a great American victory and a historic triumph for Kennedy, the great achievement of his Administration. This may be true, but it is also true that to get the Russian agreement to remove their missiles, Kennedy had to promise that the United States and other Latin American nations would not invade Cuba. Even if Khrushchev had other purposes for putting his missiles in Cuba, the protection of Cuba from invasion was surely also a reason. And in this he succeeded. The United States did make a major concession, one which it has observed up to this writing.

It has also been argued that Russia backed down—the term "chickened out" has often been used—because of fear of American might. This is the kind of oversimplification that has made the cold war so perilous. Obviously Russia was aware of America's strengths and weaknesses in the Caribbean. But that makes it no more "chicken" than the United States was in regard to Hungary. Russia simply faced the facts. It is only to be regretted that it did not face them sooner. But the United States also faced the facts. It knew that Russia, once having engaged its prestige in defense of Cuba, could not back down without a substantial concession from the United States, and it made that concession in the form of the no-invasion pledge.

This American victory thesis also ignores the important, perhaps vital, role played by the United Nations in the person of Secretary General U Thant. At the least, his appeal to Khrushchev and Kennedy that both nations take steps to avoid a physical confrontation in the Caribbean gave Khrushchev the opportunity to back away with relative grace. But it is arrogance to think that only America wants peace. Is it not also possible that Khrushchev —even if his definition might be somewhat different—responded genuinely to Thant's appeal? To foreclose such a possibility is to cast Russia, or any Communist nation, in the devil's role—as many Americans have, most with complete sincerity—and to condemn the world to a perpetual crusade against such nations. Indeed, most of our neighbors on this tiny planet increasingly view us as ideological crusaders, uncomfortable neighbors at best and dangerous at worst. But however one interprets Thant's role, he did provide a framework other than the toe-to-toe posture that often seems to force one nation to knock the chip off the other's shoulder. Thus, even if the ultimate decisions had to be reached in the Kremlin and the White House, Thant's intervention helped make those decisions easier. One can doubt that the United States ever fully appreciated his contribution.

Out of those dark October days there did come some light— the realization by both Khrushchev and Kennedy that they had come intolerably close to the brink and a determination to see that it did not happen again. Both nations reexamined the world and discovered, as Adlai Stevenson had been saying for a decade, that it would be in the interests of each to seek an accommodation, to take steps to end, or at least slow down, the dangerous arms race. So the months following the near collision over Cuba saw the pendulum swing away from war toward peace, culminating in the Moscow Treaty of August 1963, which banned the testing of nuclear weapons in space, the atmosphere and underwater. Although a ban on underground testing was not included because of disagreement over inspection (the other environments posed no detection problem), this was a major step, demonstrating what the two superpowers could achieve when they recognized their common interest in peace. It was, of course, a great satisfaction for Stevenson, who had taken the first step in this direction in the 1956 campaign, only to be accused by Richard Nixon of something approaching treason. This test ban treaty was indeed a great achievement for Kennedy—and for Khrushchev as well.

Although the worst was over by the end of October, Adlai Stevenson had not finished with the missile crisis, nor had it finished with him. For weeks Stevenson visited U Thant's office almost every day, trying to tie up the loose ends of the crisis, but before he had, he was subjected to a cruel and unfair attack for his role in the Washington discussions in October, when the Administration was frantically trying to find the right way to get the missiles out of Cuba. Stevenson first heard about it from Arthur Schlesinger.

"On December 1, 1962, the President called me over to his office and said, 'You know that Charlie Bartlett and Stewart Alsop have been writing a piece on Cuba for the *Saturday Evening Post*. I understand that Chalmers Roberts is planning to do a story on the Alsop-Bartlett piece for *The Washington Post* and that he is going to present it as an attack on Adlai Stevenson. You had better warn Adlai that it is coming.' I asked what the article said. The President replied that he understood that it accused Stevenson of advocating a Caribbean Munich. He said, 'Everyone will suppose that it came out of the White House because of Charlie. Will you tell Adlai that I never talked to Charlie or any other reporter on the Cuban crisis, and that this piece does not represent my views.' " [18]

The President's message was not enough to allay Stevenson's concern, nor could it have been, because the *Saturday Evening Post* story became a sensation, not only at the UN and in Washington but all over the country. Kennedy was right in assuming that everyone would think the story came from the White House, and the assumption was that despite Stevenson's brilliant presentation of the United States' case in the missile crisis, Kennedy wanted him out. And the press, which trumpeted the story on the front pages for days, lost no time in pointing out that it was a piece by Bartlett, one of Kennedy's closest friends, that had given the first indication that Chester Bowles was on his way out as Under Secretary of State.

Before the magazine reached the newsstands, reprints of the piece were sent to news organizations, together with a press release pointing out the sensational fact that Stevenson reportedly had advocated a Caribbean Munich. The headlines on the story and the pictures accompanying it, including a huge one of an agonized Stevenson, focused on him, but actually only a short section of the piece was devoted to Stevenson, and it was two-thirds of the way down. Although the stir was as great as it was because of the way the *Post* exploited what was only a minor part of the story, the fact remains that the authors did say Stevenson alone "dissented from the Executive Committee consensus," that he wanted "a Munich" and was for trading Guantanamo and "the Turkish,

Italian and British missile bases for the Cuban bases," and would have settled for "the neutralization of the Cuban missiles" rather than their removal.

Clearly someone around the President, although there is no reason to suspect that Kennedy himself had anything to do with it, was out to get Stevenson. It is still impossible to know fully what went on in those chaotic ExCom sessions, but certain facts are clear. In an attempt to reach a consensus, many members argued all sides of the case. Stevenson certainly was not the only one to consider throwing the Turkish and Italian missiles into a deal (the British bases were evidently never mentioned), for among other reasons, they were obsolete and had been forced on those unwilling nations by the Eisenhower Administration. Stevenson, who was more sensitive to world opinion than most American political leaders and, correctly, more responsive to it, recognized that to the rest of the world our protest about Russian missiles in Cuba would sound pretty hollow with American missiles right next door to Russia in Turkey and in a number of other nearby countries as well.

However, in the constantly shifting discussion with "doves" sounding like "hawks" one minute and "hawks" sounding like "doves" the next (it was here that these words became a part of our everyday language), Stevenson first talked of a package deal in response to the earlier support in the ExCom for an air strike, the possibility of which frightened him, as well it might. Although the military (they always want to bomb first and think later) and some of Kennedy's civilian advisers were for an air strike, that would have inevitably triggered a chain of events that most probably would have ended in nuclear war. To Stevenson, anything was preferable to that. But by the end of the week, when sentiment had shifted away from an air strike to a blockade, Stevenson wholeheartedly supported the consensus. Indeed, as Dean Rusk told me, "The mix that turned out had a good Stevenson input in it. It was a place where his influence was significant. We were all doves and hawks trying to find an alternative to force." [19] Incidentally, one of the foremost hawks then, as high Johnson Administration officials point out with considerable ironic satisfaction, was J. William Fulbright, later the dove of doves on Vietnam.

But once the ExCom had decided on the blockade—and Stevenson contributed to this decision—he did offer his thoughts on the political negotiations that must inevitably follow. Theodore Sorensen, Kennedy's intimate aid, was at those ExCom sessions and has recorded what Stevenson said. Although he does not identify him, it is unmistakable from the context that it is Stevenson.

"On Saturday and earlier, the author [Stevenson] . . . fully endorsed the blockade route, although casting doubt on any unilateral action we took without OAS approval. He wanted this military action accompanied, however, by suggested diplomatic actions which the President found wholly unacceptable. He wanted the President to propose the demilitarization, neutralization and guaranteed territorial integrity of Cuba, thus giving up Guantanamo, which he said was of little use to us, in exchange for the removal of all Soviet missiles on Cuba. Alternatively or subsequently, he said, we could offer to withdraw our Turkish and Italian Jupiter missile bases if the Russians would withdraw their Cuban missile bases, and send UN inspection teams to all the foreign bases maintained by both sides to prevent their use in a surprise attack. He also talked of a UN-supervised standstill of military activity on both sides—thus leaving the missiles in with no blockade—and of a summit meeting, and of UN inspection teams investigating not only Cuba but possible U.S. bases for attacking Cuba. The offer of such a political program, he would later write in a follow-up memo, would avoid comparisons with the Suez invasion. The offer would not sound 'soft' properly worded, he declared. It would sound 'wise,' particularly when combined with U.S. military action.

"There was not a hint of 'appeasing the aggressor' in these plans, as some would charge, only an effort to propose a negotiating position preferable to war and acceptable to the world. Even the synopsis prepared by the air strike 'hardliners' earlier in the week had included not only a call for a summit but a pledge that the United States was prepared to withdraw all nuclear forces based in Turkey, including aircraft as well as missiles. The Joint Congressional Committee on Atomic Energy had also recommended the Jupiters' withdrawal the previous year." [20]

Before Stevenson could explain what timing he had in mind for this program, the hard-liners leaped at him scornfully in a bitter attack that implied he was not man enough for this real world. From all accounts, the attack was personally insulting. No doubt the physical exhaustion and the extreme tension contributed to this, but these were men who had long disliked Stevenson. One of them was reported to have said, "Adlai's not soft on Communism; he's just soft." But Stevenson stuck to his guns, and after the long, tense meeting was over, Kennedy said, "You have to admire Adlai. He sticks to his position even when everyone is jumping on him." However, Kennedy decided that any specific political program was premature, that the United States should concentrate entirely on putting the blame on the Soviet Union and insisting that they remove the missiles. Yet at the same time, according to Sorensen, Kennedy agreed that "we should beef up the political side of the speech."

Examining Stevenson's suggestions, one cannot see anything that smacks of appeasement, only reasonable accommodation. And certainly the President was entitled to expect his advisers to suggest anything that might help. To have done otherwise because he did not want to be accused of being "soft" would have been an act of cowardice on Stevenson's part. True, he would have been more conciliatory than many of Kennedy's advisers, but that was to his credit. His course would also have gotten the missiles out of Cuba and with much less risk of nuclear war, and it would have taken a giant step toward a *detente*. Further, his concessions would have in no way damaged American interests. The Turkish missiles were quietly dismantled in 1963; Guantanamo, although it is in fact an embarrassment, has been kept largely to save face. The United States has no right to maintain a base where it is not wanted and where it can hardly be considered secure.

Kennedy, of course, knew all this, and Stevenson was distressed that he did not offer a more effective defense of Stevenson's role during the crisis. Pierre Salinger issued a statement, approved by Stevenson, expressing the President's full confidence in Stevenson and adding that nothing said during the Executive Committee meeting would be made public. The reporters found this unsatisfactory, pointing out that the Bartlett-Alsop allegations had not been refuted. And citing Bartlett's intimate relationship with Kennedy, they argued that he wouldn't have taken that tack unless he were confident he was saying what the President wanted him to say. Stevenson was convinced by some of his journalist friends that this was so, and he told Schlesinger that if Kennedy wanted to get rid of him, he didn't have to do it in such a roundabout way; all he would have to do was to say so.

Schlesinger decided that he had to go directly to the President.

" 'Mr. President, everyone in town thinks that the Bartlett article is a signal from the White House that you want to get rid of Stevenson. You know that if you really want Stevenson's resignation, you have only to say the word now and he will resign immediately without any fuss or controversy.' The President, swearing briefly, said, 'Of course, I don't want Stevenson to resign. I would regard his resignation as a disaster. Look at it logically. What in the world would I have to gain from his resignation? In the first place, where could I possibly find anyone who could do half as good a job at the UN? Look at the alternatives—Adlai would do a far better job than any of the others. In the second place, from a realistic political standpoint, it is better for me to have Adlai in the government than out. In the third place, if I were trying to get him out, Charlie Bartlett is a good friend, but he's the last medium I would use.' " [21]

Schlesinger met Stevenson that night at Averell Harriman's home and told him what the President had said. But Stevenson, who seemed profoundly depressed, said, "That's fine, but will he say it publicly?" Later that night, Stevenson and Clayton Fritchey, his confidant and press aide, took the overnight train back to New York, only to be greeted there by a headline in the tabloid *Daily News:* "ADLAI ON SKIDS OVER PACIFIST STAND."

First thing next morning, Fritchey telephoned Schlesinger and told him that Stevenson's morale was lower than ever. At the UN, where, of course, the story was an absolute sensation, the universal feeling was that the hawks had brought down the dove. Schlesinger went back to the President, who said, "I'm not impressed by the *Daily News.* They spend all their time attacking us. This goes on all the time. Just tell Adlai to sit tight, and everything will subside.

This is one of those forty-eight-hour wonders. Tell them about all those fights in the New Deal. Just get them to relax."

But the story had really caught on and showed no signs of subsiding. Now the Stevenson forces began to counterattack in defense of their man. And Stevenson, who had characterized the story as "inaccurate and grossly misrepresenting my views" and called the authors "irresponsible," was becoming the object of sympathy. All this threatened to become a political embarrassment to the President. Furthermore, after a trip to New York, Harlan Cleveland reported that Stevenson's effectiveness at the UN was in jeopardy and needed public support from the President. Kennedy had written a personal letter to Stevenson which he had asked Schlesinger to deliver and which referred to the problems of having a newspaperman as a friend. But now the President decided that the letter should be made public, and the references to Bartlett were dropped. In a phone conversation with Schlesinger and Fritchey, Kennedy strengthened the letter, terming of "inestimable" national importance Stevenson's work at the UN. After that the story dwindled away, although it was revived briefly a few weeks later, when a reporter asked U Thant at a press conference what he thought of Stevenson. Thant could have ducked the question by saying legitimately that he did not want to comment on the domestic political affairs of a member nation, but he didn't. He spoke in the fullest possible praise of Stevenson as a man and as representative of his country. The controversy, so blazing an affair then, has had little lasting significance other than to have dubbed Stevenson as the original dove, not a bad image to carry through history. But as the Stevenson story was to end, it might have been better for him and for the nation had he resigned then.

# ~~ II ~~

## *The Congo*

E VEN though Cuba was the dominant crisis in Adlai Stevenson's first two years at the UN, it was by no means the only one. Indeed, during his four and a half years there, Stevenson was continuously juggling several crises at a time, any one of which would have been sufficient to tax an experienced diplomat. He was engaged in almost constant negotiations on the frequent flare-ups along the Arab-Israeli frontiers, the continuing bitter dispute between India and Pakistan over Kashmir, the conflict between the Greek and Turkish communities on Cyprus, anti-American riots in Panama over the Canal agreement, the persistent wrangle with Portugal over its diehard control of its African colonies, the Dutch-Indonesian dispute over West New Guinea, colonial questions in Africa and the Middle East, white racism in Southern Rhodesia and South Africa, and disarmament. But demanding as they were of thought and energy, none of these plagued him and the United Nations as much as the Congo. From the day he presented his credentials to Secretary General Dag Hammarskjold on January 23, 1961, until Stevenson's death on July 14, 1965, the Congo and its effect on the United Nations were a constant preoccupation. The UN may have succeeded in saving the Congo, but it almost died in the attempt.

The United Nations had gone into the Congo at the request of its first premier, Patrice Lumumba, when, just days after its independence from Belgium on June 30, 1960, the infant state collapsed into utter chaos. But although the dispatch of UN troops

70

—contributed by a number of UN member states other than great powers—prevented further deterioration of the situation, there was at first little improvement. Although the difficulties during the first months would demand at least a book to sort out—and to do it might be beyond the ingenuity of man—there were disputes between Hammarskjold and Lumumba, the latter wanting UN forces used directly to end the secession of mineral-rich Katanga Province; between the UN and Britain, France and Belgium, which tried to limit the UN's intervention, clearly because they did not want to lose their grip on the Congo's vast mineral resources; and between the UN and the Soviet Union, which both supported the more radical policies of Lumumba and saw a chance to gain a foothold in the heart of Africa. In all this, the United States played a rather equivocal role, supporting Hammarskjold against Russia, yet at the same time advocating a go-slow policy for the UN. Although philosophically the United States was committed—or at least said it was committed—to independence in Africa, in practice, the State Department generally supported the colonial powers: Britain, France, Belgium and Portugal.

Although Lumumba, whom I had met in the Congo shortly before independence, was indeed volatile and totally ill-prepared to lead his nation, there was no one else more qualified. Belgium had long carried out the cynical policy of training Africans to work in the mines, even at a fairly high level, but it had never permitted any African to learn about government. If Lumumba were ill-trained and perhaps psychologically ill-equipped, he was the only man who had attempted to establish himself as a national rather than a tribal leader. He was, however, entirely distrusted by Britain, France, Belgium and the United States, which were looking for someone more "realistic," which means, of course, someone who would not upset Western domination of the Congo's mineral riches. After not getting the help he expected—no doubt unrealistically—from the United States and the UN, Lumumba turned to the Russians, who were only too happy to help. This disturbed Joseph Kasavubu, leader of the tribe dominating the area around Léopoldville, who had become the Congo's first president. Shrewd but unimaginative, Kasavubu dismissed Lumumba as premier, and Lumumba dismissed Kasavubu as president. In the resulting confusion, the army, headed by Colonel Joseph

Mobutu, took over the country, or at least those parts of it where there was even tenuous central government control. It must be understood, although the degree of chaos may be beyond comprehension, that the Congo, a country the size of the United States east of the Mississippi, was entirely fragmented. It existed as a country only on the map, and Belgium, during its decades of exploitation, had never made any serious attempt to unify it. There were dozens of rival tribal leaders contesting for authority; the country was perpetually on the edge, or just over it, of civil and tribal war. The UN itself didn't know what to do about it, enduring continual internal struggle on what its policy ought to be. The Soviet Union, Britain, France, and particularly Belgium were all intervening for their own purposes, and the United States couldn't make up its mind, either. No leader, not even a Solomon, could have been effective, although Lumumba, tried, however ineptly and irrationally.

At any rate, by the time Adlai Stevenson had taken his post at the UN, Lumumba had somehow fallen into the hands of his brutal archenemy, Moise Tshombe, who as leader of the secession in Katanga was the most divisive force in the Congo. Lumumba had been under house arrest, with UN troops guarding the house. In November 1960 he vanished. Some say he fled, others that he was spirited away. Whatever the case may be, a few days later, on December 1, he showed up in the hands of troops of the Central Congolese government. Then somehow, even though Tshombe's secessionist regime in Katanga was the mortal foe of the Central government, Lumumba was handed over to Tshombe.

It was at this point that Adlai Stevenson made his first appearance at the Security Council, which had met to hear charges of brutal treatment of Lumumba and two of his aides. An angry, vituperative series of meetings lasted from February 1 to February 21, reaching a climax on February 12, when Dag Hammarskjold announced the death in Katanga Province of Lumumba and two of his supporters, Maurice Mpolo and Joseph Okito. On February 14, Russian Ambassador Valerian Zorin, who had been attacking Hammarskjold for months, dropped a diplomatic bombshell:

"Dag Hammarskjold must be dismissed from the office of Secretary General as an accomplice and organizer of the murder of the leading statesmen of the Congo Republic, who has stained the name of the United Nations. For its part, the Soviet government will not maintain any relations with Hammarskjold and will not recognize him as an official of the United Nations."

This was indeed an extraordinary occasion; the second most powerful nation in the UN demanding that its Secretary General be fired and accusing him of being an accomplice to murder. The Soviet Union also called for an end to the UN military operations in the Congo. And the Soviet Union introduced its concept of the *troika* (a Russian vehicle drawn by three horses abreast), in which the office of the Secretary General would be filled by three men: one representing the Western bloc, another the Communist, and the third the nonaligned nations.[1] It's hard to know what the Russians hoped to accomplish. Obviously they were furious that the UN under Hammarskjold had helped keep the Russians out of the Congo, where Kasavubu had closed the Communist missions and dismissed from the country all Communist nationals, relying entirely on the UN. But a three-headed UN Secretariat simply would not have worked, and they must have known it. Perhaps it was sheer spite, born out of the frustration caused by the continued Western domination of the UN. But we must also recognize the possibility that there was a genuine belief that the UN, in helping shunt Lumumba aside, was not working in the best interest of the Congo.

On February 15, in one of the great dramatic moments in UN history, Dag Hammarskjold told the Soviet Union that he could not resign unless the small, nonaligned nations of the UN asked him to. But although they were not unanimously in support of his Congo policy, the small nations were convinced of Hammarskjold's devotion to the UN. Furthermore, they realized that an independent UN was the only one that would work in their behalf. And on February 15, Stevenson made his first major speech, one in which he defended Hammarskjold:

"I pass lightly over the Soviet government's petulant attack on Secretary General Dag Hammarskjold and his great office. He needs no defense from me, nor does the institution. His record is an open book, a book which all peace-loving peoples recognize as the record of a dedicated international civil servant whose only loyalty is to international justice and international peace. Let the Soviet government, if it wishes, pretend that he does not exist; it will find he is far from a disembodied ghost; and it will find that peace-loving states will continue to support his patient search for the right road to security and peace in the Congo and for all peoples. The United Nations may have made mistakes in the Congo—as who has not?—but nothing justifies an intemperate and unjustifiable attack on the integrity of the office of the Secretary General." [2]

Turning to the Soviet statement that it was "ready to render all possible assistance and support" to the Lumumba followers who had proclaimed a Congolese government in Stanleyville, capital of Orientale Province, Stevenson declared:

"The injunction of the General Assembly resolution adopted with the support of all members of the United Nations, except the Soviet bloc, against any unilateral military aid whatever, whether direct or indirect, should be adhered to fully by all United Nations members. This applies to those Belgians who are providing military advice and assistance to the Congo. It applies equally against military assistance to the forces in Orientale.

"The United States, for its part, does not intend to sit by if others consciously and deliberately seek to exacerbate the present situation. We are prepared to use all of our influence, if other members of the United Nations do likewise, to prevent such assistance from coming to the Congo, no matter from what quarter it comes."

Finally, Stevenson examined the Soviet proposal that the UN end its intervention in the Congo.

"What does this mean? It means, my colleagues, not only the abandonment of the Congo to chaos and civil war—to, if you please, the cold war—it means abandonment of the principle of the United Nations itself.

"... Do we want to withdraw the only elements that stand foursquare against civil and tribal war? Does the Soviet government really want Africans to kill Africans? The United States does not, and it devoutly hopes that the Soviet government does not, too, and that it will join the United States and other peace-loving states in supporting and strengthening the only force that can prevent Congolese civil war—the United Nations.

"... we declare that, so far as we are concerned, Africa shall never be the scene of any war, cold or hot. But we also declare that Africa for the Africans *means* Africa for the Africans, and not Africa as a hunting ground for alien ambitions. And we pledge our full and unstinted support against any attempt by anyone to interfere with the full and free development by Africans of their independent African future.

"We believe that the only way to keep the cold war *out* of the Congo is to keep the United Nations *in* the Congo, and we call on the Soviet Union to join us in thus ensuring the free and untrammeled exercise by the Congolese people of their right to independence and to democracy."

There was an interesting sidelight to the Stevenson speech, although perhaps it was more than a sidelight. While he was praising Dag Hammarskjold, his speech was interrupted by screams from the public gallery, and seconds later there was a brief outbreak of violence, the worst inside the UN to this writing. It was a shocking scene: the solemn decorum of a Security Council meeting shattered by screams and then by scuffling in the gallery between spectators and UN guards. It was all over in a matter of minutes, but this is what apparently happened. In the gallery were about fifty black nationalists from Harlem and a few Africans, among them singer Abby Lincoln, wife of the leading jazz drummer, Max Roach; Vouse Make, deputy vice-president of the Pan African Congress of South Africa; and Daniel Watts, the Columbia University-trained architect who became editor-publisher of the *Liberator*, an influential voice of the militant Negro intellectuals.

While Stevenson was defending Hammarskjold, the nationalists stood up, the women wearing black veils and the men black armbands. When they stood, the guards rushed over to them, presumably to ask them to resume their seats. But when the guards approached, a few of the women screamed, and the men, thinking perhaps that the women had been attacked, started grappling with the guards. Within a couple of minutes, reinforcements had arrived and the black nationalists were hustled outside. This outbreak, incidentally, led to the UN guards being authorized to carry black-jacks. As soon as the disturbance ended, Stevenson, obviously shaken by this unprecedented outburst, resumed his speech.

Daniel Watts later explained to me how the incident, which some at the time called Communist-inspired,[3] came about. It seems unlikely, however, that Watts, one of the organizers, was follow-ing a Communist line, for he is as deeply skeptical of Russian policy as he is of American. Watts explained that a group of mili-tants—this was in 1961, when militancy was still relatively new—hung around together at the Michauz Book Store in Harlem. They supported Patrice Lumumba as a symbol of African freedom from white domination, and in December of 1960 and January and February of 1961, they followed developments closely. As Watts put it, "Each day, rumors in the white press built up tension among the nationalists in Harlem: he's captured, he's escaped, he's beaten in Katanga, he's dead." Then when Dag Hammarskjold announced that Lumumba had been murdered, they decided to go to the UN. "We planned to stage a silent, standing protest against the murder of Patrice Lumumba." Watts said that the demonstration was not directed against Stevenson or the United States, but against Ham-marskjold. They believed that the UN should have prevented both Lumumba's arrest and his murder. But according to Watts, when Stevenson began to speak so persuasively in defense of Hammar-skjold, the nationalists stood up spontaneously. "Stevenson turned them on."

At the time, the demonstration seemed no more than an isolated incident in which the black nationalists were trying to "equate the struggle of the Negro for freedom and equality in the United States with the struggle for liberation in Africa." This is a phase long since past, as the Negro Americans became deeply disillusioned with the Africans who sought—and got—political and financial help from Negro Americans but who were unwilling to reciprocate when the Negroes asked help from them. The Africans were most reluctant to jeopardize their relations with the United States, a major provider of foreign aid, to help the Negro Americans, who, according to Watts, were regarded by many Africans as being inferior not only to Africans but to white Americans as well. But all this aside, Watts is convinced that the spontaneous demonstration in the Security Council gallery marked the beginning of the departure of Negro militants from passive, peaceful, largely legalistic protests. He regards it as the turning point.

Stevenson's speech was a good summary of America's policy toward the Congo and Africa as it developed in the Kennedy Administration, which, of course, had to pick up where the Eisenhower Administration left off. It is possible, although by no means certain, that if the UN and the Eisenhower Administration had given more support to Lumumba, the Congo situation, although still dreadful, might not have deteriorated into sheer chaos. In any case, supporting Lumumba was worth a try, but the State Department prefers to deal with gentlemen, and if there are none available, they try to find the next best thing. Lumumba was no gentleman—he had even been in prison for theft—and he didn't much care whether he got aid from the United States or from Russia, proof positive that he was no gentleman. And Lumumba alienated Hammarskjold by asking the UN to do precisely what it eventually had to do—to use force to end the secession of Katanga. Moreover, he was not solicitous of the British, French and especially Belgian financiers. On top of this, he was the object of tribal enmity from dozens of powerful Congolese. So it was hardly surprising that Lumumba did not survive.

All this was of academic interest by the time Kennedy took office, but the situation was so desperate that he had to develop a Congo policy—fast. The State Department was, as usual, preoccupied with NATO and did not want to do anything that would disturb the British, French and Belgians, who were doing everything they could to hamper the UN in the Congo. But Kennedy, who had enraged the State Department some years before by advocating independence for Algeria while France was still attempting to hold onto its North African colony, wanted a policy more adventurous than merely backing the *status quo*. He recognized, even though much of the State Department didn't, that vast and rapid changes were taking place in Africa and that American policy had to keep pace. Although Stevenson was not nearly as

NATO oriented as most of the State Department and had a great sympathy for the peoples of the developing nations, he did not get deeply involved in the Congo question. Of course, he vigorously supported the recommendation of the U.S. Mission that the United States back UN intervention, and he carried out superbly his role as American spokesman, but he seemed more interested in the effects of the Congo crisis on the UN than in the crisis itself.

From the beginning, Kennedy sensed that if the UN intervention did not succeed in filling the postcolonial vacuum in the Congo, there would be a Russian-American confrontation there. This view was shared by G. Mennen Williams, the former Governor of Michigan who became, by sheer determination and by sympathy for the Africans, a first-rate Assistant Secretary of State for Africa, and by his deputy, the extremely competent Wayne Fredericks. Fredericks, in particular, believed that the UN could be successful in the Congo only if the Congo were reunified and argued, against the stand of the pro-European group dominating the State Department, that Katanga's secession could be ended only if the United States vigorously supported the UN.

Kennedy undoubtedly would have come to this conclusion ultimately, but a little-known incident helped. Edmond Gullion, who had hit if off well with Kennedy twenty years before, when both were very young and new to Washington, had risen through the ranks of the Foreign Service and was the new Ambassador to the Congo. He, too, felt strongly that the United States should help end Katanga's secession and wanted to make his case directly with Kennedy. He visited Clayton Fritchey, Stevenson's confidential aide, and slept on the floor of his apartment. During this trip he called Kennedy's sister Patricia, whom he had dated before she married actor Peter Lawford. He asked her if she could get him in to see Kennedy. She agreed, and the appointment was arranged. It was a fairly daring maneuver for a career Foreign Service officer to go over the head of the State Department. Kennedy welcomed Gullion's views, and they reestablished a personal rapport that permitted Gullion to have great influence throughout his stint as Ambassador to the Congo.

During 1961 the Congo crisis lurched from one disaster to another, and often it seemed as if there were no earthly means of preventing the complete disintegration of a nation that had been born in fragments. In September there was sporadic fighting in and around Elisabethville, the capital of Katanga, between UN forces and white mercenaries hired by Tshombe with money from the Union Minière de Haut Katanga, the fabulously rich, Belgian-owned mining concern. When the fighting grew heavy, Secretary General Hammarskjold, who was in Léopoldville at the request of the Congo's new premier, Cyrille Adoula, cabled this message to Tshombe:

"I suggest that I should meet you personally so that together we can try to find peaceful methods of resolving the present conflict, thus opening a way to a solution of the Katanga problem within the framework of the Congo." [4]

Tshombe accepted, and they agreed to meet on neutral soil— Ndola, Northern Rhodesia—the next day, September 18, 1961. But the meeting never took place. The UN airplane carrying Dag Hammarskjold crashed, killing all aboard. This threw the Congo crisis into another phase, affecting not only the Congo but the UN itself, for the Soviet Union took this chance to revive its proposal for a *troika*. This was, of course, a major threat to the independence of the Secretariat, for any action would require the consent of all three Secretaries General. Adlai Stevenson, who had been instrumental in the London Preparatory Commission in establishing the structure of the UN, devoted countless hours of negotiation to turning back this Soviet threat to the UN. Mostly he concentrated on the nonaligned nations, patiently trying to convince them that it was in their interest that the UN Secretariat preserve its independence, for the great powers could take care of themselves, whereas the less powerful nations had strength only through the UN. Most of the nonaligned nations recognized this even without persuasion, for their dedication to the UN—by necessity and usually by conviction—is greater than that of the great powers. But it was not easy for them to oppose the giant Soviet Union. Finally, however, after weeks of negotiation that completely dominated the first half of the General Assembly convened just the day after Hammarskjold's death, acting upon the unanimous recommendation of the Security Council, the assembly elected U Thant as Acting Secretary General. Thant, the quiet, thoughtful, able and well-respected ambassador from Burma, thus began a tenure of office that has seen one major crisis after another. But he has maintained the independence of his office, often to the dismay of the United States and the Soviet Union and many other states, large and small, as well. Stevenson played no little part in his selection and in rallying support to sidetrack, perhaps permanently, the Soviet *troika*.

Thant immediately had to turn his attention to the situation in the Congo. Again there was heavy fighting between UN forces and the mercenary-led Katangese gendarmes, and Thant instructed the UN force to take whatever action was necessary to ensure the freedom of movement of UN personnel and the restoration of law and order in Elisabethville. But even while the situation in the Congo defied solution, the UN was beginning to face a situation that would, for a few anxious months, threaten its very life and pose a dilemma that was to be a constant concern of Stevenson until his death.

In March of 1961, the Soviet Union and France had both announced that they would not pay their assessments for the UN force in the Congo, and both advanced somewhat similar arguments: that only the Security Council had the authority to levy assessments for peace-keeping forces. It was not an inconsistent argument for the Soviet Union, for Gromyko and Stevenson had often clashed on this point during the 1945 London conference. The Soviet Union, knowing that it could always be outvoted in the General Assembly, where it could muster only about 10 votes to 40 from the West and Latin America, had always argued that the strength of the UN should be concentrated in the Security Council, where it could veto any acts it did not like. And France, which had never forgotten the continual General Assembly attacks on it during Algeria's fight for independence, was also reluctant to see too much power concentrated in the assembly.

At the time, these statements did not seem so serious, but as the Congo crisis staggered from one calamity to another and the UN force mushroomed in size to about 20,000 men, the expense became prohibitive, even though the United States was paying about half the cost. By January 10, 1962, only two months after he had taken office, Thant had to ask the membership to subscribe to a $200 million bond issue to meet the past and future costs of

Ambassador Adlai E. Stevenson.
*United Nations*

On January 23, 1961, Adlai E. Stevenson, the new Permanent Representative of the United States to the United Nations, presented his credentials to Secretary General Dag Hammarskjold.

*United Nations*

*United Nations*

While Stevenson was making his first major speech at the United Nations, during the Congo crisis of 1961, an angry demonstration of black nationalists and Africans erupted in the public gallery.

Stevenson addresses the Security Council during a tense moment in the Cuba missile crisis.

*United Nations*

During the Bay of Pigs, Stevenson presented photographs substantiating that the planes participating in dawn bombing raids on three Cuban airports bore the markings of the Cuban air force. Later he learned to his dismay that the photographs had been doctored by the CIA.

*United Press International Photo*

In August, 1963, Stevenson accompanied Secretary General U Thant to Moscow for the signing of the nuclear test-ban treaty that marked the fulfillment of one of Stevenson's oldest dreams.

*United Nations*

Back in New York, Stevenson joined U Thant, Dr. Nikolai Fedorenko, the Permanent Representative of the USSR (second from left), and Sir Patrick Dean, the Permanent Representative of the United Kingdom (right) in a brief ceremony as the test-ban treaty was registered with the United Nations.

*United Nations*

joying one of the pleasant aspects of
UN post, Stevenson welcomed Mrs.
queline Kennedy to the United Na-
s on February 7, 1963, where she
ended a private luncheon given by
ambassador in her honor.

*United Nations*

*United Nations*

Stevenson in conference with his longtime friend and special adviser, Mrs. Marietta P. Tree.

Throughout his ambassadorship, Stevenson enjoyed excellent relations with his large and talented staff at the U.S. Mission to the United Nations.

*United Nations*

*United Nations*

Despite President Johnson's optimistic remarks, the twentieth anniversary of the signing of the United Nations Charter, commemorated in San Francisco on June 25–26, 1965, was a melancholy occasion for a disillusioned Stevenson.

As world crisis followed crisis, Stevenson tried, at least temporarily, to forget the terrific pressures of his office in a ceaseless round of partying in the glittering world of New York society. Here he is pictured attending a dinner with Dame Margot Fonteyn.

*United Nations*

The United Nations flag at UN headquarters was lowered to half mast on July 14, 1965, in memory of Ambassador Adlai E. Stevenson, who died that morning in London.

*United Nations*

the UN operation. And a day later, in his State of the Union address, Kennedy urged Congress to authorize U.S. purchase of up to half of the bond issue on a matching basis, one dollar of American purchases for every dollar purchased by other countries. Clearly, the UN and the United States had collaborated on this proposal, and Kennedy thus demonstrated his determination to back the UN. On February 6, as the financial pinch grew tighter, Thant asked member states to pay their assessments to the regular budget and to the Congo and Middle East (established after the Suez crisis) peace-keeping forces.

The financial crisis, which was at heart a political one, reached another stage on July 20, 1962, when the International Court of Justice rendered an advisory opinion that expenses for the Congo and Middle East peace-keeping forces were "expenses of the organization" and "in conformity with the Charter" (Article 17, Paragraph 2).[5] The vote was 9 to 5, with the judges from the Soviet Union and France among the minority. This advisory opinion had been requested by the General Assembly on December 20, 1961. And with this decision that the peace-keeping assessments were mandatory, the United States hoped that the issue was closed. But the worst was yet to come.

In the Congo there continued to be clashes between UN forces and Katangese mercenaries, as Thant authorized increasingly tougher actions by the UN command. Then in August, U Thant visited the Soviet Union and made a truly extraordinary remark. Speaking over the Soviet radio, Thant told the Russian people that if they knew all the sides, they would "revise their opinion of the United Nations' involvement in the Congo and decide to shoulder their share of the responsibility." [6] This statement, which surely must be unprecedented, should be sufficient answer to those who believed Thant was prejudiced in his later critical statements of U.S. actions in Vietnam. Quiet though he is, Thant is an independent man who believes in speaking his mind and calling the shots as he sees them.

The focus continued to swing back and forth between the Congo and the UN. On September 20, 1962, two days after the opening of the seventeenth regular session, Adlai Stevenson addressed the General Assembly and urged the members, now 108, to "accept and act upon" the World Court opinion or otherwise "doom our organization to impotence." And on December 3, after being elected to a full term as Secretary General, Thant also appealed to the assembly to respect the World Court opinion that the Congo and the Middle East peace-keeping assessments were mandatory. But the Soviet Union that day and France the next refused to pay. On December 19, by the overwhelming vote of 76 in favor, 17 against, and 8 abstentions, the assembly accepted the World Court opinion. Now the General Assembly itself was asserting that peace-keeping assessments must be paid. And the assembly established a twenty-one-nation working group to study the question. It was to examine special methods to finance future peace-keeping operations and to look into the situation caused by the failure of some nations to fulfill their peace-keeping obligations. The committee was to recommend to a special session of the assembly arrangements within the spirit and letter of the Charter to bring such payments up to date. The assembly wanted to find some way to convince Russia and France and a dozen or so other countries to pay their peace-keeping assessments before they became subject to Charter provisions depriving them of their vote in the assembly.

Again the focus swung to the Congo, where the crisis was approaching still another climax, but this turned out to be the ultimate one. In early December, at UN request, the United States airlifted UN personnel and equipment to Katanga. The Katangese forces were in retreat, and the head of the UN operation informed Tshombe on December 10 that the UN would take steps to implement Thant's Plan of National Reconciliation and would use arms "wherever and whenever it might be attacked." [7] Tightening the vise, Thant announced on December 13 that he was asking Britain, Belgium, Portugal and South Africa to halt imports of copper and cobalt from Katanga. On December 18 the United States agreed to supply military equipment for the UN force, and from December 21 through the 26th, a U.S. military team visited the Congo "to find out what United States aid might be effective for the United Nations troops." [8] Then suddenly, events in Katanga took on a momentum all their own and swept out of control. And although Thant continued to insist that he was not using UN troops to force a solution, the UN troops found themselves in pitched battles with Katangese mercenaries and gendarmes.

By December 29, Tshombe had fled to Southern Rhodesia, and the next day the UN occupied Elisabethville. Britain and Belgium asked the UN to stop military operations without delay, but by then it was virtually all over. On January 9, 1963, Tshombe flew back to Elisabethville, telling a press conference that his men had placed explosives under the dam and power station at Kolwezi, the last stronghold under his control. The UN replied by saying it must enter Kolwezi. Tshombe fled house arrest for Ndola, where he chartered a plane for Kolwezi to make his last stand. But the UN refused to be bluffed and on January 14 entered Kolwezi. The explosives were not set off; Tshombe capitulated and asked for amnesty. However, it was not the end of the story for this extraordinary man. Months later, in July 1964, he was to return in triumph to the Congo as prime minister, not of Katanga Province but of the entire country he had once almost split into tiny pieces. Tshombe's triumph was, however, short-lived, and he again sought exile, a rich man. All of the names that were so familiar in the early days of the Congo—Lumumba, Kasavubu, Adoula, Gizenga—vanished from the front pages and now only that of Colonel, now General, Mobutu remains.

Now attention shifted from the military to the civilian, and on January 29, 1963, Kennedy sent Assistant Secretary Harlan Cleveland to the Congo to "assess" with Premier Cyrille Adoula "Congo needs for the nation-building phase." [9] On March 2 the Soviet Union called for the withdrawal of UN forces, but two weeks later, Adoula told the UN that the forces were needed to preserve the precarious unity. On March 20, Thant began the gradual phasing out of UN troops, and by July 7 he had announced that he intended to complete the troop withdrawal by the end of 1963, partly because of the financial crisis caused by the refusal of the Soviet Union, France and a number of other countries to pay their peace-keeping assessments. Although there seemed to be little realization of what was coming, the scene was set for the Soviet-American confrontation over financial obligations that would imperil the very life of the United Nations. On August 22, Congolese Premier Adoula asked that the UN maintain a highly mobile force of 3,000 men to deal with civil disorders in various parts of the immense, sprawling nation. The United States agreed that they should be kept on. Thant reluctantly asked the General

Assembly to authorize one final extension of the UN force through June 30, 1964. And on September 20, just two months before his assassination, Kennedy addressed the General Assembly, calling on the Soviet Union to end the payments impasse. He also supported the extension of the UN force, which was authorized by the assembly a month later.

But if the UN was almost through with the Congo, the Congo was by no means through with the UN. By the beginning of 1964, the United States had begun to drift into a position on the financing of the peace-keeping operations that made all but inevitable a direct confrontation with the Soviet Union. Yet this situation, known at the UN as the "Article 19 question," has been almost entirely ignored in all that has been written about Adlai Stevenson, even though it became an overriding preoccupation with him, hamstrung the work of the General Assembly for nearly a year, and threatened the very existence of the United Nations. Little by little the United States, without much thought by the State Department or by Stevenson, had worked itself into a public posture of insisting that the Soviet Union and, less importantly, France back down from the public positions they had taken much earlier. In retrospect, it seems almost incredible that the United States could have done so, however legally and philosophically justified their stance, without examining carefully the consequences of such an act.

No doubt acting out of conviction based on its reliance on the Security Council, where it had the veto, the Soviet Union steadfastly persisted in its refusal to pay the Congo and Middle East peace-keeping assessments. The General Assembly's twenty-one-nation working group, established under the able chairmanship of Chief S. O. Adebo of Nigeria to try to work out a solution, had met on and off during 1962 and 1963. However, it was unable to effect a compromise. On March 21, 1964, the Soviet Union reiterated its position, insisting that any attempt to enforce payment could cause "great and irreparable damage to the United Nations." Obviously the American and Soviet positions were mutually exclusive; one side or the other had to give way. The question was not only which side was right—most of the UN members, as demonstrated by the vote accepting the World Court opinion, clearly shared the American view—but what would happen if the issue were pushed to a confrontation. And this confrontation, should it take place, would be on the first day of the 1964 General Assembly and would focus on (what became the famous) Article 19 of the UN Charter, reading:

> "A Member of the United Nations which is in arrears in the payment of its financial contributions to the Organization shall have no vote in the General Assembly if the amount of its arrears equals or exceeds the amount of contributions due from it for the preceding two full years. The General Assembly may, nevertheless, permit such a Member to vote if it is satisfied that the failure to pay is due to conditions beyond the control of the Member."

Because of its refusal to pay, the Soviet Union came within the scope of that article in 1964. Because France had paid the Middle East assessments (as "voluntary" contributions, it was to argue later), that country would not be affected until 1965. Thus, the United Nations would have to decide on the first day of the forthcoming General Assembly session whether or not to try to enforce the unmistakably clear language of Article 19.

The American view of what should be done was made plain on March 23 by Adlai Stevenson, speaking in a Dag Hammarskjold Memorial Lecture at Princeton University. Stevenson said that talks were underway to avoid a recurrence of the situation and that "it should be possible to give new emphasis to the position of the Security Council by providing that all proposals for initiating a peace-keeping operation would first be presented to the council, and that the General Assembly should not have the right to initiate such an operation unless the council had shown it was unable to act." But although the United States was willing to compromise on future peace-keeping operations, it was not willing to do so on the immediate question. Stevenson said that the United States and all other members of the UN did not want to see the Soviet Union and other members deprived of their vote in the General Assembly. But he believed they all wanted to avoid such a disaster "in the only way it can be avoided, namely by a Soviet payment—in whatever form. . . . It is our earnest hope that the overwhelming sentiment of the members will prevail and that the Soviet Union and others will find the means, in one way or another, to provide funds that will make unnecessary any Article 19 confrontation." Stevenson was thus suggesting that if the Soviet Union were to make a voluntary contribution, even if it were to some other part of the UN budget, the issue would not be forced. However, the Soviet Union wanted the problem met head on.

Stevenson continued. "Let me make it quite clear that it is the [UN] Charter that imposes the penalty of loss of voting privileges for non-payment of assessments. The United States has never presumed to think it could negotiate this requirement of the Charter with the Soviet Union, and it has not entered into these exploratory talks for this purpose." It was clear that the United States and the Soviet Union were on a collision course, accelerated when Congress passed a resolution insisting that the Soviet Union pay up.

Neither side deviated an inch from its proclaimed positions as they approached the annual session of the General Assembly, which had been postponed from its customary opening in late September until November 10, in order that the UN would not figure in the American Presidential elections. On October 8, Stevenson sent a memorandum to the General Assembly expressing the hope that the nations in arrears would meet their obligations, but adding, "If on November 10 the plain and explicit terms of Article 19 become applicable, there is no alternative to its application." In short, the United States was saying that if the Soviet Union and other members in arrears, mainly Communist nations, did not pay, they would be deprived of their vote in the General Assembly, an extreme and unprecedented action. Once again the Soviet Union and the United States were engaged in a game of international "chicken," although this time the scene was the UN and not the Caribbean and the terms were political, not military.

The Secretary General and many members of the UN frantically sought a compromise, but neither side would budge. At a press conference on October 22, Thant said his efforts to prevent a confrontation had not been successful, and he suggested a postponement of the General Assembly, saying that if a majority of member states were to ask for one, he would act accordingly. Anxious also to avoid a showdown, forty-one nations the next day did request a postponement from November 10 to December 1. The Secretary General polled the entire membership and announced on November 2 that the session would be postponed. During all this time, Stevenson was, of course, engaged in constant negotiations, for the last thing in the world he wanted was a collision with the Soviet Union—a collision that, whatever its result, would only harm the UN. After meeting with U Thant, Stevenson made one last try on November 13 to avoid a confrontation by saying that "voluntary payments could be made without prejudice to the Soviet's or anyone else's legal views." And he added, "Any arrangements for such payments consistent with the Charter and satisfactory to the Secretary General will be satisfactory to the United States." [10] But the Soviet Union continued to stick to its position of principle, even though an overwhelming majority of the UN shared a different conviction. The United States hope that, in view of this majority, the Soviet Union would back down or seek the face-saving alternative of making a "voluntary" contribution simply did not pan out. By now it was too late, and December 1 arrived without any settlement. Thus began the strangest General Assembly in UN history—hopefully the strangest it will ever know.

But before December 1 arrived, the Congo again exploded in a brief but harrowing experience that rocked the UN and had a profound effect on the Article 19 crisis. Again the Congo acted as an albatross around the UN's neck. The first inkling of crisis came on November 20, 1964, when Belgium announced that 600 Belgian paratroopers had been flown in American planes to British-ruled Ascension Island off the coast of the Congo, seven hours from Stanleyville, where Congolese rebels were holding hundreds of white hostages. The next day, in a letter to the Security Council, Belgium said that "nearly 1,000 men, women and children have been arrested" in Stanleyville. "Preliminary measures have been taken, in consultation with the Congolese government (Tshombe's Central Government) and at its request, against the possibility that it might prove necessary to evacuate the hostages." And Belgium reported that by the action of thirteen governments, a radio appeal from Geneva had requested that "the immediate and safe arrival at Stanleyville of [the] staff of [the] International Red Cross" be permitted. Belgium further urged "each member of the UN to issue a pressing appeal that, in accordance with the Geneva Conventions, the hostages be immediately released." [11] In a Stevenson letter to the council, the United States associated itself with the Belgian appeal, notifying the council that the previous day it had received a message from Christophe Gbenye, leader of the rebels, suggesting preliminary discussions in Nairobi. The United States said it had accepted, setting November 21 as the date, but Gbenye's representative had not turned up, and so no meeting had taken place. That same day the Congolese rebels, perhaps fearing a swift attack by paratroopers or nearby government troops, threatened to put the Belgian and American hostages to death.

On November 24, Britain notified the Security Council that it had authorized the use of facilities on Ascension Island, and Tshombe notified the Secretary General that he had authorized the intervention of Belgium and the United States for a limited time in order to evacuate foreign civilians whose lives were threatened by Congolese rebels. The situation climaxed when U.S. military transport planes carried the Belgian paratroopers to Stanleyville to free the hostages. But the rebels killed eighteen of them before the Belgian troops could occupy the city. The rest of the hostages were flown by U.S. planes to Léopoldville.

In letters to the Security Council, the United States and Belgium reported that "all efforts at negotiation and all humanitarian appeals made by government and by the highest authorities to secure the rights and release of the hostages had been ineffective." Both countries reiterated that the operation was not military but humanitarian, and that once action was completed, troops would withdraw immediately from Stanleyville.[12] And Stevenson wrote that the necessity for the emergency rescue carried out against threats of mass execution was illustrated by the murder of an American missionary, Dr. Frank Carlson. Stevenson quoted the American consul at Stanleyville, among the rescued, as saying by telephone that the hostages were convinced "that only the airdrop had saved them."

On November 25, the Soviet Union charged that the landing of Belgian paratroopers was a "flagrant act of armed interference by Belgium, the United States and the United Kingdom in internal affairs of the Congo" and called for the "immediate cessation of military intervention and withdrawal of all Belgian troops and foreign mercenaries." [13] The UN plunged into a series of Security Council meetings as bitter and acrimonious as any in UN history, during which Stevenson was sorely beset by a number of Communist and militant African delegates. At one point Stevenson was attacked in racist terms by the representative of the Congo (the other Congo, the one with the capital in Brazzaville) and he lost his temper.

"I have served in the United Nations from the day of its inception off and on for seventeen years. But never before have I heard such irrational, irresponsible, insulting and repugnant language in these chambers—and language used, if you please, contemptuously to impugn and slander a gallant and successful effort to save human lives of many nationalities and colors."

Angry words were no novelty at the United Nations, and racism, white and colored, was often implicit, but never before these meetings had I heard such bitter, angry racist language. As with all things involving the Congo, however, this whole affair was complicated; it is too facile to let this series of Security Council sessions —which lasted through Christmas Eve and right up to December 30—go as simply racist.

There is no doubt that the hostages were in jeopardy, for they were in the hands of undisciplined rebels, many of them still tribal Africans. No doubt the rescue mission was justified. And no one who was at the UN can deny that a few (but only a few) of the African attacks on Stevenson were deeply and shockingly racist. But there's more to it than that. The American and European fears for the hostages were doubtless tinged with racism, too. If the hostages had been in European rather than African hands, it is possible that the terror would not have been so great. Unquestionably the hostages were in real danger, but this danger was quite probably magnified because of white racial fears. And there might be something—although no one can know how much—to the argument of some African delegates that the Belgian preparations to land paratroopers, which were of course revealed to the rebels by shortwave radio reports, stirred them to panic, thus increasing the hostages' peril. Also it must be remembered that Belgian paratroopers had been sent to the Congo in the first days of its independence, when the country was disintegrating, and were thus symbols of Belgian attempts to reassert colonial authority in the infant nation. Further, although Belgium had been authorized, even requested, to rescue the hostages by the Central Congolese government, that authorization was given by Moise Tshombe, who had sabotaged the Congo's attempt to survive as a unified country from the start. Tshombe was hated (the word is not too strong) by most African governments and was regarded, no doubt justly, as a front for Western financial interests who were still trying to wrest huge profits from Congolese mines. And the African critics of the rescue mission had a point when they said that the intervention destroyed the efforts of the Organization of African Unity to establish an effective coalition government in the Congo. Although Belgium and the United States repeatedly asserted that the mission was purely humanitarian and not military, the fact remains that the arrival of the Belgian paratroopers routed the rebels in Stanleyville and gave a great advantage to government troops, who immediately launched attacks on the rebels. Finally, the Africans were completely convinced that the mission was undertaken only because the hostages were almost entirely white. The Africans were particularly sensitive to this double standard and could not help remembering that the white colonialists had never hesitated to fire on colored subjects in Asia and Africa but always found it impossible to use force against whites in, say, Southern Rhodesia when these whites defied the authority of the home government.

But, and there are always *but*'s in discussing the Congo, it was also true, as some more moderate African governments pointed out, that it was not right for other countries to meddle in the Congo's domestic affairs and that, like it or not, Tshombe was the duly constituted head of the Congolese government. For it was true that the Soviet Union, mainland China and such militant African states as Algeria, Ghana and the United Arab Republic were helping the rebels, even if only because the hated Tshombe headed the Central government.

Whatever the circumstances, and historians might find it impossible ever to sort them out entirely, the dispute over Stanleyville poisoned the atmosphere at the UN as the General Assembly was preparing to meet on December 1, and bitter recriminations, many of them directed at Stevenson, continued during the early weeks when the Assembly was attempting to effect a compromise on the payments problem. Thus, when the session was convened, the United States did not know whether it had sufficient votes to enforce Article 19. A two-thirds majority would be required, and the United States had been counting on many African votes which might have been lost to it because of the Stanleyville affair. Moreover, Stevenson and the State Department did not know whether or not they wanted to force the issue even if they had the votes.

In short, at this climactic moment, the United States knew neither what it could do nor what it wanted to do. Consequently, it went along—to Stevenson's great relief—with those nations (most of the membership) that wanted to avoid a confrontation on opening day. In order to evade the question of whether or not the Soviet Union should lose its vote, the General Assembly began a curious session in which votes simply were not taken. No vice-presidents were elected, no committees were set up and no business was considered beyond a handful of budgetary and institutional items necessary to keep the UN going. The rest of the agenda— scores of items, many of them urgent—was simply ignored. Alex Quaison-Sackey of Ghana was "elected" president by acclamation, three new nations were admitted by acclamation, and three countries were given rotating seats on the Security Council by consensus. Otherwise, the General Assembly was effectively crippled. It could take absolutely no action on any world problem, but of course the speechmaking continued.

Meanwhile, frantic efforts went on behind the scenes to work out some kind—any kind—of compromise, but neither the United States nor the Soviet Union would give in. Neither dared bring the payments question to a vote, so the great world body lay inert, another victim of the cold war. By December 30 the General Assembly had decided, again without taking a vote, to recess and come back on January 18, 1965, in the hope that things would be better then. But there was no improvement, and when the General Assembly reconvened, Secretary General U Thant reported that the UN was almost broke and appealed for a settlement of the Article 19 crisis. Within a few days the Soviet Union and France, at that point the equivalent of two years behind in their payments, again insisted the assessments were illegal and that they wouldn't pay. By this time it was perfectly clear, despite the many ingenious plans offered for a solution, that there was none in sight, and Stevenson began to work within the State Department for a plan that would let the Soviet Union—and the United States— off the hook. But Rusk and Johnson remained obdurate. The Soviet Union would have to pay. Also by this time the African and Asian states were getting restive. There were many issues they wanted discussed, yet nothing requiring a vote could be brought up until the Article 19 dispute was settled. Now they began to blame the United States, even though most of them had voted with the United States to accept the World Court opinion that the peace-keeping assessments were mandatory. They realized that the Soviet Union wouldn't back down, they feared that a confrontation would irreparably damage the UN, the only place where they had any real influence, and so they began to urge the United States to agree to some compromise. But the United States continued to argue that there was no way to reinterpret the unmistakable language of the Charter, and on January 26, Adlai Stevenson told the General Assembly that the issue was "whether or not we intend to preserve the effective capacity of this organization to keep the peace." The next day the assembly again adjourned, this time for a week, in the hope that something could be worked out. It couldn't, and when the assembly reconvened on February 1, it was only to adjourn for another week.

The spectacle was painful to UN supporters. Stevenson became increasingly distressed over the impasse, but neither the Kremlin nor the State Department would give an inch. Then the day before the assembly again reconvened, the United States began the bombing of North Vietnam, and Stevenson sent a letter to the Security Council calling the raids "prompt defensive action" in response to Vietcong raids on Pleiku and other areas in South Vietnam. Stevenson told the Security Council, "We seek no wider war."

Now the war in Vietnam was added to Stevenson's burden as well as the Article 19 impasse, and the Dominican Republic invasion was just around the corner. These final months would be bad months indeed for America's leading peacemaker. Adding to the terrible strain was the fact that he was forever being summoned back from his short and infrequent vacations to meet still another crisis at the UN. It must have been tiring indeed to interrupt a vacation in Europe, fly for hours, rush by car to the U.S. Mission, get quickly brought up to date, and then walk across the street to a Security Council meeting that often lasted well into the night. One of his deputies, Francis T. P. Plimpton, recalls bumping into Stevenson at the Milan Airport. Stevenson gave him a smile and a cheery wave and then hurried off to his New York-bound plane. This might have seemed merely another jet set coincidence, except that Plimpton had just flown from New York to be Stevenson's host at the Plimpton villa at Lake Como. But Stevenson had been summoned back to New York, another brief respite aborted.

The assembly met on and off in February to dispose of a few essential housekeeping items by consensus, and then suddenly disaster loomed. In a statement before the assembly on February 16, Albania presented a "formal request" that the assembly resume its "normal work," that is, return to the normal voting procedure. This, of course, would have meant an end to evasion. The United States would have had to decide immediately whether or not to try to enforce Article 19 and deprive the Soviet Union and France of their assembly votes, and the other nations would have had to decide whether to back the United States—and the letter of the law—and perhaps see the Soviet Union walk out, or to vote against penalizing the Soviet Union and thus vote against the UN Charter, publicly humiliating the United States, the UN's most powerful member. It was a Hobson's choice, the very thing that virtually all the members, including the United States and the Soviet Union, had been so determined to avoid. The crunch now seemed inevitable, and a shaken President Quaison-Sackey appealed to Albanian Ambassador Halim Budo "not to insist on his proposal" because of the "overwhelming desire" of the members to avoid a confrontation on Article 19. But Albania, no doubt acting as *agent provocateur* for mainland China, blandly insisted not only that the assembly vote but that it be a roll-call vote (in which each nation must publicly commit itself) "as a matter of priority over all other questions." All through the huge domed chamber, delegates frantically flipped through their rules of procedure, desperately seeking a way out. A procession of delegates went to the podium to plead with Budo to withdraw his request or at least permit them a couple of days to get instructions from home. But Budo was unmoved. While Quaison-Sackey sat in agony behind the tribunal, Sweden asked for the floor, saying it believed that the president had the discretionary power to adjourn the meeting at any time. Quaison-Sackey hastily examined Rule 35, grasped at the straw, and declared the meeting adjourned until February 18.

For the rest of that day, all the next and on February 18 until the assembly reconvened, Albania's Budo was put under incredible pressure to withdraw his request. The delegates, particularly those from the smaller nations, were desperately trying not to be forced to choose publicly between the United States and the Soviet Union. But Budo wouldn't budge, and when the assembly reconvened, it was all up to Quaison-Sackey. As soon as the president opened the meeting and began a statement, Budo demanded the floor on a point of order. Quaison-Sackey said Budo would be allowed to speak after he had finished, but in a scene never before witnessed at the UN—and never since—Budo left his seat and hurried up to the podium. He addressed the astonished assembly through dead microphones (they are not turned on until the speaker has been recognized), while Quaison-Sackey pounded the gavel and called down to the Albanian to return to his seat. This extraordinary scene continued for some minutes until Ambassador Jamil Baroody of Saudi Arabia stepped forward and began to whisper into Budo's ear. After a whispered conversation, Budo returned to his seat, and a stunned assembly listened to Quaison-Sackey rule that the assembly had agreed "by its decision, by its consent, and by the procedure it has consistently followed" to use a no-vote procedure to "avoid a confrontation." And, he declared, "there is a consensus against reconsidering that decision."

This was another one of the great dramatic moments in UN history. The president was exerting his authority, the entire membership had pleaded with Albania not to force a confrontation, and all eyes were on Budo as he requested the floor. He walked slowly up to the microphone. Would he give in or would tiny, politically isolated Albania take on the entire UN? His procedural rule book in his hand, Budo calmly challenged Quaison-Sackey's ruling under Rule 73 ("A representative may appeal against the ruling of the President. The appeal shall be immediately put to the vote and the President's ruling shall stand unless overruled by a majority of the Members").

Now Adlai Stevenson waved for attention, and Quaison-Sackey gave him the floor. Stevenson bustled up to the front of the expectant chamber. He wanted to salvage whatever might be salvaged from this incredible situation, but even while he was speaking, the normally mild-mannered Budo shouted from his seat. Stevenson asked to be allowed to continue, but Budo kept shouting that Rule 73 specified that a challenge to the president's ruling must "be immediately put to the vote." He insisted that Stevenson not be permitted to continue, that the question be voted on immediately. A distraught Stevenson looked up at a distraught Quaison-Sackey. The president frantically consulted his rule book. The arrangement agreed to by 115 member states was about to fall apart with untold repercussions because a single member had changed its mind. If there should be a vote right then, the assembly would have to decide immediately whether or not the Soviet Union had the right to vote. The confrontation was imminent.

Quaison-Sackey looked helplessly down at Stevenson and began to say that Budo was right, that the challenge would have to be voted on immediately before Stevenson could make whatever point brought him to the podium. The feeling in the assembly chamber was electric. What would the members do? They were going to have to commit themselves publicly.

But then another extraordinary thing happened. Richard Pedersen, one of Stevenson's top aides, came rushing up to the podium, the rule book in his hand. All the delegates, of course, rely on their aides for expert advice, but it is usually given unostentatiously. Here was Adlai Stevenson, one of the best-known figures in the world, put on the spot by the obscure Halim Budo, standing alone in front of the assembly, helpless, with political disaster just seconds away. Pedersen had made a difficult decision, choosing to embarrass Stevenson rather than have the American position lost. A splendid tactician with an extraordinary knowledge of the UN, Pedersen had come up with another rule. He whispered into Stevenson's ear, pointing to the rule book as the entire membership looked on. Stevenson turned to Quaison-Sackey, citing a rule permitting a point of order on the actual conduct of the voting. A relieved president allowed Stevenson to continue. But the assembly wondered what Stevenson would say. Would the United States insist that the assembly enforce Article 19? Stevenson said, however, that since the procedural vote dealt only with the issue of whether the assembly should or should not continue on a non-voting basis, and since the vote was not on the substance of the assembly's business, the United States considered that such a vote would not involve or prejudice the Article 19 question and that the question could in no way be affected by the procedural vote. And Stevenson said that in order that the overwhelming majority of the assembly not be frustrated by one member, and in order that the assembly might complete its business on a consensus basis, the United States would not raise any objection to the procedural vote. You could feel the relief. The United States had let the other members off the hook. It would not challenge Russia's right to vote.

A grateful assembly quickly sustained the ruling that it continue on a no-vote basis, passed by consensus a few more housekeeping items and adjourned until September 1, three weeks before the convening of the next General Assembly. It was hoped that the five-month interval would allow adequate time for a compromise to be worked out. Clearly, the United States had lost this round. There had been a vote, and the Soviet Union had been permitted to participate. But the fight was not over, nor was it to be in Stevenson's lifetime. And to the deep distress of Stevenson and many other delegates, the assembly was still paralyzed.

Behind the scenes, talks continued but it soon became apparent that Russia was not going to relent, no matter how much time there was. There was now no way to avoid the postponed confrontation on September 1 unless the United States modified its position. Stevenson was convinced, as he had been for some time, that it was no longer profitable for the United States to be unyielding. He felt deeply that the General Assembly must be permitted to resume its normal work, and he realized that if the Soviet Union was originally the villain of the piece, sentiment had now swung against the United States as the obstacle to the normal functioning of the UN. He believed that the United States had to make a gesture of accommodation and that the best possible time would be in June in San Francisco at the twentieth anniversary of the founding of the UN. With increasing gloom over Vietnam, with the widespread revulsion over the U.S. invasion of the Dominican Republic, Stevenson felt that a concession by President Johnson would be gratefully and enthusiastically welcomed and would turn what promised to be a melancholy occasion into something of an American triumph. Therefore, he pushed hard for an American concession, and he believed he had convinced Johnson to announce in San Francisco that the United States would be willing to reach some agreement on the Article 19 question that would allow the General Assembly to resume its work. As the June 25 anniversary date approached, Stevenson became convinced that he had carried the day, despite Dean Rusk's stubborn advice to the President that Congress would not stand for an American backdown on Article 19. Then a couple of days before Johnson's San Francisco speech, Assistant Secretary Harlan Cleveland gave a background (not to be attributed) briefing to New York *Times* columnist James Reston, who wrote a piece saying that Johnson would announce such a compromise in San Francisco.

Stevenson had been asked to draft Johnson's speech, and in the draft such a compromise was included. However, when Johnson got the draft, he ordered it rewritten by Richard Goodwin, Kennedy's former aide, who had not yet left the White House. This must have been a terribly embarrassing situation for Goodwin, later the author of a tribute to Stevenson, who had first caused him to be interested in public service. He was instructed by Johnson not to let anyone, especially Stevenson, know the content of the speech, and when Stevenson called the White House to have the final version read to him, Goodwin had to refuse him. This was clearly an unprecedented situation, when the President's UN Ambassador was not permitted to know what the President would say to the UN.

The reason soon became apparent. Johnson's speech was a collection of platitudes about American devotion to the UN and a defense of U.S. intervention in Vietnam. There was no compromise on Article 19. Stevenson was later to say bitterly something to the effect that the literature that remained in the speech was his; all the meat was taken out. Apparently what had happened was that Johnson became furious when he read the Reston column predicting a compromise, so he changed signals. As he has done so often in similar cases of press disclosures, he let lesser concerns outweigh greater ones. So the United States lost its last chance to make a gracious retreat, one that would have been considered not as a backdown but rather as a wise and graceful decision. And so the UN's anniversary became even further steeped in gloom, and Stevenson, already deeply distressed by Vietnam and the Dominican Republic, became even more depressed. Of course, as soon as Arthur Goldberg went to the UN, he found that the U.S. position on Article 19 was untenable, and he convinced the President that it had to be modified. And Congress, despite Rusk's prediction, raised little fuss.

What then went wrong, causing the United States to take a position on Article 19 that set it on a collision course with the Soviet Union and causing the UN General Assembly to be paralyzed for an entire year? Clearly, the United States was on solid ground. The World Court and the General Assembly had ruled that the peace-keeping assessments were mandatory. And the language of Article 19 was unmistakable. If a nation were in arrears for the equivalent of two years, it was to lose its vote in the General Assembly. Further, the principle of collective responsibility is basic to the UN. But the problem was that the UN is not a judicial body; it is a political body where the rules are interpreted not by legal standards but according to political considerations. And the fact that the United States seemed unable to comprehend was that the Soviet Union, after the United States the most powerful member of the UN, had, for whatever reasons, an entirely different interpretation of the Charter.

It seems plain that the United States simply drifted into a position of absolute inflexibility without ever really considering the question. Usually budgetary matters—and this was long considered merely a budgetary matter—were left to budgetary specialists at the U.S. Mission and at the State Department. And even when it should have been apparent at both places that it was becoming a major political issue, neither paid much attention. Stevenson simply didn't even want to discuss what seemed to him at first a routine budgetary question. And no one else at the U.S. Mission or the State Department was interested enough to make sufficient fuss to have the question given high-level consideration until it was too late. Little by little, standing entirely on legalistic grounds, the United States had maneuvered itself into such a position with Congress that the payments problem developed into a major issue in the cold war. And this was done without any high-level consideration of whether a two-thirds majority of the UN would back the United States, without any consideration of what the repercussions would be in the various possible circumstances, or without any thought as to what Russia and France might do. Thus, the United States and Russia found themselves at a stalemate, the Administration had committed itself to Congress to insist on application of Article 19, and the General Assembly was paralyzed for a year without the United States ever really knowing what it was doing, or even what it wanted to do. And the major responsibility for this incredible situation rested with Adlai Stevenson.

By the end of 1964 it was apparent to Stevenson that Russia was adamant. Up to then, Stevenson and the State Department may have thought that the overwhelming assembly vote in favor of the World Court opinion would force Russia to change its position, possibly by the face-saving tactic of making "voluntary" contributions. But Stevenson, above all others because of his clashes with Gromyko in London, should have realized that Russia was unshakably committed to the belief that the UN's real power resided in the Security Council, where it had the veto. (The Soviet Union had been afraid in 1945. This fear was confirmed in 1950 during the Korean crisis, when the General Assembly passed the "Uniting for Peace" resolutions, which Russia argued were attempts to undermine the authority of the Security Council, and in 1964 it continued to fear that it would be at the mercy of the West if substantial powers were given the General Assembly, where it was so terribly outnumbered.) Russia regarded this position—however unjustified it might have seemed to Western eyes—as essential to its national interest. So Stevenson wanted a change, not only because he was distressed to see the UN paralyzed but because he felt a Soviet-American confrontation would be a serious setback to the developing *detente* between the two nations that had been his goal ever since 1952. But his efforts to get the Administration to change its position were unsuccessful in the months of life he had remaining.

It can be argued, of course, that the American position was a sound one and that there should not have been then, or later when Goldberg recommended it, a retreat from the American position. But as attractive as it seems at first, this proposition is simply unworkable. The Soviet Union—whether out of genuine conviction or through a narrower concern for its self-interest—did not accept the majority opinion. The question then became one of practical international politics. Could the majority view, even if shared by the Secretary General, even if supported vigorously by the United States, be imposed on another powerful nation? The answer was no, and the United States should have realized that because it, no less than the Soviet Union, would never accept a UN decision that it saw as a substantial threat to its national interest. There can be no doubt about this, for the United States has on a number of occasions clearly violated the UN Charter to which it had subscribed and of which, indeed, it was substantially the author.

In retrospect, Francis T. P. Plimpton, the deputy under Stevenson responsible for the question, said that the United States should have forced the issue on the first day of the General Assembly and gotten it over with.[14] But Plimpton readily concedes that that would have been a difficult decision to make and that Stevenson didn't want to make it. Stevenson was, he said, as he was himself, almost overeager for any compromise with Russia. Plimpton said that before Stanleyville, the United States thought it just barely had the two-thirds majority to enforce Article 19 but that "the United States had taken a terrible battering on the Stanleyville" incident and was no longer sure whether it had the votes. And as others have made plain, the United States was not sure whether it wanted to deprive the Soviet Union of its vote, even if it were *able* to. Nor was the United States certain it would have been able to force a showdown. Plimpton agrees with the many others who think that the smaller nations would have been able to avoid a confrontation by one parliamentary means or another. Thus, Stevenson was "delighted" at the no-vote device but, as Plimpton points out, the African and Asian nations "got more and more irritated at not being able to vote. The Russians got tougher, and it became obvious that the United States was unable to get support for applying Article 19."

Chief S. O. Adebo of Nigeria, the respected diplomat who headed the twenty-one-nation group that tried to work out a compromise, said he didn't think the United States had ever had sufficient votes to carry the Article 19 battle. He also said, "Many of us shared the position that everyone should contribute, but we

didn't think it should be made into a cudgel to beat out of the
UN those who didn't contribute." [15] Adebo believed the United
States should have let like-minded nations, of which Nigeria was
one, carry on the effort to convince Russia to contribute. And
he said the United States "converted the majority view into a cold
war position" by the congressional resolution demanding that the
Soviets pay up. "The character of the controversy changed. Then
those for the majority opinion became U.S. satellites and the others
became satellites of the USSR." The United States did try to make
it seem like a dispute between the Soviet Union and the UN majority. For instance, in my "Voice of America" broadcasts on the
subject, I was instructed to put the story in a UN-versus-the-Soviet
Union context, but this was totally transparent. It was the United
States that was trying to force Russia to back down, and everyone
at the UN knew it. Most of the others would have been willing to
settle for any reasonable compromise from the very beginning.

Adebo shares Stevenson's view that President Johnson should
have abandoned the vain fight and announced American willingness to compromise in his San Francisco speech. He thought Johnson could have given way gracefully and thus received the gratitude of the UN membership. But when Goldberg announced
readiness to compromise some months later, there was no applause.
As Adebo observed, "Do it when it's gracious. If you do it when
you're beaten, there's nothing left."

However, Adebo's view that the United States should have left
the fight in the hands of the Afro-Asian nations that shared the
same view of the Article 19 question is vigorously disputed by one
of Stevenson's top aides at the U.S. Mission. He claims the idea
that the congressional resolution made it into a cold war controversy was a lot of nonsense. "People are always saying that the
United States shouldn't take the lead and make things into a U.S.-
Soviet controversy, but if the United States doesn't take the lead,
nothing happens. We can't win either way."

But the fact remains that the United States did take a licking
on the question. It is one thing to stand fast on a principle but quite
something else in international politics to commit yourself to an
untenable position. In theoretical terms, the American position
was doubtless right. But that is no excuse for going into a major
political battle totally unprepared, as were Stevenson and the State

Department. Without adequate consideration of the problem, the United States publicly took an inflexible position, defended it implacably long after this defense had begun to do serious damage to more important concerns, and then had to back down anyway. This was something less than a triumph for Adlai Stevenson in particular and American diplomacy in general, for it was botched from beginning to end.

# ❧ III ❧

# *Disarmament and Other Matters*

ADLAI STEVENSON was one of the few top-ranking American
political figures who had a genuine interest in disarmament.
Indeed, he may have been the only one. The others generally regarded it as a utopian scheme, unlikely ever to be achieved and
something to be manipulated solely for propaganda purposes. It
is true, of course, that significant disarmament has never been
achieved for any lasting period of time. Disarmament and peace
fall into the which-came-first-the-chicken-or-the-egg category. Is
peace possible without disarmament or is disarmament possible
without peace? Yet if the world waits for peace before there is
disarmament and for disarmament before there is peace, there will,
of course, be neither. This has always been, yet man, however blood-
ied and degraded, has always survived. Now, with five nations
possessing nuclear weapons and many more capable of their possession, never in man's time on earth have the stakes been so high.
Stevenson had always proclaimed as a first priority the establishment of a *detente* between the United States and the Soviet Union
that would make possible a step-by-step inching toward genuine
and lasting peace. If there were, as he saw it, a little more peace,
then there could be a little more disarmament, and then a little
more peace and then a little more disarmament, so that man could
edge gradually away from the precipice. The need for disarmament
was a constant theme in his speeches.

Stevenson's great talent in his last years—as his eloquent advocacy of disarmament revealed—was speechmaking. He was for-

tunate that he had a number of writers who were in tune with his style and produced speeches that could have been his.

So many people contributed to Stevenson's speech writing during his UN years that it would be impossible to say in what proportion they did so. But, in general, it was something like this. His formal statements of policy before UN bodies were usually, but not always, drafted in Washington by the State Department's Bureau of International Organization Affairs, headed by Assistant Secretary Harlan Cleveland, the longtime Stevenson supporter. Most often the speech was drafted by Thomas Wilson, Cleveland's right-hand man. Then, if there were time, the draft was kicked back and forth between Washington and New York until it was satisfactory to all concerned. But often there wasn't time, and to the dismay of Stevenson and his public affairs staff, a speech would be coming in over the teleprinter in sections within hours, or sometimes even minutes, of when it was to be delivered. Other times, major speeches would be drafted by the senior U.S. Mission official for the subject area, say colonialism or economic affairs.

Speeches to be given outside the UN—and Stevenson was forever speaking at commencements or before national organizations—were generally written by his personal speech writer at the U.S. Mission, in the early days Wally Irwin and later, for most of Stevenson's time, Robert L. Schiffer. Both were first-rate speech writers who knew how to craft Stevensonian prose. Sometimes outside speeches were written by his friends in the academic or journalistic communities—Barbara Ward, Arthur Schlesinger, William Attwood, to mention only a few of his volunteer speech writers from his political days.

Those outside speeches were often his best ones, partly because they did not have to hew quite so closely to policy lines as those written at the State Department and partly because they were written by men closer to him, both personally and geographically, with whom he could exchange thoughts and make suggestions. For example, one of his finest speeches during his UN period was one given at Harvard not long before his death, in which he seemed to be chiding the cold warriors at the State Department and in the Pentagon. Clearly, such a speech could never have been written by someone in State.

All this is not to say that Stevenson did not care about his speeches. He had a great pride in his skill and reputation as a speechmaker and could be quite testy if he were given what he regarded as a graceless text. Sometimes he would reenact his campaign days and tinker with a speech, although now he did not write the original draft, making little changes to conform to his style and marking it so that he could read it better. This drove his public affairs staff wild and, when it was a major speech, UN correspondents as well. Stevenson got so bad at holding up speeches so he could make last-minute changes that Francis W. Carpenter, his enormously able press officer, finally persuaded him to allow the speeches to be released in advance to the press in their final draft form, with changes to be released later if they were substantial.

Perhaps Stevenson never quite forgave himself for having his speeches written by others, for he was so grateful—"pathetically grateful," one colleague said—when he got a good one that he would send off touching little notes to the writer.

Of course, they didn't always reach that standard, and when they fell short, Stevenson was quite capable of giving a poor reading or even of bumbling his way through a speech as if his mind were somewhere else, which it probably was. Even more noticeable, if he were forced to say something in which he didn't believe, as he had been during the Bay of Pigs crisis, he could make as many fluffs as a novice. Sitting in my broadcast booth, listening to him speak (and I heard most of his speeches at the UN), I used to feel I could tell how much he believed in a speech by how well he delivered it. This may well have been fanciful, but that was the impression he gave.

But when Stevenson was in form, as he was throughout the test ban negotiations, there was no political speechmaker of his time to match him. His voice, his diction, his measured cadence, his dignity made him a joy to listen to, even in that great hall of winds, the United Nations, where correspondents soon develop a necessary immunity to speeches. Often, when I heard him speak, as he did now, on something in which he really believed—the vital importance of disarmament and peace—I found myself on the verge of tears, thinking, why, oh, why, were the American people so blind as to reject him in favor of Eisenhower?

One can say, of course, what did it matter that Stevenson was so superb a speaker? It is deeds, not words, that count. True perhaps, yet America's Ambassador to the UN is not merely the representative of the government; he is a spokesman for the entire nation. He represents not only the current Administration but the whole people and its ideals, for the United Nations is more than a practical body; it represents man's aspirations as well. If the UN were to be judged solely as a machine, it would inevitably be found wanting, but it must be judged as a hope as well as a reality. Indeed, it is as the embodiment of a hope that the UN is most real. Thus, America's representative must be more than a diplomatic mechanic (there are many of those); he must represent as a man the ideals the UN represents as an institution—and paramount among these is world peace.

The best place to make a start toward peace, thought Stevenson, was in ending nuclear testing. A test ban would not only inhibit the growth of nuclear arsenals, it would end the poisoning of man's environment, which has been, in so many ways, the great legacy of the industrial revolution. As early as April 1956, before he had been nominated for a second vain attempt at the Presidency, Stevenson had advocated an end to nuclear testing. And on October 15, 1956, as his second campaign was reaching its climax, he said on nationwide television, against the counsel of his political advisers, that if he were elected President, he would make "the first order of business" an attempt to halt nuclear testing. Eisenhower termed Stevenson's proposal a compound of "pie-in-the-sky promises and wishful thinking," while Vice-President Nixon, in characteristic fashion, suggested that anyone who made such a proposal was somehow suspect, not fit to deal with the Communists. There was still the smell of McCarthyism in the air.

Between 1956 and 1961, Stevenson saw no reason to depart from his belief that a test ban was urgently needed, for tests on both sides of the Iron Curtain continued to increase the pollution of land, sea and air. And in July of 1961, Stevenson wrote to President Kennedy, "I can think of no better position for the United States in the forthcoming General Assembly than the earnest advocacy of disarmament as our top priority national interest. . . . [We must] seize the initiative in disarmament which the Russians have held too long. . . . The United States must appear second to none in its desire for disarmament." [1]

During the first half of 1961 Washington grappled with this incredibly complex problem, with the military opposing the civilians, the idealists opposing the realists, as they tried to sort out levels of deterrence, categories of armaments (nuclear weapons, delivery vehicles of various sorts, conventional arms and forces), stages of disarmament, balancing of American nuclear strength against Russian conventional superiority in Europe, the degrees and shades and nuances of which could be understood only by a medieval theologian. By early August, as an American proposal for "General and Complete Disarmament in a Peaceful World" was taking shape, Stevenson visited Kennedy in Hyannis Port on Cape Cod with Harlan Cleveland and Arthur Schlesinger to discuss the General Assembly, which was to begin in September.[2] Stevenson again suggested that disarmament be the major American theme. Kennedy responded that disarmament did not seem to be a popular issue, either with the American people or with Congress. On the other hand, he recognized how much disarmament meant to the rest of the world, and he realized it was an issue that could be used effectively against the Soviet Union. "We are ready for inspection; they aren't, and we should take all the advantage of this we can."

Stevenson agreed but went beyond the political advantages. "We can't do this effectively if we ourselves equivocate. Your first decision, Mr. President, must be to make sure that you yourself are genuinely for general and complete disarmament. We must go for that. Everything else in our program derives from it. Only total disarmament will save the world from the horror of nuclear war as well as from the mounting expenses of the arms race. Your basic decision must be to identify yourself with a new approach to disarmament. This must be our principal initiative in the United Nations."

Kennedy was interested but skeptical. He saw little chance of significant progress and thus thought of disarmament in political terms. At the same time, he recognized that if it were to be effective in these terms, any new American proposal, unlike those under Eisenhower, must offer a genuine basis for negotiation. When Stevenson finished, Kennedy said he understood the "propaganda" importance of an American campaign for disarmament.

Schlesinger writes:

"This casual remark stung Stevenson; he seemed seized for an instant as if by an anguished feeling that Kennedy did not really care about disarmament at all. While Cleveland and I, both anxious to keep our principals together, watched a little helplessly, Stevenson returned to the attack, telling the President in effect that he just had to have faith. This was not an argument likely to move Kennedy, and I never felt so keenly the way these two men, so united in their objectives, could so inadvertently arrive at cross-purposes." [3]

But then Cleveland intervened, and the uncomfortable moment passed. This whole question assumed not only philosophical but practical urgency when, amidst rising tensions over Berlin, Khrushchev announced on August 30, 1961, that the Soviet Union would end the nuclear testing moratorium, which had been in effect since October 1958. The Russians resumed testing on September 1. This, of course, put enormous pressure on Kennedy to resume American tests. Within a couple of weeks the United States began underground tests but held off tests in the atmosphere that would further contaminate the environment. And a week later, President Kennedy made his first appearance at the UN, paying tribute to Secretary General Hammarskjold, who had just died in the plane crash en route to the Congo: "Let us here resolve that Dag Hammarskjold did not live, or die, in vain." Calling on the General Assembly to reject the Russian *troika* proposal, he said its establishment would only serve to "entrench the cold war in the headquarters of peace." This, he maintained, would paralyze the United Nations at precisely the moment when it was needed more desperately than ever before, in this precarious age when "a nuclear disaster, spread by wind and water and fear, could well engulf the great and the small, the rich and the poor, the committed and the uncommitted alike. Mankind must put an end to war—or war will put an end to mankind. . . . Let us call a truce to terror."

Then, reflecting the view Stevenson had long held, Kennedy said that the goal of disarmament "is no longer a dream—it is a practical matter of life or death. The risks inherent in disarmament pale in comparison to the risks inherent in an unlimited arms race." And Kennedy told the delegates assembled from the world over—with the single and momentous exception of mainland hina—that a nuclear test ban treaty was the place to start. One nnot know whether he was speaking with the conviction of a evenson or at least partially as a political tactician, but Ken-:dy's appearance was a triumph—an appearance that Stevenson d been right in advocating so forcefully. For the moment, per-ps, Kennedy's words may have seemed no more than conven-onal speechmaking, but they were soon to be underlined dra-atically by the Soviet Union, when it announced that it would plode a nuclear bomb of some fifty megatons. An alarmed Gen-al Assembly quickly passed a resolution asking the Russians to frain. But despite the overwhelming vote (87 to 11, with 1 ostention), the Soviet Union proceeded to detonate the bomb on ctober 30 at Novaya Zemlya. It was even bigger than fifty egatons. As Khrushchev was to say the next day, his scientists ad made a mistake: "Instead of fifty megatons it proved to be ore, but we will not punish them for that."

Immediately the pressure on the United States to resume atmos-heric testing intensified. Kennedy gave the word to begin prep-rations, but still he delayed the actual testing. However much the :alists and the military wanted tests, Kennedy was reluctant to t them in motion, and there were advisers—Stevenson among em—who believed that tests were not, for the moment at least, ssential to national security. British Prime Minister Harold Mac-illan did all in his power to convince Kennedy to make one last y at ending the testing before ordering American tests. He wanted summit meeting in Geneva so that Kennedy, Khrushchev and e could make a final try.

But the advisers who feared for national security carried the ay, and on March 2, 1962, Kennedy announced that the United tates would resume atmospheric tests with all precautions pos-ble to restrict radioactive fallout. "I still exceedingly regret the ecessity of balancing these hazards against the hazards to hun-reds of millions of lives which would be created by a relative ecline in our nuclear strength." But Kennedy made one last bid, nnouncing that the United States would present at the disarma-ent talks in Geneva a comprehensive test ban treaty. If the Soviet Jnion were prepared to "accept such a treaty, to sign it before e latter part of April, and apply it immediately—if all testing an thus be actually halted—then . . . there would be no need for our tests." But the Soviet Union rejected Kennedy's offer. Perhaps they regarded it as an unacceptable ultimatum, or perhaps the military men, just as ours, felt that testing was essential to the national security.

So on April 25, the United States began a new round of atmos pheric tests and the two superpowers took another giant stride the arms race, polluting the earth in the process. It was only the fearsome days at the edge of the abyss in October of 1962 durin the Cuban missile crisis that would cause them to pull back. How ever, Stevenson and others in the Administration continued push for disarmament measures, as did Great Britain. On Augu 9 the two countries presented alternative draft treaties to th disarmament conference in Geneva, one calling for a total ba on nuclear tests, the other for a ban on tests in the atmospher outer space and underwater, but not those underground. Althoug the United States and Britain preferred the comprehensive treat it offered the partial ban to meet the objections of the Sovi Union, which continued to oppose on-site inspection to dete possible underground tests, contending that this was just anothe Western attempt at espionage.

Discussions were continued after the Cuban missile crisis, wit the Soviet Union saying it would accept a partial test ban treat on the understanding that underground tests should not be carrie out while negotiations continued. So, still trembling from th Russian-American confrontation in the Caribbean, the Genera Assembly passed a resolution on November 6 condemning a nuclear tests and asking that all such tests cease, immediately possible and no later than January 1, 1963. The Soviet Unio agreed to a cessation by then, but the United States and Grea Britain, conscious that the Soviet Union had once before broke a moratorium, shortsightedly did not. Fortunately the questio soon became academic. Sobered by the precipitous approach t the nuclear brink, both Kennedy and Khrushchev recognized tha a test ban treaty was in their mutual interest. In the exchange c letters that ended the missile crisis, Khrushchev suggested a examination of the differences between them. Kennedy agree and, in his famous American University speech of June 10, 196 suggested that both the Soviet Union and—an almost revolu tionary thought—the United States reexamine their attitudes.

This met with ready response by the Soviet Union, and in mid-July, Averell Harriman made another mission to Moscow, and this time he came back with the greatest achievement of the Kennedy Administration, the Moscow Treaty banning nuclear weapons tests in the atmosphere, outer space and underwater. But it must not be forgotten that this treaty was an equally historic achievement for Khrushchev—it would not have been possible without his agreement—and a long overdue vindication of Adlai Stevenson. Stevenson was a member of the American delegation that went to Moscow to sign the treaty on August 5, 1963, and this was surely one of his happiest moments. That day marked one of the most significant steps toward world peace of the postwar years, and it had all begun in 1956 with the Stevenson proposal that Nixon had termed "catastrophic nonsense."

So momentous was this step that there was reason to hope—indeed, to believe—that others would follow, and surely Stevenson must have hoped so. But soon Kennedy's intervention in Vietnam, tentative at first, then firmer, would lead, after his death, to the resumption of the cold war. Again, one can only regret that Kennedy had not been perceptive enough—or big enough—to have made Stevenson his Secretary of State, for if he had, it is impossible to believe that the United States would have moved so inexorably toward the impending catastrophes.

Just as Stevenson was one of the few leading political figures who was genuinely dedicated to disarmament, so was he one of the few who was not obsessed by NATO. Although the United States spoke endlessly about its revolutionary heritage and its commitment to self-determination, in practice the State Department under Truman and Eisenhower regarded colonial matters as though they were sitting in London, Paris or Brussels rather than in Washington. So fearful were they of a rift in NATO and thus a weakening in the common front against the Soviet Union that they would seldom do anything to embarrass the colonial powers. Justice, morality, even the United States' own words meant nothing; NATO must not be jeopardized.

But this policy began to change under Kennedy. Despite the fact that the State Department and the "foreign policy crowd" in Washington and New York still saw the world through the eyes of cold warriors, Kennedy himself and some of his top advisers were more sympathetic to the Third World. While a Senator, Kennedy had supported Algerian independence, to the horror of the State Department and the shocked outrage of Paris. Chester Bowles, Paul Hoffman, G. Mennen Williams, Harlan Cleveland and particularly Adlai Stevenson recognized that the underdeveloped nations were no longer mere pawns to be shoved around on the international board by the great powers. Stevenson had visited most of these new nations—perhaps more than any other American political figure—and he had a deep human understanding of them as people. Furthermore, he was one of the very few to recognize that it was within the frontiers of the crumbling empires that the main political, and perhaps military, struggles would be fought. Stevenson, and those who shared his beliefs, realized that if these new nations were not helped, and helped generously, even greater dangers would arise than those in the now-traditional arenas of the cold war. And of course, neither Stevenson nor Kennedy shared Dulles' simplistic view that those countries that weren't with us were against us.

Although Kennedy had real sympathy for the views of the Stevenson-Bowles camp, he was also greatly influenced by the counsel of the realists. Idealists were always at a disadvantage in arguments with realists, particularly when the referee was the pragmatic Kennedy. Idealists always seem to be dealing in "maybes," whereas the realists brandish "facts." And despite the observable fact that the policies of the realists have led from one disaster to another, the realists believe, with an exquisite self-confidence, that the failure of their last policy is proof positive of the undoubted success of their next, a trend that at this writing shows no sign of altering.

Yet Stevenson always persevered, despite the fact that the realists got Bowles out of his job as number two man at the State Department and succeeded in hemming in Stevenson himself. Although he had little success in influencing Kennedy on Latin America and Asia, Stevenson's viewpoint had considerable success in the case of Africa, perhaps because Kennedy, for some reason, had a particular sympathy for the African leaders. It may in part have been because Africa was not contiguous to either of the cold war's main camps. Indeed, if the Kennedy Administration had a major success in foreign policy beyond the Moscow Test Ban Treaty, it was in Africa, where the United States backed the UN in the Congo, supported—although, as it eventually turned out, almost entirely in words—the African position on the Portuguese colonies and on South Africa. But there is a psychological aspect in foreign relations as in all others, and one of the first moves by the Kennedy Administration convinced the new African leaders that Kennedy was on their side.

The issue was Angola, one of Portugal's three African colonies. Unlike Britain, France, and Belgium, Portugal not only was taking no steps toward preparing its colonies for independence, but it refused even to recognize their right to eventual freedom, maintaining the transparent fiction that these territories were not colonies but overseas provinces of Portugal itself. Just a month before Kennedy's inauguration, the Afro-Asian members of the UN had submitted a draft resolution on "the granting of independence to all colonial countries and peoples." The resolution declared that "immediate steps shall be taken" in all colonies "to transfer all powers to the peoples of those territories, without any conditions or reservations, in accordance with their freely expressed will." Although this draft was written in fairly sweeping language, it was clearly a statement of principle with no specific action immediately called for. The principle was in accord with views expressed many times by the United States. Indeed, the resolution was drawn up by the Afro-Asian delegations in close consultation with the United States, which wanted to block a tougher Soviet draft. The U.S. Mission, of course, intended to vote for it, and even the Europeanists in the State Department were prepared to go along. But British Prime Minister Macmillan called Eisenhower directly and asked him not to back it. Eisenhower agreed, giving instructions to abstain to James Wadsworth, who had succeeded Henry Cabot Lodge at the UN after the latter had received the Republican Vice-Presidential nomination. Wadsworth tried but was unable to get his instructions changed, and so the United States joined only 8 other nations in abstaining, while the resolution swept to victory with 89 votes in favor and none against. As far as the Third World was concerned, Washington, despite its professions, was no better than London or Paris.

But shortly after Stevenson took up his post at the UN, the

United States had a chance to redeem itself in the eyes of the nonaligned nations, and Kennedy and Stevenson took it. This was not solely on Stevenson's initiative. The entire U.S. Mission was in favor of supporting an Afro-Asian resolution in the Security Council that would establish a subcommittee to look into the situation in Angola, where African rebels were fighting the Portuguese authorities. And there was also support in the State Department from Harlan Cleveland, G. Mennen Williams and Williams' able deputy, Wayne Fredericks. Even though the resolution was defeated by the council—only the three Afro-Asian sponsors, the United States and the USSR voting for it—there was a wave of jubilation in the UN. The new American Administration had lived up to its promise; it had voted with the Afro-Asians. And it did so again in the General Assembly, where the same resolution this time passed.

Stevenson, joined by G. Mennen Williams and others, also pushed for stronger American action against South Africa's loathsome policy of apartheid, or racial separation. As a matter of course, and not much more than that, the United States had always verbally condemned apartheid, while declining to support any strong UN measures against it. No doubt South Africa's strong anti-Communist stance (a peculiar posture, since Communism was something less than a major threat in South Africa), its predominance as a supplier of gold and its rich opportunities for economic investment (eagerly seized by American business) had something to do with this. But by 1963, South Africa was becoming even more repressive, and African fury against the racists was growing. Williams suggested an embargo on American arms, and a few days later, in June 1963, Stevenson wrote to Kennedy, "It seems clear that we are approaching a decisive situation from which the Africans will draw conclusions about the long-run nature of our policies."

Neither Kennedy nor Rusk nor Stevenson liked the idea of UN-imposed sanctions against South Africa. They were not prepared to take such an extreme step, nor did they want to be forced to vote against them. So Kennedy proposed that the United States make a unilateral declaration that it would not sell arms to South Africa after January 1, so long as that nation practiced apartheid. Stevenson announced this on August 2, 1963, while the Security

Council was discussing a resolution, soon to be passed, condemning apartheid and calling for an arms embargo against South Africa. But Stevenson also said that the United States would oppose sanctions as "bad law and bad policy." For the moment at least this appeased the African militants, for it was indeed stronger action than the United States had ever taken before. However, it had limited practical effect, since South Africa could buy weapons elsewhere and was developing its own arms industry. Eventually the United States would be asked to take more effective political and economic measures against South Africa, but by 1963, despite its continued professions of abhorrence of apartheid, the United States had gone about as far as it would go.

One of Stevenson's lesser hours came early in his UN years, when he bitterly attacked India for its one-day conquest of the Portuguese colony of Goa, which had, almost literally, been a thorn in India's side for centuries. Nor was this incident much of a triumph for the State Department or for India or Portugal. Goa was a small colony on the west coast of India established by the Portuguese in 1510 and, as with the rest of their colonies, they had no intention of giving it up. India, of course, insisted from its earliest days of independence that the colony be surrendered to it, but although the subject was discussed sporadically, no progress had been made, nor did it even seem that India was terribly upset about the situation. Then in mid-December 1961, Prime Minister Nehru ordered his troops to take the tiny, ill-defended colony. It is hard to say why Nehru picked that particular moment; perhaps it was frustration over India's inability to cope with Chinese troops in the border dispute over its northern frontier. American Ambassador John Kenneth Galbraith heard of the order and prevailed on Nehru to postpone the invasion for a few days. He then asked Washington to give India assurances that it would make serious efforts to get Portugal to give up the territory that it couldn't, in any case, hold. But in exchange for a six-month postponement of India's move, Washington offered only some unspecified pressure on Portugal, not the necessary assurance that it would get Portugal out of Goa. This wasn't enough for Nehru, and in the middle of the night on December 17 his army struck.

Immediately the Security Council was summoned into emergency session at Portugal's request. And Stevenson launched an attack that stunned India for its bitterness. It was one of Stevenson's most compelling performances, yet paradoxically it was an extraordinary exercise in hypocrisy. He began—and there were few at the UN who did not take a perverse pleasure in his words— with a scathing attack on Krishna Menon, "so well known in these halls for his advice on peace and his tireless enjoinders to everyone else to seek the way of compromise." He drew a picture of the sarcastically eloquent advocate of peace urging his troops on in the midnight attack on tiny Goa. Other than Stevenson himself, Menon was the best-known figure in UN history. He was justly famous for his brilliant marathon speeches, many of them scornfully anti-American. And there was no more dramatic figure at the UN than Menon, his white hair crowning his arrogant, handsome face, stalking the corridors, his hands clasped at his back, a cane dragging behind. Stevenson doubtless spoke for many at the UN who had long since been sickened by India's self-righteous lectures on international morality. Stevenson called on India to withdraw its forces and declared that "if the United Nations is not to die as ignoble a death as the League of Nations, we cannot condone the use of force in this instance and thus pave the way for forceful solutions of other disputes." These words angered the Indians, for hypocritical as India was, the United States was no less so. It must have wondered how the United States could take so Olympian a point of view when only months before it had organized, financed and launched the Bay of Pigs invasion of Cuba. And Stevenson's concern over the "forceful solutions of other disputes" must later have seemed hollow indeed in view of Vietnam and the Dominican Republic.

Indeed, this was a clash of the two great international hypocrites of the mid-twentieth century: India assuming a moral stance based on the ancient wisdom of the East, and America taking the same position based on the self-evident superiority of American democracy. Yet, offensive as was India's sudden attack, the fact remains that it had every legal and moral right to Goa. Its fault was not in getting Goa, but in its methods. And Stevenson's speech made no reference to Portuguese colonialism of so retrograde a nature that it had offended most of the world. India was not surprised by the U.S. attack; it must have expected that. But it had not imagined that the United States would completely ignore the Portuguese intransigence that probably made a clash inevitable, if not immediately, then later.

Stevenson was, of course, entirely aware of the injustice of such a one-sided speech and wanted, as Galbraith had urged, to call on Portugal to end its anachronistic occupation of Goa. But it turned out that the Portuguese dictator, Salazar, had asked the United States to focus entirely on the issue of aggression, and the State Department, without consulting the White House, had instructed the American ambassador in Lisbon to assure Salazar that this would be done. Thus, the State Department instructed Stevenson to delete any reference to Portuguese colonialism. This, of course, weakened the impact of Stevenson's speech, for without reference to Portugal's contribution to the crisis, it seemed like one more American defense of the colonial powers. And if he was unable to be fair in his speech, Stevenson should at least have toned down his attack on India.

Stevenson's attack struck New Delhi with magnified impact, because he had always been considered one of India's staunchest friends and a particular, personal friend of Nehru. C. S. Jha, who represented India in the Security Council debate, said that although he realized Stevenson was speaking on instructions, he thought that his statement and attitude were "not entirely explained by instructions." Jha believed that Stevenson had projected his own feelings, perhaps spontaneously in the stress of the debate. Jha said that Stevenson went far beyond what anyone else said, even others who did not agree with India's action. The Stevenson speech, observed Jha, "seemed to gloss over Portuguese intransigence and the basic issue of colonialism." And Jha added that in the debate Stevenson had a chance to clarify the U.S. position on colonialism but was evasive, saying only that America's position was well-known. Jha, of course, had heard the reports that Stevenson soon felt he had been carried away and gone too far in his attack, perhaps out of great disappointment in Nehru, whom he had always admired. But if this were so, said Jha, Stevenson never mentioned it to him. However, Jha said, he and Stevenson later became "very good friends, and that may have been his way of making it up."

As his reconciliation with Jha indicates, Stevenson had a truly extraordinary capacity for friendship and for interest in others, a capacity not always possessed by men in high position, whose overpowering preoccupation is often themselves. He was reluctant ever to turn away a friend or, as several of his intimates reported, "anyone who had given him a nickel" during his political campaigns. Because he was unable to restrict an interesting visitor to the allotted time, his appointments schedule was always a shambles, and his appointments secretary, David Guyer, had to make it a practice to break in whenever an ambassador had been kept waiting for ten minutes. But his interest in others was not boundless. Whenever he learned that a bore wanted to see him—and diplomats are not always stimulating—he would make a face and ask Guyer, "Do I have to?" [4]

When Guyer answered, as he usually did, "You'll be sorry if you don't," Stevenson would reluctantly give in.

So, even during times of crisis, he was always trying to squeeze into his impossible schedule one of his friends or someone who had helped in the campaigns or someone he had met abroad. This often meant they'd be sandwiched in between appointments or ride with him from the Waldorf to the U.S. Mission or to the airport on one of his frequent trips to Washington. There was almost always someone staying at his apartment that he'd have to entertain, even if only for a drink before his evening engagements or a drink afterward. And he was undeniably the most sought-after single man in New York. It's unlikely that there was ever a night when he didn't have a choice of invitations from the rich, the famous and the talented. If any one person could be called "the toast of New York," it was Stevenson. And of course, there was the incessant round of diplomatic parties, but he did his considerable best to avoid as many of these as he could, regarding them as frightful bores, as indeed they were. He simply hated the UN parties, although he could not avoid them all, and there is one marvelous story, probably essentially true, of his sitting on the floor at a party given by one of the African delegations, banging on a drum. He was wise to have attended an African party, for the Africans, new to the ways of diplomacy, considered a party something at which people had fun, and not a dreary, crowded extension of the working day. But his reluctance to attend diplomatic parties was something of a trial to his senior aides, who were forever making excuses for him. It would be an overstatement to say that his infrequent attendance caused resentment in the other delegations, but it did bother them enough to cause some concern at the U.S. Mission.

But if he didn't like UN parties, he loved New York parties, and if he heard of a good one he hadn't been invited to or hadn't been able to attend, he was genuinely upset. Perhaps he was, as he liked to claim, really a small-town boy from the Midwest who couldn't bear to miss anything. Whatever the reason, he was out just about every night. He'd stay out late, then when he got back to the Waldorf, he'd usually have a drink and a chat with his houseguests.

Some might say that a discussion of Stevenson's social life is not really relevant here. That might be so with some men, but it is of great importance in any assessment of this remarkable man. It seems true, as some associates have suggested, that in his final years Stevenson led an increasingly empty social life, that he would find himself in the middle of a lively party with a glass in his hand and not really know why he was there. To be sure, he often gained sustenance from quiet evenings with close friends, but if friends were a help, they could also be a handicap. Unquestionably Stevenson became something of a trophy to be displayed at parties. If you had him, you were one up on the others in New York's fierce, unending social contest. Stevenson was the best catch in town, and often he was invited and pressed to attend more for display than for companionship. He must have sensed this, yet he couldn't resist. He was forever saying that he didn't have time to read and to think. He could have made the time, but he didn't really want to or wasn't able to. One of his oldest and closest friends said Stevenson "had the adulation of an awful lot of rich people" and that he "was sure Stevenson got awful tired of sycophants."

Perhaps. But he was not able to tear himself away. He enjoyed the society of rich people. Perhaps he was not unlike a fellow Princetonian of his generation, F. Scott Fitzgerald. He knew all about the emptiness of that life, yet he couldn't resist it. Many of his friends kept hoping he would marry again, that his life would be less frantic if he could find a good woman who would make a home for him. That might have helped, for Stevenson was, as the friend said above, "a lonely kind of fellow." But there is no evidence that, during his UN years at least, Stevenson contemplated remarriage.

Stevenson simply liked to bring together his friends from different circles, and many of them have commented happily on the friendships they formed because of him. And he was, of course, famous for squiring attractive women. Many of his male friends have spoken with admiration—and no little envy—of how attractive women seemed drawn to him. There's no doubt that was so. There is no real point in listing them here, but the ladies were a formidable group indeed, and they certainly did pursue him. He was no Adonis. In fact, with his girth, his slightly protuberant eyes and his curious waddle, he had a slightly comic aspect, in a very pleasant sort of way. But his warmth, his wit, his gaiety, his courtesy, his vitality and, it must be faced, his celebrity made him uncommonly attractive.

Stories vary as to how the ladies regarded one another. Some claim that there was no envy or jealousy, that they formed a sort of club based on a common interest—Adlai Stevenson. That seems rather unlikely, however, and it seems more credible that Stevenson, as some of his friends reported, was always juggling the ladies, telling whoever arranged his dinner parties, "My God, I don't care who else you invite but you've got to have so-and-so." This, no doubt, to redress the social balance.

If Stevenson was trying to escape loneliness in his ceaseless round of partying, he was also trying to escape the pressures of his job. Particularly in the last months, he wasn't happy in his work, and he sought relief in the gaiety of New York social life. It was no doubt a relief, but it was also a strain. He didn't get enough sleep, he was smoking and drinking more than his doctors wanted him to, and he wasn't spending the time he should have on his homework. There's simply no doubt that Stevenson was not as well prepared on detail as he should have been, certainly not nearly as well prepared as Henry Cabot Lodge before him and Arthur Goldberg after him. This, too, we must take into account in our final evaluation.

Not surprisingly, Stevenson's many friends and admirers were concerned not so much with Goa, Cuba, the Congo and disarmament, important as these issues were to Stevenson, the UN and the United States. What they wanted most to know in Stevenson's last months—and since—was how he stood on the frightening direction American policy took under Lyndon Johnson. This, and a closer look at Stevenson the ambassador and even the historic figure, will occupy the rest of this book.

# ❧ IV ❧

## *Vietnam*

T<small>HE</small> great question at the death of Adlai Stevenson was: how did he really stand on Vietnam? This was the question that his former supporters had been asking for months, at least since the Gulf of Tonkin incidents in August 1964 clearly indicated a turning of the corner in what had been until then an ugly, but still limited, war. Just hours after his death, the well-known broadcasters Eric Sevareid and David Schoenbrun reported that Stevenson had told them privately—and separately—only days before that he intended to resign. These reports inevitably increased the speculation that Stevenson strongly disagreed with President Johnson's Vietnam policy.

Such speculation was a serious political threat to an Administration already beleaguered by the academic and intellectual communities which substantially, and often dramatically, opposed growing American involvement in the Vietnamese civil war. Indeed, although President Johnson, like President Kennedy before him, had almost completely excluded Stevenson from the decision-making center of government, he, also like Kennedy, was aware of Stevenson's diminishing but still powerful political appeal. Thus, the Administration was always careful to listen to Stevenson more or less politely, so as not to drive him out of government to head the Democrats-in-exile. And Stevenson did have his uses to Johnson. More than likely, however, Stevenson's acquiescence with policy had caused the Administration to feel fairly confident that he would not break openly with President Johnson and serve as the rallying point of antiwar opposition that might then become irresistible. Obviously, then, the Administration was determined not to allow Stevenson to become, after his death, the antiwar focus he had consciously avoided becoming during his life.

Immediately the Administration moved to stop such speculation by asserting that Stevenson had given absolutely no indication that he planned to resign, and it further declared that his complete support of American foreign policy was demonstrated by his many public statements to that effect. In an attempt to discredit the resignation reports, the Administration also suggested that it was unethical for reporters to attribute statements to a man no longer able to verify them. Moreover, Johnson moved quickly to embrace the memory of Stevenson. There is no certainty here that Johnson's sincerity must be questioned, for although he has been a tough man, he has often proved to be a sentimental one as well. But it must be pointed out that Johnson had had little use for Stevenson during the period between the 1952 Presidential campaign and 1960 (nor did Stevenson have much regard for Johnson) and that Johnson had ignored Stevenson's counsel on several crucial matters, relegating him to the post of advocate for policies which he had little or no part in formulating. And it is demonstrably true that any split between Johnson and Stevenson, even a posthumous one, would have been a major political embarrassment to the Administration.

Then, four months later, on November 15, Sevareid published in *Look* magazine a detailed account of his long and searching conversation with Stevenson only two days before his death, documenting further his conviction that Stevenson was on the verge of resigning. He also reported that Stevenson had told him that the Administration had declined to respond to a message from UN Secretary General U Thant, passed on by Stevenson, that North Vietnam was willing to meet with American emissaries to discuss the terms for ending the Vietnam War. This article, which severely challenged—and not for the first time—the credibility of an Administration that had claimed time and again that Hanoi had shown no interest in peace talks, will be discussed in more detail later. For the moment, however, suffice it to say that the Administration again tried to end speculation that Stevenson had been about to quit. Asked for comment on the Sevareid article, Bill

D. Moyers, then Johnson's press secretary, told White House correspondents, "I follow the President's advice given a long time ago on not commenting on what dead men might have said or might not have said."

A month later, on December 14, columnist Clayton Fritchey, Stevenson's press adviser at the UN and a longtime confidant, wrote that Stevenson essentially supported Johnson's foreign policy. "Mr. Stevenson," he maintained, was " 'troubled' by some aspects of foreign policy, including Vietnam and the Dominican Republic, but so is nearly everybody, including the President himself."

Fritchey went on in his new column in *Newsday,* a Long Island newspaper, to cite as evidence what the New York *Times* in its story that day termed an "unposted letter" by Stevenson to a group of artists, writers and scientists rejecting their proposal that he resign as U.S. Ambassador to the United Nations in protest against the Administration's foreign policy. This letter was released to the press the same day by Adlai Stevenson III, then an Illinois state representative. He reported that he had received it from Philip Kaiser, minister in the American Embassy in London. It had been among Stevenson's papers at the time of his death. But when the "letter incident" is examined closely, it becomes apparent that it was anything but what it seemed at first glance and what Adlai III wanted it to seem.

However, before looking at the considerable, and previously unavailable, evidence of Stevenson's views on Vietnam—and on the Johnson Administration's foreign policy generally—it is necessary to establish in some detail the context in which Stevenson privately, but often freely, expressed these views. First, like most Democratic politicians, Stevenson did not have much of a record on Vietnam in particular and Southeast Asia in general, for that had been largely a Republican problem. It was not until the Eisenhower years that Indochina had become a major U.S. preoccupation, although it is true that American aid actually began under President Truman in 1950. His was the Administration to decide that the anti-Communist crusade, now extended to a newly Communist China, was more important than the anticolonial struggle carried on against the French by Ho Chi Minh.

American dollars began to flow to the French military effort to put down the Ho-led nationalist rebellion. From $150 million that year, the aid grew to more than a billion in fiscal 1954. By that time, the year of the French disaster at Dienbienphu and the subsequent Geneva Conference, aid to Indochina, which is to say, aid to the French attempt to defeat the Vietminh, accounted for approximately one-third the entire American foreign aid program. And it was in 1954 that Secretary of State John Foster Dulles, Vice-President Richard Nixon and much of the military leadership advocated committing American planes to a last-ditch effort to save the French at Dienbienphu and to prevent the Vietnamese "domino" from toppling over, imperiling the rest of Asia.

Interestingly, during these years one of the few American political figures to challenge U.S. policy in this area was the then-young Congressman from Massachusetts, John F. Kennedy. As early as November 1951, Kennedy said such things as: "In Indochina we have allied ourselves to the desperate effort of the French regime to hang on to the remnants of empire." [1] It is one of the ironies of history that the inept Eisenhower, who didn't think much about such things as colonialism and anticolonialism, kept American forces out of the military morass of Indochina, whereas the sophisticated Kennedy began a policy of military intervention that allowed Johnson to say legitimately that he was carrying on a policy inherited from his slain predecessor.

During these years Stevenson did not have a great deal to say about Indochina, although on April 11, 1955, in a radio address primarily devoted to one of the periodic Quemoy-Matsu crises, he alluded briefly to the problem in what was a clear and effective effort to score some political points against Eisenhower, who would surely be his opponent again in the 1956 election. While asserting that he would not "belittle some recent achievements in the foreign field," Stevenson argued that there was a "yawning gap between what we say and what we do." Referring to Nixon's eagerness to send American forces to Indochina to help the French, he said that all this talk had ended in nothing, while half of Vietnam had been lost. This certainly implies that Stevenson's sympathies were with the discredited French colonial masters and not with the Vietnamese nationalists seeking their independence. Stevenson was not suggesting that he would have sent American military assistance but was merely playing the politician's game of blaming his opponents for something that could not have been helped. Although Stevenson's political campaigns were essentially of a high level that dignified the American political process, in this instance he was doing no different than the Republicans who had blamed Truman for "losing" China. However, unlike the Republicans, he did not imply that there was any lack of patriotism involved. And in any case, America was not then terribly interested in Indochina—and there were few indeed who had even heard of Vietnam.

When Kennedy took office in 1961, Vietnam was just one of several major foreign policy problems left on his desk by Eisenhower. Almost immediately, he became preoccupied with another of them, Cuba, and as the months hurried on, Vietnam never received Kennedy's full attention—a great pity, for Kennedy had been one of the very few political figures to recognize that an anticolonial revolution completely in accord with the principles of the American Revolution was being transformed into another unfortunate episode in America's continuing crusade against Communism. For whatever reason, Kennedy turned over the direction of Vietnam policy largely to such sophisticated but implacable cold warriors as Secretary of State Rusk, Defense Secretary McNamara and White House aides McGeorge Bundy and Walt Rostow.

However, as early as 1961, Stevenson had warned Kennedy not to get drawn into the quicksands of Indochina. This was Stevenson at his best, for more than any other leading American political figure, he was convinced that political problems could be solved only by political action, not by military action—and that military action would not only fail to solve the problem at hand but could raise others perhaps even more dangerous. Not surprisingly, the hard-nosed realists (as they apparently liked to regard themselves) around Kennedy greeted Stevenson's advice with scorn. He was, in their estimation, a soft-boiled egghead, not up to making the tough decisions the real world demanded. To them, he was in the right place, the United Nations, a make-believe microcosm, a place for lofty thoughts and eloquent language, but not the place where the real decisions were made. Here, then, is another of those ironies with which history abounds. As with the Bay of Pigs, the pragmatic realists—the Rusks, the McNamaras, the Bundys, the

Rostows—got us into the deepest kind of practical trouble in Vietnam by actions that the unrealistic idealists—the Stevensons, the Bowles', the Fulbrights—would have dismissed out of hand as absurd. One is often forced to conclude that there is nothing so unrealistic as a realist.

Thus, little by little, Kennedy increased American involvement in Vietnam, shifting it in degree and kind from economic to military. From time to time, whenever Stevenson had the chance—which wasn't often, because it simply never occurred to Kennedy to consult Stevenson on matters not of direct concern to the UN —Stevenson cautioned on Vietnam. But since both men were preoccupied with other matters, Vietnam did not become a major concern until shortly before Kennedy's death, and by then it was too late. The coup that removed dictator Ngo Dinh Diem and presented the chance for a change in direction didn't take place until the same month as Kennedy's assassination.

In his brilliant apologia for Kennedy, *A Thousand Days,* Arthur Schlesinger writes: "I saw the President soon after he heard [President] Diem and [his brother, Ngo Dinh] Nhu were dead. He was somber and shaken. I had not seen him so depressed since the Bay of Pigs. No doubt he realized that Vietnam was his great failure in foreign policy, and that he had never really given it his full attention." [2]

There has, of course, been a great deal of speculation as to what Kennedy would have done had he lived. Many have argued that eventually, when he saw things simply weren't working out, he would have cut his losses in Vietnam as he had at the Bay of Pigs and in Laos. This is what Schlesinger says: "But the fact that the Vietnamese seemed ready to fight had made him feel that there was a reasonable chance of making a go of it; and then the optimism of 1962 had carried him along. Yet, with his memory of the French in Indochina in 1951, he had always believed there was a point at which our intervention might turn Vietnamese nationalism against us and transform an Asian civil conflict into a white man's war."

Although there is some reason to believe that Kennedy would indeed have decided to pull out, the indisputable fact remains— and President Johnson never allowed it to be forgotten—that it was Kennedy who introduced American troops into Vietnam in substantial numbers, increasing them from the 2,000 under Eisenhower to 16,000. This permitted Johnson to argue, as he did continually, that he was merely carrying on the policy of his predecessor, trying to cloak his actions with posthumous Kennedy approval. But can anyone doubt that there is a great—and significant—difference between increasing troops from 2,000 to 16,000 and increasing them from 16,000 to a half million or so by the end of 1967? Or can anyone doubt the significance of Kennedy's words on September 2, 1963, less than two months before his death:

> "In the final analysis, it is their war. They are the ones who have to win it or lose it. We can help them, we can give them equipment, we can send our men out there as advisers, but they have to win it—the people of Vietnam—against the Communists. . . . All we can do is help, and we are making it very clear. But I don't agree with those who say we should withdraw. That would be a great mistake." [3]

Although it was perfectly legitimate for the Johnson Administration to cite the last two sentences, they clearly depended on the earlier ones. Kennedy did not envision a war in which the Americans were dominant.

In any case, President Johnson soon demonstrated that he was not going to take the opportunity afforded by his succession to end the Vietnam conflict by negotiation. In a New Year's message to the South Vietnamese government of the day (a term not normally meant to be taken literally but often just that in Vietnam at that time; the General Duong Van Minh government lasted another twenty-nine days), President Johnson declared:

> "Neutralization of South Vietnam would only be another name for a Communist take-over. . . . The United States will continue to furnish you and your people with the fullest measure of support in this bitter fight. . . . We shall maintain in Vietnam American personnel and material as needed to assist you in achieving victory." [4]

Stevenson could hardly be faulted for assuming, as would most, that this was just the normal diplomatic rhetoric appropriate to such occasions, but before too many months had passed, it became abundantly clear that Johnson meant every word of the above statement. However, during these few months it was Stevenson's job as the Administration's chief spokesman to echo and reecho Johnson's words: "We want no wider war." And it was the chore of the man who had dedicated himself to the belief that negotiation, not military action, was the way to settle international disputes to reject publicly time and again overtures for another Geneva Conference. They came from UN Secretary General U Thant and French President De Gaulle, as well as from Moscow, Hanoi, the National Liberation Front in South Vietnam and, it must be emphasized, from Peking. There is simply no doubt about this crucial fact: the United States could have had negotiations in 1964 merely by saying yes.

But as on many occasions, Stevenson declared on May 21 before the UN Security Council that there was no need for another Geneva Conference such as the one in 1954 that presumably had provided for a peaceful settlement to France's long, costly and disastrous attempt to hold onto its Indochinese empire. Such a conference, said Stevenson, "if it reached any agreement at all, would prove no more effective than the agreements we already have." What was needed, he asserted, was that the agreements already in existence be respected. Inasmuch as Stevenson—and the Administration—were to say repeatedly that the conflict was caused by North Vietnam's refusal to observe the Geneva Agreements, this is clearly a key point that merits close examination.

Since Adlai Stevenson was not only a student of international affairs but a lawyer, he surely knew from his examination of the documents that it was not North Vietnam but the United States and South Vietnam that were the major violators of the Geneva Agreements. The victorious Vietminh would never have agreed to the Geneva Conference Agreements, which they thought did not give them as much as they had won from the French on the battlefield, were it not for the elections guaranteed by the agreements to be held throughout Vietnam, North and South, in 1956. Ho Chi Minh's negotiators reluctantly accepted the agreement— after prodding by Moscow and Peking (the fact that Moscow and Peking both eagerly sought a negotiated settlement to the Indochinese conflict was never mentioned by the United States)—

because of the certainty, shared by President Eisenhower, among others, that Ho's forces would win overwhelmingly in the internationally supervised elections.

However, South Vietnam refused to allow these guaranteed elections, a refusal possible only with the support—if not at the suggestion—of the United States. Since the United States has always professed its belief in free elections, *betrayal* of its fundamental principles is not too strong a word to describe American action. Further, the United States sent men and equipment to and established military bases in South Vietnam in clear violation of the Geneva Agreements.[5]

Further, Hanoi, instead of ordering the insurrection in the South, tried to prevent it while it sought by peaceful, political approaches to arrange the guaranteed elections. The NLF began the rebellion in the South because it believed that it had been abandoned by Ho's government in the North. Thus, it was only after events in the South threatened to cost Hanoi any influence it had on the rebels that Hanoi began to assist the NLF, and its assistance was paltry compared to that given the dictatorial Ngo Dinh Diem regime by the United States.

All this Adlai Stevenson knew as he stood before the United Nations and solemnly declared that it was North Vietnamese violations of the Geneva Agreements that had caused the Vietnam War. One can only wonder if such untruths were what he bargained for when he reluctantly agreed to take the job.

Speaking after his death, almost all his friends and colleagues cited as one of Stevenson's great virtues his integrity. And certainly his integrity—and his courage—had been demonstrated many times in the past, often at great political risks, such as the ones he took in giving a deposition favorable to Alger Hiss and in opposing Senator Joseph McCarthy at the height of his terroristic powers. Further, it can be argued that when a man departs from the truth in fulfilling his job as a diplomat, he is not compromising his personal integrity.

Yet some of Stevenson's friends went so far as to say he never knowingly told a lie during his service as UN Ambassador. Such a statement is wholly untenable, and it is difficult to believe that Stevenson himself would have ever made so incredible a claim. The clear, observable fact is that Stevenson often departed from the truth—about so decent a man who had contributed so much to raising the level of public debate, one is reluctant to use the word *lie*. The fundamental question, and it will be examined later in evaluating his United Nations years, is whether these departures were so flagrant and so inimicable to the principles of peace and justice in which he believed that they were a violation of his personal honor.

This clearly was not a question that a man like Stevenson could dismiss lightly. For although there are always many, in and out of government, who believe that any action is justified by the national interest (or by what they interpret to be the national interest), he was preeminent among those political figures to whom personal integrity was important and who regarded the national interest in broad rather than narrow, short-range terms. This fundamental dilemma should be borne in mind as we watch Stevenson during his last year.

Worse was yet to come. In the months between May and August 1964, the Johnson Administration indisputably decided that rather than seek peace by negotiation when the NLF and Hanoi held all the cards, it would attempt to swing the situation in favor of the United States—and only incidentally, South Vietnam—by escalating the war. The only thing needed was the occasion for escalation (this term, now a part of our everyday language, was relatively new then). The occasion was not hard to find, and Adlai Stevenson played a leading role in the charade.

The Tonkin Gulf events as they actually unfolded bear little resemblance to those reported and interpreted by the Administration, particularly by Stevenson before a series of tense meetings of the UN Security Council. As precisely as it can now be reconstructed, the course of events went like this: On July 25, 1964, Hanoi Radio charged the American Navy with firing on North Vietnamese fishing vessels and filed a formal complaint with the International Control Commission established by the 1954 Geneva Agreements. On July 31, Hanoi filed another formal protest with the ICC, alleging that South Vietnamese naval vessels under the protective cover of an American destroyer had bombarded two North Vietnamese islands the day before. Then on August 2 occurred the first of the incidents that changed the course of the war and with it the course of American history.

That night three North Vietnamese torpedo boats launched what the United States termed an "unprovoked" attack on the destroyer *Maddox* while it was on "routine patrol in international waters in the Gulf of Tonkin ... about 30 miles at sea from the mainland of North Vietnam." [6] According to the United States, two of the attacking craft fired torpedoes which the *Maddox* avoided, and all three directed machine-gun fire at the destroyer. The torpedo boats were driven off by the *Maddox,* aided by four planes from the aircraft carrier *Ticonderoga,* which had been alerted by the destroyer. The ship and the planes escaped without damage, whereas the *Maddox* reported that it had hit at least one of the attacking PT boats. Hanoi freely admitted the attack, saying it was in reprisal for the bombarding of the nearby North Vietnamese islands, Hon Me and Hon Ngu. According to the New York *Times* of August 3, the Administration did not regard it as a major crisis. Government officials, reported the *Times,* "said the United States Seventh Fleet had been patrolling the area for some time, would continue its patrols and had sufficient strength on hand." And Secretary Rusk, speaking characteristically, observed, "The other side got a sting out of this. If they do it again, they'll get another sting."

The second of these historic incidents took place on August 4, when the United States claimed that North Vietnamese torpedo boats had launched another attack, this time sixty-five miles at sea and against the destroyer *C. Turner Joy* as well as the *Maddox.* This time, according to the United States, two of the patrol boats were sunk before they were driven off. This time, however, Hanoi insisted that the PT boat raid never took place.

Whatever the true facts, President Johnson went on the air at 11:30 on the evening of August 4 in a television broadcast reminiscent of President Kennedy's chilling report to the American people about the introduction of Russian missiles into Cuba in 1962. Solemnly Johnson reported, "Air action is now in execution against gunboats and certain supporting facilities in North Vietnam which have been used in these hostile operations." This bureaucratic language meant that heavy American air attacks had been launched against North Vietnam and were taking place as he spoke, attacks that hit three major naval bases and, according to the Pentagon, demolished all three, destroyed or damaged twenty-five boats, and almost totally destroyed the local fuel depots.

Just before going on the air, Johnson had met with the congressional leaders of both parties and informed them, "I shall immediately request the Congress to pass a resolution making it clear that our government is united in its determination to take all necessary measures in support of freedom and in defense of peace in Southeast Asia." And he reported that the leaders of both houses had given him assurance that "such a resolution will be promptly introduced, freely and expeditiously debated, and passed with overwhelming support." [7]

At the same time, Stevenson was summoned from his vacation on an island off the coast of Maine. A boat took him to the mainland and an Air Force jet rushed him to Washington, where he was instructed to request an emergency meeting of the Security Council. This meeting, convened on August 5, was certainly intended to provide international justification for the extreme retaliation against North Vietnam and, perhaps more, through the glare of publicity at the United Nations, to increase the pressure on Congress to act swiftly—and without asking too many questions —to pass the Johnson resolution.

At this first meeting of the Security Council, Stevenson, with all his unique skill, used the standard American rhetoric: that the United States wanted "no wider war," that North Vietnam with Communist China's backing was the cause of all the trouble, and that peace would return to Indochina when Hanoi and Peking observed the Geneva Agreements. And referring to the specific occasion for the Security Council meeting, he said, "There no longer could be any shadow of doubt that this was a planned, deliberate military aggression against vessels present in international waters. One could only conclude that this was the work of authorities dedicated to the use of force to achieve their objectives regardless of the consequences." Stevenson went on to describe the American air attacks as "positive but limited and relevant measures to secure its naval units against further aggression." Stevenson declared that in an earlier intervention that same day, the United States had "sought to dampen the explosive potentialities . . . and to reduce the likelihood of expanding the conflict." [8] This latter statement has an Orwellian ring. The United States sought to "reduce the likelihood of expanding the conflict" by responding to a minor and unsuccessful attack by large-scale bombing that represented a significant and, as it turned out, historic escalation of the war. Then, on August 7, Stevenson termed the attacks on North Vietnam "a relevant response of self-defense." He was careful then, as two days before, not to use the word *retaliation,* because retaliation is against the United Nations Charter, and Stevenson himself on several occasions in that very Security Council chamber had said so.

At the time of the Tonkin crisis, Stevenson took time out to preside over what turned out to be a surprising social event, one that revealed something about the man. Some months before, he had met folk singer Joan Baez, who had long been an admirer. Miss Baez, a supporter of the UN (her father had worked for UNESCO), offered to do anything she could to help Stevenson in his work. Delighted, he replied that he hoped to be able to take her up on her offer. Then, some time later, her agent called Stevenson's office, said that Miss Baez was going to be in town, and repeated the proposal. Stevenson happily accepted, asking if she would sing at one of the affairs he held from time to time in the handsome, glass-walled hall atop the U.S. Mission, overlooking the UN grounds and the East River.

Stevenson was a little late for the gathering of foreign diplomats and U.S. Mission officials because he had been across the street at the Security Council meeting on the Tonkin Gulf incidents. Miss Baez included in her program such Bob Dylan protest songs as "God on My Side," "Times They Are A-Changing," and "Blowing in the Wind." This should not have surprised anyone, since that was the kind of song Miss Baez was famous for singing, but somehow hearing such bitter words—words less than admiring of America at a time of national crisis—shocked the audience, particularly the young Foreign Service officers. People who were there said there was a stunned silence. Even if some of them might have shared the criticism in Dylan's songs, the foreign diplomats didn't know where to look, and the young Americans were distressed.

The awkward silence continued until Stevenson stood and said with complete composure, "That was very nice, Joan. Now perhaps you'd sing us one last song." His casual, gracious words broke the tension, Miss Baez did sing another song, and the moment passed. Despite the circumstances, Stevenson, a believer in free expression, was clearly not distressed by the songs and probably enjoyed them.

Later, via her secretary, Pauline Marden, Miss Baez wrote me that she had chosen the Dylan songs "because they were appropriate at the moment." And Miss Marden went on to report, "Mr. Stevenson was quite exhausted, a little late, having stomach trouble, and pretending nothing was wrong in the world. Joan says that Mr. Stevenson was not reacting to anything that night, since he was so exhausted from having spent the day on TV telling lies. For example, she asked him what we were doing in Vietnam, and he said we were doing things like putting up hospitals and doing good things, and then he would leave the table because his stomach was bothering him.

"Joan said she liked Mr. Stevenson, felt a great compassion for him, but she cannot trust people in office. She felt badly because he had to put up a front for the United States' *faux pas,* the involvement in Vietnam. At one point she remembers asking him, 'What do you mean? The world's about to be blown up!' "

These Tonkin incidents, so eloquently described by Stevenson as "deliberate aggression," are worth closer examination, inasmuch as they were the turning point of the war and the occasion of a congressional resolution which President Johnson often said authorized the subsequent escalation of the conflict. In the first place, in view of the Administration's repeated misstatements on Vietnam, to phrase it as gently as possible, misstatements that have led to what came to be known as the "credibility gap," one cannot dismiss out of hand Hanoi's contention that American naval vessels participated in prior strikes against North Vietnamese territory. If this were true—and although it cannot be said with certainty that it was, neither can it be said that it was not—then it was the United States, not North Vietnam, that established the state of naval belligerency, thus providing to an extent that would have satisfied any government justification for North Vietnamese counterthrusts.

But there is more to consider. When the United States first reported the attack on the *Maddox,* it asserted that the destroyer was in international waters thirty miles off North Vietnam. However, the New York *Times* reported on August 11 that on the previous day Rear Admiral Robert B. Moore, commander of the task force that hit North Vietnam, "indicated that the destroyer *Maddox* might have been two or three miles inside the twelve-mile limit set by Hanoi for territorial waters. The United States, he pointed out, recognizes only the traditional three-mile limit." If this statement—which appeared in the last paragraph of a story on page 15, a curious place for information about an absolutely crucial point in the American justification—is true, it all but demolishes the American contention of North Vietnamese aggression in the Gulf of Tonkin.

That day, despite the obscure placement of the item, the Pentagon did not miss its significance, and the next day's *Times* carried a story in which a Defense Department spokesman said, "The destroyer was not closer than twelve miles from the North Vietnamese shore at the time of the first incident. . . ." The spokesman went on to say, as the *Times* reported, that "while the *Maddox* and other patrol warships occasionally went inside the twelve-mile limit set by Communist countries, because the United States recognizes only a three-mile limit, this was not the case on the day of the patrol-boat attack." There is no way of knowing now whether Admiral Moore, presumably a seaman of great experience, was wrong (and there's a considerable difference between nine or ten miles and thirty) or whether the Pentagon was trying to cover up what could have been, to say the least, a major embarrassment. Whichever, the inconsistency was not picked up, no doubt much to the Administration's relief.

However, two questions remain. Was it the United States and not North Vietnam that initiated naval warfare in the Gulf of Tonkin, and did the *Maddox* violate North Vietnamese territorial waters at the time of the first incident? Then, too, there is the flat and oft-repeated denial by North Vietnam that the second incident ever took place.

Senator William Fulbright was among the many who felt uneasy about the Tonkin incident, declaring:

"But this Gulf of Tonkin incident, if I may say so, was a very vague one. We were briefed on it, but we have no way of knowing, even to this day, what actually happened. I don't know whether we provoked that attack in connection with supervising or helping a raid by the South Vietnamese or not. Our evidence was sketchy as to whether those PT boats, or some kind of boats, that were approaching were coming to investigate or whether they actually attacked. I have been *told* there was no physical damage. They weren't hit by anything. I heard one man say there was one bullet hole in one of those ships. One bullet hole!" [9]

Fulbright's doubts persisted, as did those of many others, and little by little evidence has been filtering out—although the Administration has attempted to keep classified any information that might embarrass it—that casts the severest doubts on the truth of the Administration's original story. It now seems clear that the *Maddox* was within the twelve-mile limit claimed by North Vietnam, probably at the time it was attacked and certainly on a number of previous occasions. Also the *Maddox* and the *Joy* were not on "routine patrol" as reported at the time; they were carrying on electronic spy missions similar to those carried out by the *Liberty,* which was attacked by Israel in the June 1967 war, and by the *Pueblo* until it was captured by North Korea in January 1968. As Senator Wayne Morse has said, this was clearly a provocative action. Further, it now seems evident that President Johnson ordered the air raids against North Vietnam before the Navy had been able to verify that the *Maddox* and the *Joy* had been attacked on August 4, if indeed they were attacked.

Even assuming the American reports of the incidents were true (an often risky assumption where Vietnam is concerned), Stevenson, the dove of the Cuban missile crisis, must have wondered whether two feeble, totally unsuccessful PT boat attacks merited the overpowering response that he had to tell the Security Council and the world was "limited and relevant." Perhaps it occurred to him, as it did to many, that Johnson had seized the first convenient pretext to plunge deeper into war.

But Stevenson had more to be concerned about than an examination of the facts of the Tonkin incidents. It was their result that must have troubled him deeply. For the events in which he played so public a part had indeed led to swift passage of the resolution

Johnson had sent to Congress. On August 7, by a vote of 98 to 2 in the Senate (only Senators Morse and Gruening voted "nay") and 416 to 0 in the House, the resolution gave Johnson the "blank check" he was seeking. Or perhaps the event would be better described as opening Pandora's box.

In brief, the resolution gave congressional approval and support to the President's "determination . . . to take all necessary measures to repel any armed attack against the forces of the United States and to prevent further aggression." It also said that the United States was "prepared, as the President determines, to take all necessary steps, including the use of armed force, to assist any member or protocol state of the Southeast Asia Collective Defense Treaty requesting assistance in defense of its freedom."

Not since the Quemoy-Matsu situation in early 1955, when the United States feared a Chinese attack on these offshore islands, had a President asked for sweeping military powers—in advance. Then, as nine years later, Congress had proved easily swayed, and with Lyndon B. Johnson, then Senate majority leader, backing Eisenhower all the way, the Formosa Resolution passed. Then, as in 1964, Congress acted in haste and repented at leisure. But there was one major difference between 1955 and 1964. In 1955 Adlai Stevenson was against such a "blank check" resolution. "Stevenson thought the resolution unnecessary and ill-considered, since it seemed to commit the Democratic majority to supporting in advance almost any line the President might choose to follow. They had given Eisenhower a blank check. Indeed, it was already difficult for Senators disturbed by the tension over Quemoy and Matsu to speak out against the Administration." [10] Who more than Stevenson could have appreciated this latest in the series of ironies that seemed to characterize his career in public life? Only the proper names had to be changed to bring the above statement up to date.

And in the April 11, 1955, speech referred to earlier, Stevenson had discussed the Quemoy-Matsu situation in terms that could have applied equally well to Vietnam. He said the gravest peril to the American position in the offshore islands was the risk of losing allies who could not agree to a belligerent policy by the United States:

"I know some politicians tell us we don't need allies. Life would certainly be much simpler if that were so. But it is not so. We need allies because we have only six percent of the world's population. We need them because the overseas air bases essential to our own security are on their territory. We need allies because they are the source of indispensable strategic materials. We need, above all, the moral strength that the solidarity of the world community alone can bring to our cause. Let us never underestimate the weight of moral opinion. It was a general, Napoleon, who wrote that: 'In war, moral considerations are three-quarters of the battle.' "

The Stevenson of 1955 deplored the "rattling of the saber" and an American stance that made the country "appear hard, belligerent and careless." And he said, "As best we can, let us correct this distorted impression, for we will win no hearts and minds in new Asia by uttering louder threats and brandishing bigger swords."

One wonders what the Stevenson of 1964, in effect the leading salesman for the Tonkin Resolution, thought about the Stevenson of 1955, a leading opponent of the Formosa Resolution. And no doubt Stevenson, like many others at the UN and in Washington, had heard the widespread reports that Lyndon Johnson had been carrying the Tonkin Resolution around in his pocket for weeks, just waiting for a likely occasion to produce it. Testimony before the Senate Foreign Relations Committee in September 1966—two years later—tends to confirm these reports. Assistant Secretary of State William P. Bundy, one of the Administration's Vietnam gurus, told the committee in secret session that he had prepared several contingent drafts some time before the Tonkin incidents. He told the Senators that this was simply normal planning. But since Dean Rusk did not mention this to the committee when he testified after the Tonkin incidents, Senators began to wonder whether the Administration had already decided to escalate the war and was merely waiting for its chance to push the resolution through Congress when not too many awkward questions would be asked.[11]

There is an interesting, almost amusing, sidelight to the Tonkin Resolution affair. The New York *Times*—which later thundered against congressional haste in giving Johnson a blank check—had a somewhat different view then. According to an editorial on August 6, the *Times* felt that Johnson had made it clear that we want "no wider war." And it went on to declare, "The President has rightly asked that the resolution express a determination that 'all necessary measures' be taken." One wonders if that editorial view had any influence on placing at the end of a story on page 15 the indication by Admiral Moore that the *Maddox* had been inside the twelve-mile limit for territorial waters claimed by North Vietnam. But one shouldn't focus indignation on the New York *Times*. Virtually the entire American press lay supine before the Administration, adding further to the melancholy evidence that the press, on fundamental matters, is slow to ask fundamental questions.

But things were happening rapidly, and Stevenson no doubt had little time to dwell on the ironic or amusing aspects of the Tonkin Resolution, for at about this time, UN Secretary General U Thant approached him with a plan for secret talks between American and North Vietnamese emissaries. This approach was kept undercover for months, and even by mid-1968 the principals had not spoken about it publicly. But the essentials of the story—which has been a constant source of irritation to Dean Rusk—can now be told in considerable detail.

For a full understanding of the Thant initiatives, it is necessary to go back a bit. Thant had always thought that American intervention was not only morally wrong but could lead to the wider war that Johnson and Stevenson were later to say again and again the United States didn't want. As early as January 29, 1963, he said in a press conference in response to a question about a reported Soviet military buildup in Cuba:

"If one says that the presence of Soviet technicians on Cuban soil constitutes a threat to peace in the area, others may say —they are actually saying it—that the presence of American troops in South Vietnam also constitutes a threat to peace in that particular area. Of course, if you go on discussing these phenomena, there will be no end to this debate. What we should do now, in the context of the developments in Cuba or South Vietnam or in Ruritania or anywhere, will be to explore the means of easing tensions and bringing about better understanding between the Powers primarily involved. I think this is the only sensible thing to do." [12]

Later, after the coup that killed dictator Ngo Dinh Diem, Thant hoped, as did many Americans, that the situation in Vietnam would improve. But the assassination of Kennedy, just three weeks after the same fate had befallen Diem, precluded any immediate amelioration. However, in talks with Stevenson, Thant advocated the establishment of a broadly based government in Saigon that would include political leaders brought back from exile. But the United States, as events would prove, wanted not a representative government but one that would carry on the fight against the Vietcong.

Subsequently Thant joined leaders in Hanoi, Moscow, Peking, Paris and elsewhere in calling for the reconvening of the Geneva Conference. This, as we saw, was turned down by Washington, with Stevenson carrying the public burden of trying to prove that a reconvened conference was not necessary.

When the Tonkin Gulf incidents demonstrated that the already serious situation was on the verge of getting out of hand altogether, Thant took another initiative. In Washington as the guest of Johnson and Rusk, he suggested to Rusk in Stevenson's presence that private talks be held between Washington and Hanoi. Thant had the feeling, according to those close to him, that the Delphic Rusk was receptive to the idea.[13] Using the Russians as intermediaries, Thant therefore passed the proposal on to Ho Chi Minh, assuring him that if talks were held, it would be in complete secrecy. Within three weeks Hanoi let Thant know that it had accepted the proposal, and Stevenson notified the State Department to that effect.

However, Stevenson was told that nothing could be done until after the November elections. Presumably Washington was afraid that if word leaked out, Senator Barry Goldwater could accuse Johnson of planning to sell out South Vietnam. The election came and went, U Thant went into the hospital with an ulcer and came out, and on January 10, 1965, Stevenson went to the Secretary General and, clearly disturbed, had to inform Thant that after nearly five months there was still no response, one way or the other, from Washington. One of Stevenson's closest colleagues has wondered why Stevenson waited so long, why he didn't insist that Rusk say whether or not the United States would meet privately with Hanoi.

But now Stevenson decided to take action on his own, without authorization from the unresponsive State Department. He asked Thant where he proposed the talks be held. Thant suggested his native Burma. Stevenson then asked Thant to find out if Burma would agree to such talks being held in Rangoon. On January 18, within forty-eight hours, Ne Win, the Burmese head of state, agreed to secret talks as long as his country would not be directly involved. Stevenson passed this on to Washington and finally, at the end of January, got an answer.

Washington argued that news of the talks would reach Saigon and destroy that government's morale. Thant's response was that the Saigon government was falling every two months anyway. Washington also said that it had learned, through the Canadian representative on the International Control Commission in Hanoi, that Ho Chi Minh was not interested in such talks. Thant knew otherwise, and later the Canadians told him that they had made no such check.

Stevenson was deeply disturbed by Washington's decision and, as he reported to Eric Sevareid, Thant was furious. However, neither man said anything publicly, although Thant did allude to his private efforts at a press conference on February 24, a couple of weeks after the United States had started the regular bombing of North Vietnam. He told correspondents in the enormous conference room that the situation in South Vietnam had "gone from bad to worse" and that the "prospects for a peaceful settlement of this problem will be more and more remote as time goes on and as the aggravation develops. But still I do not believe it is too late to try diplomatic and political methods of negotiation and discussion." [14]

Thant went on to say that he had never advocated the immediate withdrawal of the United States from South Vietnam:

> "I am fully conscious of the fact that such a step will naturally involve questions of face and prestige, and questions of abrogation of previous commitments, and so forth. But I feel that once the diplomatic and political methods have been

tried and if there is any perceptible improvement in the situation, if an agreed formula is at hand, if some sort of stability can be restored in the country, then at that time, of course, the United States can withdraw its troops with dignity."

The Secretary General then told the international press corps that he had presented "certain ideas on my own to some of the principal parties directly involved in the question of Viet-Nam. I have even presented concrete ideas and proposals. But up to this moment, the results of these consultations and discussions have not been conclusive." But although Thant did identify the United States as one of those to whom proposals had been made, he would not make them public.

The State Department in general and Dean Rusk in particular had long regarded Thant as a meddler. It was bad enough, in their view, that he was clearly opposed to U.S. intervention in Vietnam, but they were angered that he made public statements damaging to the American image as the champion of world peace. They thought that, as an international civil servant, he should keep quiet on Vietnam. The Administration could never understand that Thant thought it his duty to evaluate things as he saw them. However, the United States was never reluctant to seize on statements by Thant and his two predecessors, Trygve Lie and Dag Hammarskjold, when they were favorable to the American position on any issue, as they often were.

It was during this press conference that Thant made a statement for which he was never forgiven, either by Rusk or by Johnson. After paying ritual respect to President Johnson's "wisdom, moderation and sensitivity to world opinion," he said:

"I am sure the great American people, if only they know the true facts and the background to the developments in South Viet-Nam, will agree with me that further bloodshed is unnecessary. And also that the political and diplomatic method of discussions and negotiations alone can create conditions which will enable the United States to withdraw gracefully from that part of the world. As you know, in times of war and of hostilities the first casualty is truth."

Thus Thant demonstrated that he was aware of the "credibility gap" long before the term become commonplace in American political discussion. And Washington's response proved the point. Needless to say, reporters rushed to the White House press office to find out about Thant's "concrete ideas and proposals." But George Reedy, President Johnson's press secretary, denied that any proposal had been received from Thant or anyone else, in effect saying that Thant was lying. Stevenson, of course, knew that it was his government that was lying about events in which he had played a direct part.

However, it must be said in defense of Rusk and the State Department that they did have a reason for being angered with Thant—a reason beyond the fact that he made public his belief that the United States was wrong in Vietnam and that its people were being misled by the Administration. During this same press conference Thant cited his own country, Burma, as an example of one that had been able to handle its own problem of Communist insurrection without outside help, even though it has a thousand-mile border with China. Pointing out that the Communist party was "still underground after seventeen years and still illegal," Thant said:

"If only the Burmese government had decided at some stage to seek outside military assistance to suppress the internal insurrections and revolts, then I am sure that Burma would have experienced one of the two alternatives: either the country would be divided into two parts or the whole country would have become Communist long ago. This proves one point: that Burma's attitude and policies both in regard to domestic affairs and foreign affairs have been very appropriate in the circumstances prevailing in Southeast Asia.

"Not one American life has been lost in Burma. Not one American dollar has been spent in Burma in the form of military assistance in the last seventeen years. We should ask the great question: Why? I just present these facts to you just to set about thinking: Why?"

Bitterly American State Department men asked privately how Thant could have any credibility as an authority on events in

Southeast Asia when he didn't even know, after his experience as a high Burmese official, that the United States had secretly provided his government with millions of dollars in arms to fight the Communist rebels.

Thant's belief that the American supply of arms to South Vietnam had precipitated the situation was mentioned to Rusk at their meeting the previous August. Further, according to high American sources, Thant tried to convince Rusk that Ho Chi Minh was not really a Communist. All this, it has been said, persuaded Rusk and the State Department that Thant's views could not be taken seriously. To be sure, his ignorance of the supply of American arms to Burma did make that part of his argument sound foolish. But it is indisputable that without American aid, South Vietnam would have been unable to prevent compliance with the Geneva Agreements and that the problem, as it came to exist, would never have developed. And events have proven that despite the fact that Ho Chi Minh is one of the world's most celebrated Communists, he is first and foremost a nationalist, as Stalin was and Mao is—although Washington tragically has never recognized it.

Thus, despite this apparent justification for some of Rusk's bitterness against Thant, the conclusion is inescapable that the Johnson Administration simply did not trust Thant's opinions, particularly on Vietnam, and regarded him as a stubborn and formidable obstacle to its efforts to convince the world of the justice of its cause in Vietnam. This conclusion is not the author's alone; it has long been widely held in the United Nations press corps.

In April 1965 there was a brief flurry of hope. On April 1, seventeen nonaligned nations called for negotiations on Vietnam without preconditions. And on April 7, President Johnson at Johns Hopkins University in Baltimore declared that the United States was ready for such "unconditional discussions." [15] Perhaps overeager to detect an American change of heart concerning what he considered a dangerous policy, U Thant welcomed the speech, saying that he regarded Johnson's "indication of a readiness to enter into 'unconditional discussions' as both constructive and statesmanlike. . . . It may well be, Mr. President, that your speech will make a turning point in the long-standing Vietnam conflict." [16] And Thant described as "positive, forward-looking and generous"

Johnson's proposal for a gigantic Southeast Asia development program, for which he would ask Congress for a billion-dollar contribution and in which North Vietnam could participate.

Thus, when Premier Pham Van Dong of North Vietnam indicated on April 8, as reported in the press, that talks might be possible, this hope seemed justified, causing Thant to declare: "I strongly hope that there will be a prompt follow-up on the stated willingness of the parties directly involved to enter into discussions and that no effort will be spared to get discussions started with a minimum of delay. The world, which is gravely threatened by this conflict, is certainly due this much." Also during this hopeful period, the Secretary General drafted an appeal for a cease-fire, gave a copy to Stevenson and said he would be willing to consider whatever changes the United States might suggest.

But whatever Washington said to Stevenson, it did not authorize him to reply to Thant. It seems Senator Wayne Morse was right when on April 10 he said of Johnson's heralded speech that he saw nothing in it that indicated the Administration had negotiations in mind. Somehow, in all the euphoria, the speech had not been read carefully. Johnson's call for "unconditional discussions" simply was not that at all. There was a vital condition in the speech. Negotiations could be held only with "the governments concerned." This meant only one thing—and why it was overlooked at the time is hard to say, perhaps due to wishful thinking —that North Vietnam could be represented, but not the NLF. This was not only unacceptable to North Vietnam and the NLF but totally unrealistic, for it would be impossible to end the fighting in the South without negotiating with the main force struggling against the Saigon government, the NLF's Vietcong. So the hope, for a few days so desperately seized by so many, dissipated, while escalation continued.

It is not hard to imagine Stevenson's reaction to all this, but, as we shall see, it is not necessary to imagine. There is considerable evidence of what Stevenson thought. And all during these months, beginning with the Tonkin Gulf crisis in which he played such a major role, there were snowballing protests by the very people who had formed the heart of his political support and with whom he felt such close ties, the intellectual and academic communities.

A book could be written about these protests—protests unparalleled in American history. Approximately 1,000 in New York heard Norman Thomas criticize the war. Senator Frank Church said the United States should never have intervened. Arnold Toynbee criticized the United States. Senator George McGovern advocated a political settlement. Educators at more than 25 New England colleges urged negotiations in a New York *Times* ad. The United Church of Christ appealed to Johnson to respond favorably to Thant's negotiation proposal. Oberlin College staged a hunger strike. A group of New York City-area professors urged negotiations. College professors in San Francisco took an ad in the *Chronicle*. The Central Conference of American Rabbis urged Johnson to negotiate. Asserting that U.S. policy was futile, the World Council of Churches urged negotiations. Delegates of the California Democratic Council and John Kenneth Galbraith criticized U.S. policy. A Wisconsin University student-faculty committee protested. More than 2,000 attended an eight-hour teach-in at Columbia University. And 23 scholars signed a petition urging Johnson to negotiate, while 2,700 clergymen urged a cease-fire and withdrawal of U.S. troops. Artists and writers called for an immediate halt in the bombing. Martin Luther King said he had no objection to civil rights workers participating in anti-U.S. policy demonstrations. A Boston-area faculty group demanded a negotiated peace. A total of 100,000 students and faculty at 100 colleges watched a televised teach-in, and 10,000 attended a Berkeley teach-in. Lewis Mumford, president of the American Academy of Arts and Letters, called U.S. policy a "moral outrage." Archibald MacLeish, who was later to speak at a Stevenson Memorial at the United Nations, said that U.S. actions had changed the conception of the United States in many minds, causing many to see this country as indifferent to public opinion and outgrowing its old idealism. And thousands of students picketed the White House and the UN.

The student protests must have been particularly hard for Stevenson to bear. One of his happiest characteristics had always been his genuine and deep interest in young people. His appointments secretary, David Guyer, said, for instance, that whenever Stevenson came to his house for dinner, he would visit with the children before going in to greet the other guests. And whenever his friends had children in school or college, he made specific inquiries about what they were doing or, if young people were present, he asked questions that demonstrated a sincere interest in what they were thinking. It was ironic, then, that at the time of his death, Stevenson was no longer the symbol of idealism he had been ten and fifteen years before. Perhaps it was the young people who had changed, but whatever the reason, young, politically minded idealists were prone to think of him as a nice old man who now belonged to that other camp. What a difference from those exciting days of 1952, when Stevenson had stirred the young idealists the same way Roosevelt had in the early thirties. Then Stevenson was a Pied Piper leading the young on to political adventures. Indeed, as many have noted, it was this reinvigoration of Roosevelt's party that made Kennedy possible. Stevenson's appeal to the young was not the physical appeal of Kennedy, whom Norman Mailer aptly termed "the first movie star President"; his was a deeper appeal, an appeal to the mind and spirit. Thus, one of the many regrets that was felt at Stevenson's death was that he, who had so often sounded the tocsin against drift and complacency, had become, however reluctantly, their defender.

Almost every day there was another protest by those who were by conviction—by instinct, even—Stevenson men. And with the U.S. intervention in the Dominican Republic, an action in direct violation of the United Nations Charter and that of the Organization of American States, the protests grew. In the UN press corps there was continual speculation as to whether Stevenson would resign and widespread agreement that he would fatally compromise his integrity if he stayed on much longer. Pickets began to march in front of the U.S. Mission across First Avenue from the United Nations. Even inside the mission, some of Stevenson's closest colleagues were advising him to leave, not in public protest, to be sure, but to escape an impossible situation. Mail began to arrive from supporters urging him to resign. For instance, writer Martha Gellhorn sent him a letter from Africa saying she was ashamed of America and that he represented the only hope of diverting the country from its disastrous course.

Then on June 21, just over three weeks before his death, an event took place that was to disturb him profoundly, one that he discussed with his intimates right up to the day he died. On

June 21 he was asked face-to-face not only to resign but to lead the opposition to President Johnson's foreign policy. This unique confrontation—which received only brief passing notice in the press—took place when Stevenson met for nearly an hour and a half with writer Kay Boyle, writer-philosopher Paul Goodman, writer-critic Dwight Macdonald, novelist Harvey Swados, the young Socialist leader David McReynolds, writer-critic Nat Hentoff, and William Meyer, the former Democratic Congressman from Vermont. During this spirited but courteous exchange, Stevenson turned aside requests that he resign in protest, but he was clearly shaken. This revealing encounter, which symbolized the growing gulf between Stevenson and the intellectual community that had been the heart and spirit of his political support, will be discussed in considerable detail when we examine Stevenson's final troubled weeks.

Stemming from this encounter was a "letter" to Paul Goodman that was not made public until months after Stevenson's death on July 14. This letter came to light only after the Eric Sevareid *Look* article appeared on November 15, saying that Stevenson was on the verge of resigning. A month later, Clayton Fritchey, in his *Newsday* column cited earlier, wrote, "Despite a number of highly publicized reports to the contrary, Adlai Stevenson did not die an embittered and disappointed man, weary with frustration and disillusioned with public office."

Fritchey went on to say that although Stevenson was "troubled" by some aspects of foreign policy, including Vietnam and the Dominican Republic, so was everyone else, "including the President himself."

"He was pleased at Johnson's increasing emphasis on a negotiated peace for Vietnam," said Fritchey, but this is difficult to reconcile with Stevenson's knowledge that the Administration had turned down U Thant's efforts to arrange peace talks and had, in fact, denied that such efforts had been made.

Then Fritchey brought up the letter written to Paul Goodman, citing it as evidence that Stevenson was basically in sympathy with Johnson foreign policy. The same day in Chicago, Adlai E. Stevenson III released the complete letter. However, unlike the New York *Times* story, Stevenson's son noted that the letter was "still in draft form and contain[ed] handwritten corrections." This, as we shall see, is important.

The younger Stevenson released the letter with this statement:

"My father's former associate and good friend, Clayton Fritchey, has published excerpts from a letter on U.S. foreign policy written by my father shortly before his death. Very recently I received this letter, still in draft form and containing handwritten corrections, from Philip Kaiser, the American minister in London.

"In the interest of history and in order to carry out my father's intentions, I am making the full text of the letter public. In June 1965 my father told me that he had received many suggestions that he resign his post as U.S. Representative at the United Nations to protest U.S. policy in Vietnam. He told me that on the contrary, he intended to restate publicly and firmly his support of our Vietnam policy in a letter to Paul Goodman of North Stratford, New Hampshire. Mr. Goodman was one of those who had urged him to resign. My father prepared a draft of this letter and gave it to Mr. Kaiser for his comments three days before he died. He died before he mailed this letter.

"By releasing this letter to the public, I am carrying out my father's intentions. Moreover, it contains some of his views on long-range foreign policy objectives, as well as his reaffirmation of support for our Viet Nam policy. It may therefore be of current interest and historical value."

Since this letter is the keystone in the Johnson Administration argument that Stevenson was really in accord with Johnson's foreign policy and since it does have some, although limited, historic interest, it may be useful to present it verbatim.

"Dear Mr. Goodman:

"Thank you for your letter. Its arguments, I think, rest on a simple presupposition: that I share your belief in the disastrous trend of American foreign policy and that I must therefore resign to underline my disagreement, rally public opinion against it and nail the 'lies' into which it is being presented to the people.

"But it is precisely this presupposition that I do not share with you, and I would like to send you my reasons for believing that whatever criticisms may be made over the detail and emphasis of American foreign policy, its purpose and direction are sound.

"Our overriding purpose must be to avoid war. Yet we still live in a state of bitter national anarchy in which each nation claims absolute sovereignty and great powers believe they can enforce the aims and interests which they consider paramount.

"I believe that the ultimate disaster of atomic conflict can be avoided in this situation only by the pursuit of two clear lines of policy.

"The first is to establish a tacitly agreed frontier between Communist and non-Communist areas of influence on the understanding that neither power system will use force to change the status quo. On the other side of it there may [be] change, of course, but not outside intervention of that line.

"The second is to move from this position of precarious stability toward agreed international procedures for settling differences, towards the building of an international juridical and policing system and toward a whole variety of policies designed to turn our small vulnerable planet into a genuine economic and social community.

"If you like, the first policy is static and defensive, the second creative and constructive. Both have to be pursued together.

"The period from 1947 to 1962 was largely occupied in fixing the postwar line with the Soviet line. It is not a very satisfactory one since it divided Germany and Berlin. But the Russians respect it in Europe. So do we.

"The Russians are perhaps not wholly committed to it since their doctrine included the right to encourage 'wars of national liberation.' These, we know, can lead to the imposition of governments which are not later answerable to any form of popular approbation or control. However, the missile crisis of 1962 may have convinced the Russian leaders that interventions of that sort beyond the tacit frontiers of the two worlds are in fact too costly and dangerous.

"We have no such line with the Chinese. Since they are in an earlier, more radical stage of their revolution, it may be more difficult to establish one. Should we try? And is the line we stand on halfway across Vietnam a reasonable line? Should we hold it?

"Let me take the second point first. I have no doubt that if France had handled the forces of decolonization in the prompt and orderly fashion of the British, the situation in Southeast Asia might be much more stable today. It can even be argued that in 1954 we should not have taken any action to guarantee a non-Communist regime to South Vietnam. Yet we did so in South Korea and it was reasonable to argue that the refugees streaming south from Hanoi had as much desire to avoid Communism as the people of South Korea. In any case, the line inherited by the Democratic Administration is the 17th Parallel. History does not always give us the most convenient choice. What sane statesman would choose West Berlin, for instance? Yet can one doubt its pivotal significance?

"Since this is the line, should we hold it? The answer depends on the assumptions made about Chinese power. In the past, some Chinese dynasties have been aggressive, claiming sovereignty over wide areas of Asia, including all Southeast Asia and even some of India. So far, the new Communist dynasty has been very aggressive. Tibet was swallowed, India attacked, the Malays had to fight twelve years to resist a 'national liberation' they could receive from the British by a more peaceful route. Today, the apparatus of infiltration and aggression is already at work in North Thailand. Chinese maps show to the world's chagrin the furthest limits of the old empire marked as Chinese. I do not think the idea of Chinese expansionism is so fanciful that the effort to check it is irrational.

"And if one argues it should not be checked, I believe you set us off on the old, old route whereby expansive powers push at more and more doors, believing they will open, until, at the ultimate door, resistance is unavoidable and major war breaks out.

"As President Johnson pointed out the other day, my country has suffered 160,000 casualties since the last war, but aggression didn't succeed—with your help—in Greece or Turkey, Iran or Formosa, Korea or Lebanon. And I think timely resistance has vastly enhanced the hope for peace and the prospects for the evolution of the principle of peaceful settlement of disputes underlined in the U.N. Charter.

"While I hesitate to draw historical comparisons with the Chinese, I remind you that the French Revolution led to prolonged war before the limits of France's power to control its neighbors were established.

"My hope in Vietnam is that relatively small-scale resistance now may establish the fact that changes in Asia are not to be precipitated by outside force. This was the point of the Korean War. This is the point of the conflict in Vietnam. I believe Asia will be more stable if the outcome is the same in both—a negotiated line and a negotiated peace—a just and honorable peace which leaves the future of the people of South Vietnam to be decided by them and not by force from North Vietnam.

"This brings me to my second point—the hope of transcending the static policy of containment and moving to the more creative task of building a world security based on law and peaceful settlement.

"I believe that we must seek a negotiated peace in Vietnam based upon the internationalization of the whole area's security, on a big effort to develop, under the U.N., the resources of the Mekong River and guarantees that Vietnam, North and South, can choose, again under international supervision, the kinds of governments, the form of association and, if so decreed, the type of reunification of the two states they genuinely want to establish.

"If we can achieve this, we begin to offer the small nations of the world an alternative to being within spheres of influence. We are more decisively beyond the age of empires. We would begin to establish procedures by which local revolutionary movements, such as the rising in the Dominican Republic, and for that matter, Zanzibar, are not automatically a prey to outside intervention.

"I believe, for instance, that the U.N. effort in the Congo

did prevent Central Africa from becoming a Southeast Asia, and I would make the strengthening of these U.N. procedures and activities a cardinal principle in a policy aimed at substituting 'due process' for violence as the basis of international life. Meanwhile, I do not believe the opposite policy of retreat in Asia or anywhere else would make any contribution whatsoever to the ideal that violence should not be the formal arbitrator in world affairs.

"It is my conviction that American policy is groping its way toward this difficult, but essential ideal, and this is the reason both for my support of the policy and for my continuance in a position which gives me some hope of assisting its advance in that direction.

"Now it is possible for honest men to differ on every aspect of this interpretation. You may believe the Communist powers are not expansive. Or you may believe that the changes they seek to support by violence are beneficent changes which can be achieved by no other way. Again, you may believe that a return to some form of non-involvement in world affairs is the best posture for America. Or you may genuinely believe that America is in Vietnam 'for sheer capitalist greed.' These are all possible attitudes and I do not impugn the good faith of those who hold different views.

"I would simply ask them, in the names of the courtesies and decencies of a free society, that they should equally refrain from impugning mine."

This, then, is the letter that proves, according to his son, Adlai III, that Stevenson supported Johnson's foreign policy. Careful investigation has discovered that this letter is fragile support indeed, for one of Stevenson's closest colleagues has asserted flatly that the content "didn't jibe" with previous discussions as to how to answer Paul Goodman. This colleague reports that Stevenson left him a draft of the letter before departing for Europe, asking him to go over it with some care. He says further that the letter was done hurriedly after the encounter with Goodman and the other intellectuals, and he feels sure that the letter as made public by Adlai III was not in its final form, that it would have been changed, and that if Stevenson had been satisfied with it, he would have sent it. This colleague also reports that the draft, which Stevenson had taken with him to Geneva and London, naturally got into the hands of the State Department and the President and that the "Administration loved it."

This evidence alone—from one who was indisputably in a position to know—is conclusive that the letter was not Stevenson's final, considered view. But there's more. Another of Stevenson's closest friends, one who had worked intimately with him since the 1952 campaign and who had held high posts under both Kennedy and Johnson, regards the letter as "terrible." He said that it represented what neither Stevenson nor his ghost-writer believed, but rather the "yellow peril" argument advanced two years later by Dean Rusk and Vice-President Humphrey. Stevenson's colleague was referring, of course, to Rusk's statement in late 1967 in which he pictured the menace of a billion Chinese armed with nuclear weapons. And the colleague suggests that the letter was not at all intended as an expression of Stevenson's own beliefs but merely as a tactical maneuver.

Since this letter has been given such importance by the Administration, it merits close examination. In the first place, it can be said flatly that Stevenson was not a Munich man. He did not share what seemed to be basic to Rusk's philosophy: the conviction that China had to be stopped or it would conquer Asia as Hitler had Europe. Not a single one of Stevenson's closest colleagues regarded him as having accepted the facile Munich analogy. Indeed, Stevenson had long recognized the need for better Chinese-American relations and that such relations were possible only with concessions by both sides.[17] Further, Stevenson was deeply concerned about Rusk's intractable antagonism toward China, an antagonism shared by much of the "bomb them back to the Stone Age" leadership in the Pentagon.

This deep concern, shared by many others then and since, received extraordinary public expression during the UN's twentieth anniversary celebration in San Francisco in June 1965. During these days—days of the greatest possible frustration for Stevenson —one of his closest aides came storming into the press room and, obviously so disturbed that he lost for a moment his normal caution with the press, blurted out, "Stevenson's going to quit when they decide to bomb China."[18] This was, of course, not a reasoned statement, but it was certainly a spontaneous expression of one of Stevenson's fears.

As to the facts cited in Stevenson's letter, he clearly must have known that some of them were dubious indeed. While calling for a negotiated peace, he knew that it was in fact the United States and South Vietnam that had violated the peace that had already been negotiated at Geneva in 1954. And while advocating an "understanding that neither power system will use force to change the status quo," Stevenson knew that it was American power that had changed the status quo in Vietnam.

Nor does this statement stand up to scrutiny: "the missile crisis of 1962 may have convinced the Russian leaders that interventions of that sort beyond the tacit frontiers of the two worlds are in fact too costly and dangerous. We have no such line with the Chinese. Since they are in an earlier, more radical stage in their revolution, it may be more difficult to establish one. Should we try? And is the line we stand on halfway across Vietnam a reasonable line? Should we hold it?" Then Stevenson goes on to defend the American thesis that such a line should indeed be established and at China's very doorstep. Such a proposal would be greeted with incredulity if Russia or China tried to establish such a line, say, in Canada or Mexico. And when he said that "changes in Asia are not to be precipitated by outside force," he knew that the Vietnam struggle was a civil war in which the United States was the outside force.

Thus, examining Stevenson the statesman and his letter, it is all but indisputable that the unmailed draft did not, no matter what was said by his son, genuinely represent his views. This assertion could perhaps be disputed were it not for the considerable body of evidence gathered by conversations with most of Stevenson's closest colleagues. Almost all agree he was deeply distressed by the bombing of North Vietnam. Not only was he disturbed by the humanitarian aspect, but from his survey of Allied bombing undertaken just after World War II, he knew that bombing simply did not have the strategic effect that Air Force leaders forever claim it has, particularly against so primitive an economy as North Vietnam's. Further, one of Stevenson's most cherished goals was the achievement of a *detente* with the Soviet Union, a goal that was on the verge of fulfillment until America began to escalate the war. Although he realized that cynicism often motivated Russian foreign policy—as it does that of all major powers—he was surely aware of the fact that Russia's support of North Vietnam and the NLF was not merely a public posture it felt it had to adopt, but a genuine conviction that the United States had transgressed the behavior permissible even to a great power. Stevenson had long and eloquently advocated an end to the cold war as being necessary to a reasonable international society, and here was the cold war being revived not by Russia but by the United States.

There is no doubt that all through the Kennedy and Johnson years, Stevenson suggested to the Administration (the singular is used because Vietnam policy was in the same hands under both Presidents: Rusk, Rostow, the Bundys, Komer and McNamara) that it try to get the Vietnam situation out of a military context into a political one and out of the Vietnamese context into a Southeast Asia one. However, he was only a "moderate dove," a term applied to him by a number of his intimates, until some months before his death. He evidently thought until fairly late that if only a small American involvement were required, it was worth a try to keep South Vietnam out of Communist hands. But in the last months, as American troop strength was rapidly increased, as American bombers began routinely to fly over Vietnam, his reservations multiplied. And curiously, it was not events in Vietnam but those in the Dominican Republic that caused him to have the gravest doubts that President Johnson knew what he was doing overseas.

As was perfectly clear at the time, Stevenson thought that the Dominican intervention was a disaster. But what was not widely known then was that Stevenson considered it a disaster not only in and of itself, but for what it revealed about Johnson's foreign policy generally. This is not mere surmise. At the end of May— just six weeks before his death—Stevenson was in Canada to receive an honorary degree from the University of Toronto. During free moments he made a series of telephone calls to Arthur Schlesinger, who was then in Washington working on his Kennedy book. For a time, whenever Stevenson called Schlesinger was out, and whenever Schlesinger returned the call Stevenson was not available. But finally they made contact, and Stevenson told Schlesinger that he had something important to talk over, asking if they could meet in Washington the next day, where he was to do the narration for Aaron Copland's *Lincoln Portrait*. And he suggested three o'clock at any convenient tennis court.

This was typical of Stevenson. Although he gave every outward appearance, to the public at least, of being in robust good health, it must be remembered that he was, after all, sixty-five and that he was under the most constant and extreme physical, mental and, in the last months, psychological pressure imaginable. And there were signs, although not widely known then, that his health was not perfect. He was exhausted in every way it is possible for a man to be exhausted. He was substantially overweight. He was not getting enough sleep. He was drinking and smoking more than was good for him; one friend said sympathetically that "he kept going on nerves and whiskey." He avoided doctors because they always told him the same things: cut down on the smoking and drinking, lose weight and get more sleep. However, once in a while he'd try to diet, and during these periods his luncheons at the Waldorf were on the skimpy side, causing his guests to remark privately with rueful humor that Stevenson was trying to starve them, too. Stevenson was normally a splendid host, but when it came to depriving himself, he acted just like a little boy. He was physically pained to sit down to an austere meal if his companions had their plates full. Evidently the only way he could force himself to cut down was to have everyone else cut down, too. He, like Oscar Wilde, could resist everything but temptation.

According to Kenneth S. Davis in his fine biography, Marietta Tree knew that Stevenson occasionally had "attacks of what he laughingly called 'the flutters'—an erratic throbbing of the heart." [19] Davis reports also that his devoted secretary, Roxane Eberline, knew that a cardiograph taken in late 1964 was not good. And he writes that Stevenson told his son Borden during the flight to Toronto, "You know, Borden, I have a heart problem." But that's all he would say to his anxious son. After receiving the degree and making the address (the *quid pro quo*), Stevenson was the guest of honor at a dinner. During the dinner party he felt ill and asked if there were some place he could lie down. But after resting a while he got up and went on to a dance because it was in his honor.[20]

That was his way: to make no concessions to his health. Maybe he simply refused to believe that his health, which had always been so good, would ever let him down. That, at least, had been something he had always been able to rely on. Not only did he refuse to take heed from the Toronto incident, but when he got to Washington, he played tennis with the vigor of a twenty-year-old, even though it was just a day or two after his indisposition.

After tennis, Schlesinger reports, Stevenson talked a lot about his disquietude over Vietnam. He kept asking questions about what the United States was up to, where it was going. He was worried about the United States trying to find a military solution to a political problem. He felt the country was overcommitted. But what was most important, says Schlesinger, was that Stevenson was profoundly disturbed by what seemed in the Dominican Republic a misuse of American power.[21] Schlesinger feels that because of the Dominican Republic, Stevenson "began to think that Johnson didn't know what he was doing in Vietnam." This view is not Schlesinger's alone, for a number of Stevenson's colleagues have reported to the author that he doubted Johnson had the depth and the sense of history basic to a sound foreign policy.

There is an interesting point that should perhaps be mentioned here. During the months immediately after Stevenson's death, his friends and colleagues respected the decision he had made—or at least had not yet unmade—to support publicly Johnson policy, and these friends did all they could to make it seem that Stevenson did in fact support this policy privately as well as publicly. However, as they themselves became increasingly disillusioned, even horrified, by the Vietnam War, they began to drop this pretense and spoke candidly, even if not always for attribution.

Stevenson also told Schlesinger that he had to get out of his job at the UN. Schlesinger dismissed this at the time, as did most of Stevenson's friends, for he was forever saying he wanted to leave, but under the circumstance of his undeniable distress, what Stevenson told Schlesinger does add weight to Eric Sevareid's absolute conviction that Stevenson was not engaged in his characteristic griping but really was on the verge of quitting, not only because of disagreement on policy but because he had lost most of whatever influence he had had.

Certainly Stevenson did try to modify somewhat Johnson's

policy toward Vietnam, but just as certainly, he was ineffective. In the first place, although he usually got a polite hearing, he was —as he had long known—simply without significant influence. Second, according to one high-level insider, he did not articulate his position well. He sometimes gave the impression of not having done his homework, a criticism made of him in other contexts. Stevenson was inclined to argue in moral terms or to appeal to the necessity of considering world public opinion. This was the sort of argument least likely to persuade Johnson, Rusk, Rostow, and their supporters. It didn't even appeal to George Ball, then Under Secretary of State, who was one of the few, perhaps the only, high Washington official to argue against the Vietnam policy. Although one of Stevenson's first and most important backers for the Presidential nomination in 1952, Ball was not convinced by Stevenson's moral arguments either. Ball was against the Vietnam involvement, not so much as a moral concern, but because it meant the United States was bogged down in Asia, demonstrating not strength but weakness. He was against Vietnam because the United States did not have an interest there worth the effort, because it made this country divert its energies from other, more important matters. And he was concerned not with the effect of Vietnam on the smaller nations but on America's important European allies. He wanted to keep the power center intact.[22]

Thus, if Stevenson were as ineffective in influencing foreign policy as he obviously was, this would seem to weaken fatally the argument of those who defended Stevenson's refusal to resign by saying that he could best serve the cause of peace within the Johnson Cabinet.

Not only had Stevenson little influence, but we have seen how Rusk had for months simply declined to respond to U Thant's proposal that secret talks with the North Vietnamese be held in Rangoon. Further investigation into this extraordinary episode discloses that Rusk simply did not put any credence in Thant's proposal. Rusk believed then, and continued to believe as late as the end of 1967, that Thant had gotten the proposal thirdhand from a Russian member of the UN Secretariat, and the State Department argues that Ne Win, the Burmese head of state, knew nothing about the proposed meeting in his capital. On the other hand, Thant continues to insist that his was a concrete proposal based on specific acceptances from Burma and North Vietnam. In any case, the incident has caused bitter feelings, at least as far as Rusk is concerned. Although one learns that at Thant's insistence the original conversation on the proposal was not back-stopped with an exchange of notes, since then all State Department dealings with Thant have been in writing. Rusk is known to believe that the accuracy of the various reports of what actually went on during the peace maneuvering depends on personal veracity alone, with the only witness, Stevenson, dead.

Some persons close to the situation from the State Department point of view term the proposal a "hallucination" of Thant's and assert that Stevenson had a habit of being "a little imprecise." Rusk, accordingly, didn't appraise the Thant proposal as meaningful and didn't do anything about it.

However, Stevenson unquestionably thought the proposal should have been pursued, even if only to find out what it *did* mean, and he believed toward the end that Rusk had not even notified Johnson of Thant's proposal. Certainly Stevenson should have pushed for an answer for Thant; even a career ambassador without Stevenson's personal authority would have done that much. Yet even without pushing, Rusk should have replied promptly. Later, it was to be argued that although Rusk hadn't told Stevenson to go ahead, he hadn't told him not to, either. A curious breakdown in communications had occurred, and who was mainly to blame, it is impossible to say.

But whatever had or had not happened concerning the Thant proposal, Stevenson knew that the Johnson Administration not only did not want negotiations but would not even admit that the possibility of talks existed. On July 13, 1965, just the day before Stevenson's death, Johnson insisted at a press conference: "I must say that candor compels me to tell you that there has not been the slightest indication that the other side is interested in negotiations or in unconditional discussions, although the United States has made some dozen separate attempts to bring that about." [23] This is the kind of candor that has characterized the Administration's statements on Vietnam.

Thus, as we have seen, Adlai Stevenson both disagreed with

Administration policy on Vietnam and knew he was powerless within the government to do anything about it. Whether he would have resigned is something we shall consider when we examine the factors other than Vietnam influencing Stevenson in the last frustrating months of his life.

# V

## *Stevenson's Last Months*

ADLAI STEVENSON'S last months were not happy ones, nor would they enhance his record as the American political leader who, more than all others, believed in talking sense to the people. His enormous vitality was exhausted. At the age of sixty-five, the strain would have been bad enough even if he had been getting satisfaction from his job. But he was not. He was harassed, frustrated and, at times, even in despair.

It is no wonder, when one considers what the man had to face in those last six tormented months. His constant efforts to devise a way to end the United Nations' constitutional and financial crises met constant rebuffs from the Russians and finally even from his own State Department. Then, with the General Assembly paralyzed by the constitutional impasse, the Russians succeeded in convening the UN Disarmament Commission for the first time in five years, primarily to give the Soviet Union a forum to attack the United States on Vietnam. This futile and often angry debate dragged on for two months. Almost simultaneously there was the long and bitter series of Security Council meetings called by the Russians after the U.S. intervention in the Dominican Republic— deeply wounding meetings in which Stevenson had to defend an action that he privately regarded as a "massive blunder." And finally, just before Stevenson's death, there was the hollow celebration in San Francisco of the United Nations' twentieth birthday, at which President Johnson's empty performance was a profound letdown, not only to Stevenson but to the delegates of all the nations, for they had been led to believe that Johnson would come with something positive to end the constitutional deadlock.

And all during these last six months there was the never-ending routine business, the briefings, the cables, the telephone calls, the countless meetings with diplomats who flocked to his eleventh-floor office at the U.S. Mission, other Security Council meetings on Southern Rhodesia, Cyprus and Senegal, new flare-ups between India and Pakistan, his private work with the Eleanor Roosevelt and Field foundations, his public appearances and commencement addresses in various parts of the country and, hanging over everything, Vietnam.

In January 1965 the UN named the countries, including Russia, that were so far behind in paying their assessments, mainly for specific peace-keeping operations, that they were subject to Article 19 of the UN Charter, under which they could lose their votes in the General Assembly. On January 26, Stevenson made a major address in the assembly outlining the American position on Article 19, declaring that the issue before the United Nations was, "in essence, whether or not we intend to preserve the effective capacity of this organization to keep the peace. It is whether to continue the difficult but practical and hopeful process of realizing in action the potential of the Charter for growth through collective responsibility, or to turn toward a weaker concept and a different system." [1] But his long, eloquent plea went for nothing. The Russians were obdurate. He knew, of course, that the speech would have no effect. It was just for the record. The real work was being done behind the scenes, but he would not live to see it finished. Indeed, he would die with no solution in sight.

Two days later, Stevenson, who had already paid honor to Winston Churchill in the General Assembly, flew to Washington to speak at the U.S. tribute to the old warrior. In the National Cathedral, where he himself was to be memorialized less than six months later, Stevenson said: "Sir Winston Churchill is dead. The voice that led nations, raised armies, inspired victories and blew fresh courage into the hearts of men is silenced. We shall hear no longer the remembered eloquence and wit, the old courage and defiance, the robust serenity of indomitable faith. Our world is thus poorer, our political dialogue is diminished and the sources of public inspiration run more thinly for all of us. There is a lonesome place against the sky." [2] Stevenson was, of course, the only choice to speak for America in saying farewell to the gallant old man, for as Churchill was the most eloquent of Englishmen, so was Stevenson the most eloquent of Americans. Yet, what a difference. When Churchill believed his party wrong, his nation wrong, he thundered defiance and quit his party, whereas Stevenson in the same situation spoke only of "playing the game."

A few days later, he was back at the UN playing the game, sending a note to the president of the Security Council informing him that the United States and South Vietnam were taking "prompt defensive action" in response to Vietcong attacks on American installations at Pleiku and elsewhere in South Vietnam. Stevenson's letter again quotes President Johnson's statement that "we want no wider war. Whether or not this course can be maintained lies with the North Vietnamese aggressors. The key to the situation remains the cessation of infiltration from North Vietnam and the clear indication by the Hanoi regime that it is prepared to cease aggression against its neighbors." [3] The American "defensive action" consisted of heavy air strikes against Donghoi, a military base in North Vietnam. According to President Johnson, the Vietcong attacks on Pleiku and a couple of other American installations in South Vietnam on February 7 were "provocations ordered and directed by the Hanoi regime." But Stevenson would not have been alone if he had thought that perhaps the Administration was looking for another pretext to escalate the war. The front page of the New York *Times* of February 8 carried a solemn story saying, "The Administration ordered the strike against North Vietnam today in the belief that it faced the most serious test so far of its will to help resist aggression in South Vietnam." The *Times,* of course, had no choice but to print such a story because that was what the Administration was saying, what it wanted the American people to believe.

But inside, the *Times* carried another story that seemed then, and certainly seems at this writing, much closer to the truth. Charles Mohr, a first-rate correspondent with experience in Asia, analyzed the Administration's claim that it was "quite clear that this was a test of the will and challenge of purpose" of the United States and Vietnam. He questioned the assertion that the raid was directed by North Vietnam, pointing out that a company or less of Vietcong was involved, that they were armed with small weapons, the largest being American-made 81-mm. mortars captured from the South Vietnamese. This was not a large Vietcong assault. In fact, it was much smaller than many made routinely by the Vietcong night after night. Why, then, would North Vietnam have had any more responsibility for this attack than for any others? Further, Mohr pointed out that all three attack carriers of the U.S. Seventh Fleet were in the South China Sea near the North Vietnamese coast at the same time. This was contrary to the usual pattern of dispersal, which involves each carrier's forming the center of an attack force operating in a separate area. In view of the Administration's record on Vietnam, particularly the Tonkin Gulf incidents, there was ample reason to believe that the Pleiku raid was merely a pretext for further American air raids on the North.

There is, of course, no way of knowing whether or not Stevenson shared this view—he probably didn't, for he must have been trying desperately to sustain his wavering faith in the Administration—but he must certainly have been alarmed that the American retaliation against North Vietnam took place when Soviet Premier Aleksei N. Kosygin was visiting in Hanoi. Despite a message sent to Moscow by the Administration explaining the Donghoi raids as merely a retaliation rather than an expansion of the war, Kosygin—and Stevenson—must have regarded them as a heavy-handed threat and one more formidable barrier against the Soviet-American *detente* that both Stevenson and the Russians wanted. And even the Administration's assertion that this was a specific response to a specific provocation must have seemed hollow to Stevenson when, less than a month later, the United States began regular air raids into North Vietnam.

During this time the Article 19 crisis was coming to a head, reaching its climax on February 18, as we saw earlier, with the extraordinary procedural jousting between Stevenson and Albanian Ambassador Halim Budo. When this was finally resolved, the General Assembly limped to an inglorious close, all but crippled, another major frustration for Stevenson that was to persist until after his death.

With the adjournment of the General Assembly until September 1, Stevenson escaped his cares for a few days by flying down to Jamaica to speak at the University of the West Indies in Kingston. (On the program with him was the Chancellor of the University, Princess Margaret.)

But his sojourn in the sun was brief. Back in New York, he could see the shadows of Vietnam lengthening across the United Nations. Vietnam, the question *not* before the UN, dominated the conversation in the halls, just as China, the country not a member, grew increasingly in influence. On February 24, Secretary General U Thant gave his startling press conference in which he said that "if only they know the true facts," the American people "would agree that further bloodshed was unnecessary." On March 2, American airplanes again roared over Vietnam. Regular bombing had begun. The last corner had been turned. There was nothing ahead but further escalation, and the Russian response to the bombing ("acts of a planned aggression," a "glaring violation of the Geneva Agreements" that undermines "peaceful coexistence") ended, for years to come, any hope of the relaxation of East-West tensions, which had been one of the most important goals of Stevenson's public life. Later that month, American officials disclosed that U.S. forces had used "types of tear gas" against the Vietcong. Whether or not such use truly violated the international agreements against the use of poison gas, the disclosure caused Stevenson considerable and recurring embarrassment at the UN. In April, there was a brief period of hope after President Johnson's speech at Johns Hopkins University, but that faded as soon as it was realized what the NLF and Hanoi recognized immediately: that Johnson's offer of unconditional negotiations was not that at all.

By April 21 the UN Disarmament Commission, on which all UN members were represented, had begun a session that was to drag on until June 16. The UN members, the United States included, had agreed to the meeting, for who could oppose a session ostensibly devoted to disarmament? But Stevenson, one of the few American political leaders who had more than a ritualistic devotion to disarmament, was grieved to see the Disarmament Commission misused. As expected, Russian Ambassador Nikolai T. Federenko immediately unleashed a savage attack against the United States, using the intemperate language that had characterized the iciest days of the cold war. Although this was the very thing he was trying to avoid, Stevenson regretfully made a stinging response.

But even while Stevenson was speaking, there was developing far from Vietnam a situation that was to magnify his already substantial doubts about that ugly struggle and indeed cause him the greatest misgivings about the direction of Johnson's entire foreign policy. At that moment in the Dominican Republic, rebels were in an early stage of a revolution to restore Juan Bosch to the Presidency, to which he had been freely elected and from which he had been ousted by a right-wing military coup. There was every reason to believe that Bosch would have been restored to his rightful office had the revolution not been crushed by a massive intervention of American troops.

Soon after the revolution began on April 24, the U.S. aircraft carrier *Boxer,* with 1,000 Marines aboard, approached the Dominican coast. On the 26th, the Administration announced that the Navy would evacuate American citizens. On the 27th, Marines using helicopters did bring out more than 1,000 Americans. On the 28th, Johnson received a panicky message from Dominican Ambassador William Tapley Bennett and made the historic decision that American Marines would again land in Latin America. Before the crisis was over, more than 20,000 Marines and soldiers would pour onto the unhappy island.

The immediate problem for Johnson was to justify the dispatch of Marines. On April 28 he appeared on nationwide television to tell the American people, "The United States government has been informed by military authorities in the Dominican Republic that American lives are in danger. These authorities are no longer able to guarantee their safety and have reported that the assistance of military personnel is now needed for that purpose. I've ordered the Secretary of Defense to put the necessary American troops ashore to give protection to hundreds of Americans who are still in the Dominican Republic and to escort them back to this country. . . . Four hundred Marines have already been landed."

Stevenson was among the high Administration officials who had met in the President's office to consider Johnson's statement. Vice-President Humphrey was also there, along with Dean Rusk, McGeorge Bundy, Bill Moyers, the Presidential press secretary, and Richard Goodwin, a holdover from Kennedy days who specialized in Latin American matters. An additional justification for sending the Marines had been included in the original draft of the Presidential statement by Rusk, who said that the Marines were needed to protect "democratic institutions," a hint that the American intervention was directed at Communists involved in the revolution. Stevenson, and only Stevenson, questioned this statement, wanting to know whether the Marine operation was solely to rescue Americans or whether it was a full-scale intervention into Dominican affairs. He looked around the room for support but got none. Everyone else seemed intimidated by Johnson. Stevenson got no direct answer to his question, but after a few moments Johnson looked up from the draft and said, "I think you're right." Thus the line hinting at the need to combat Communism was crossed out.

In Washington the United States hurriedly summoned into session the Council of the Organization of American States, seeking to get its approval after the fact of United States intervention. While the OAS Council was meeting in Washington, Stevenson at the UN notified the president of the Security Council on the 29th that American troops were in the Dominican Republic "to protect American citizens" and "escort them to safety." No mention of a Communist conspiracy was made.

On May 1, the Soviet Union called for an urgent meeting of the Security Council to consider what it termed "armed aggression" by the United States. By May 2, what had originally been justified as a rescue operation now had a new explanation. President Johnson declared on television that American intervention was necessary because "a band of Communist conspirators" was taking control of what had begun as a "popular democratic revolution." And he announced that 14,000 American troops were then in the Dominican Republic and asserted that the United States was determined to "prevent another Communist state in this hemisphere."

Johnson's speeches, not for the first time nor for the last, had Orwellian overtones. On the one hand, he could declare, "The form and nature of the free Dominican government, I assure you, is solely a matter for the Dominican Republic. . . . And neither we nor any other nation in this hemisphere can or should take it upon itself to ever interfere with the affairs of your country or any other country." On the other, he could send in troops that from the very beginning bolstered not the forces trying to restore democracy, but the right-wing generals to whom successive American governments have been partial all through Latin America.

It was clear to any observer, as it was to me sitting only a few feet away in the "Voice of America" broadcast booth, that Stevenson's heart was not in the job. But he used his considerable lawyer's skill to obfuscate the situation. He, of course, could find no defense for the American intervention so clearly contrary to the UN Charter. So instead he argued endlessly that the question was not really a UN matter, but one for the OAS, which was busily at work in Washington and later in Santo Domingo. And he resorted to uncharacteristic tactics, heaping sarcasm on the Soviet Union and on Cuba, which had asked to appear before the council. He even found himself forced to raise the bogey of "a Communist takeover," naming a number of men identified by the United States as Communists active in the leadership of the revolution. But even as attorney for the defense, Stevenson could not entirely suppress his instinctive sense of fair play. At one point on May 5 he said, "Mr. President, it may, of course, be said—I think accurately— that the bulk of the participants in the rebellion are not Communist and that even in the present leadership non-Communists are active." [4] But then he had to return to his role and add, "But I would remind you that only twelve men went to the hills with Castro in 1956 and that only a handful of Castro's own supporters were Communists." And Stevenson went on to develop the dubious case that whatever happened in Cuba must necessarily happen in the Dominican Republic.

For weeks, all through May and late into June, Stevenson had to defend American actions that found few other champions at the United Nations. There was almost universal agreement that the United States had committed a political, diplomatic and, not least, moral offense on the order of the Bay of Pigs fiasco. Stevenson, who had to repeat endlessly statements he knew not to be true and justifications he believed indefensible, agreed with the critics. And he must have been aware, and deeply distressed by the knowledge, that in defending the indefensible he was drawing heavily on his personal capital as a man of peace and integrity.

No one as sensitive as he could have failed to realize that he was tarnishing his reputation, perhaps irretrievably.

These were Stevenson's most bitter days at the UN. His deception about the American planes involved in the Bay of Pigs adventure had hurt him deeply. But he accepted the explanation that the Administration had not meant to give him the false information he passed on to the UN as true. And the Bay of Pigs— catastrophe that it was—lasted only a few days. But here was Adlai Stevenson, the biggest man at the UN, the apostle of peace, the man of integrity, under assault day after day, week after week, for telling lies and defending actions that were indefensible.

There is absolutely no doubt that Stevenson was entirely against the American intervention, despite what the Administration in general and Rusk in particular were to say later. On the evening of Stevenson's death, David Schoenbrun broadcast that Stevenson had told him shortly before in a private conversation that the Dominican intervention was a "massive blunder." Schoenbrun also quoted Stevenson as having told Averell Harriman, "I could not believe in some of the things I had to say" and that defending the Administration's action at the UN "took several years off my life."

There is plenty of evidence to indicate that this last statement was not merely rhetorical. In his *Look* article, Eric Sevareid confirmed Stevenson's distress at the Dominican invasion, as did virtually all of Stevenson's close colleagues in conversation with this author. One reported that Stevenson believed Johnson was overly alarmed at the so-called Communist threat and believed that Johnson had acted hastily without really knowing why the United States was going into the Dominican Republic. Stevenson was disturbed, said this colleague, that Johnson, like other Presidents before him, based his foreign policy on just one thought: we've got to stop the Communists. Another said that Stevenson believed the Dominican intervention "made us look like idiots." Stevenson could not understand what was wrong with a revolution to restore to office a man who had been democratically elected and then overthrown by a military coup. Nor could he understand the Administration's enormous concern over a few Communists. He realized, of course, that the best way to breed Communists in Latin America or elsewhere was to frustrate the impulse toward democratic government, as the United States consistently did with its traditional policy of supporting right-wing, militaristic regimes. In any case, he might well have agreed with the pickets outside the U.S. Mission that any country, even a country in Latin America, had the right to choose whatever form of government it wanted, even Communism.

But most important, as Arthur Schlesinger pointed out, the Dominican adventure caused Stevenson to have the most profound misgivings about Johnson's foreign policy.[5] Johnson had not only acted hastily and on the basis of incomplete and faulty information, but had also demonstrated a readiness to use military power —overwhelming military power—to solve political problems. This misuse of power disturbed Stevenson. The mere existence of such power was a danger to world peace and in the hands of an imprudent man was serious cause for alarm. Johnson, the man who had become a legend for his skillful use of domestic political power, had demonstrated his incapacity to exercise power prudently in foreign affairs. It is no wonder that Stevenson, spiritually and physically exhausted by his unhappy trial in the Security Council, was to be profoundly affected right up to the day of his death by what was about to happen.

On June 21, seven intellectuals met with Stevenson to ask him to resign, an encounter over which he brooded until his death. Various reasons for the meeting have been advanced by the participants: Kay Boyle, Paul Goodman, Dwight Macdonald, Harvey Swados, David McReynolds, Nat Hentoff and William H. Meyer. McReynolds, long a political activist and never a supporter or even an admirer of Stevenson, said "the intent was really quite brutal." [6] According to McReynolds, who is not brutal but extraordinarily humane, "We took for granted that Stevenson had committed himself. We wanted, in a sense, to discredit him with intellectuals. He was the last hold Johnson had on the intellectuals, and we hoped, by making an appeal from a number of his former supporters, to essentially destroy his role. We didn't expect him to resign; we didn't even expect to be granted an interview. We were trying to wipe out the last link between the Kennedy and Johnson periods."

Swados suggested a slightly different reason. When approached to be a member of the group, he said, "I stated that in my opinion it was already far too late for Mr. Stevenson to redeem himself morally, that although I had voted for him twice, I had been appalled and repelled by his apologetics at the UN, not only on Vietnam but on the Dominican situation as well, and that in sum I regarded him as irredeemably compromised by his willingness to front for a series of outrageous actions. The others declared that they agreed, but that inasmuch as Stevenson was still somewhat of a world figure, it would be useful for the antiwar people to seek a confrontation and to attempt to derive maximum publicity from such a meeting, even though there was no serious expectation or hope that he would do anything at all as a result of such a meeting. (In fact there was surprise that he had agreed to the meeting at all.) I felt that the gain to the peace movement would outweigh any disingenuousness involved in such maneuvering, so I went along." [7]

But if some of the seven wanted the confrontation for political and publicity reasons, some of the others certainly were hoping, although they had almost no expectation, that Stevenson would in fact resign. Goodman said they were "trying to clutch at straws. The feeling against the war lacked an official symbol, something to rally to. The ordinary Joe can't afford to have an opinion unless someone big in politics makes it respectable. It was logical to try to get him to resign." [8] And, as we shall see, Kay Boyle desperately wanted Stevenson to leave the UN.

Although the participants were all surprised that Stevenson had agreed to the meeting, it was not really so unlikely. Stevenson was deeply disturbed by the protests that were mounting all over the nation—protests by those who had been his most devoted political supporters. He wanted to know more about the protesters and exactly what they wanted. Also, he may have been aware that as a high government official he was cut off from the people and the movements that stirred them. It is hard for an outsider to realize just how isolated high government officials are. They read the New York *Times,* of course, and the Washington *Post* and a few other papers, perhaps, and maybe an occasional magazine. But they are so incredibly busy that they have little time for reading anything other than official papers. Too, they are in contact almost entirely with other government officials, most of whom tend to say what they think their superiors want to hear. They become inbred. They are the captives of their jobs. True, not being in Washington, Stevenson was not quite so aloof. He did talk to diplomats from other nations and he did have friends outside the government community, something rare indeed in Washington. Still, most of his information came from official sources: cables, briefings, government reports and telephone conversations with Washington officials. Since he did little outside reading, he was, to a considerable degree, isolated. However, unlike many in Washington, he must have realized this and hoped that an encounter with such well-known and well-informed intellectuals would help redress the balance. Also, he was more than a little vain about being considered the leading intellectual in American politics, and he enjoyed the favor of real intellectuals. Perhaps he was hoping to find out why he was losing his hold on them and possibly even to regain it.

Whatever his reason, he did agree. But if one of the reasons on the other side was to gain publicity for the antiwar movement, the mission was almost completely a failure. For some reason—perhaps the intellectuals didn't do their public relations work, although several of them were skilled publicists, or perhaps the press simply missed a good story—the news of the encounter was almost entirely ignored. However, through conversation and correspondence with most of the participants, it is possible to reconstruct this interview that so profoundly affected Stevenson. Although, naturally, the participants do not agree on every detail, the substance of the meeting is clear, since independent cross-checking verifies its main outlines.

Stevenson greeted them cordially. Dwight Macdonald reported that Stevenson "looked handsome and well—at least ruddy, perhaps a bit too burstingly pink, a little plump in the face." [9] Kay Boyle wrote, "Mr. Stevenson did not look at all well. His face was flushed and his jowls were bluish. As I had not met him before, I do not know whether or not this congested look was normal for him." [10]

All agreed that Stevenson was courteous and patient, even friendly, and that he spoke more freely after the departure of a couple of aides, who stayed for only a few minutes. The encounter lasted for almost an hour and a half, an extraordinarily long time for one whose day was always a frantic rush to fit in all those who had to see him on business.

Straightaway, Stevenson was given the declaration asking him to resign:

"We speak to you as fellow citizens. We have watched in dismay as our government—by its actions in Vietnam and the Dominican Republic—has clearly violated the United Nations Charter, international law, and those fundamental principles of human decency which alone can prevent a terrifying, world-wide escalation of suffering and death.

"We urgently ask you, as our government's representative in the United Nations and as a man who has in the past stood for the best hopes of realizing American ideals, to consider your complicity in what this government is doing. We mean not only the persistent escalation of the war in Vietnam but also the willingness of this government to resort to unilateral military intervention, thus dangerously weakening the United Nations.

"We urgently ask you to consider your complicity in the persistent misstatement of facts by this government and by you as its representative. We refer you to the numerous discrepancies between official government statements and on-the-scene reporting by responsible newsmen on such papers as the New York *Times* and the New York *Herald Tribune*.

"In the past you have expressed your commitment to a world of law and to an honest, compassionate search for peaceful solutions to conflict. Therefore, we believe this must be a time of deep inner conflict for you, and we urge you to resolve that conflict in the interest of restoring sanity to this government's foreign policy.

"*We urge you to resign as United States Ambassador to the United Nations,* and having done that, to become a spokesman again for that which is humane in the traditions and in the people of America. By this act, you can contribute immeasurably to the prospects of world peace. By remaining in your post—without speaking truth to power—you will have diminished yourself and all men everywhere.

"Bernard Bihari, M.D., Kay Boyle, George Dennison, Jules Feiffer, Betty Friedan, Mitchell Goodman, Paul Goodman, Margaret Halsey, Hilary Harris, Nat Hentoff, Paul

Jacobs, Anton Kuerti, Denise Levertov, Helen Merrell Lynd, Dwight Macdonald, David McReynolds, Eve Merrian, Hon. William H. Meyer, A. J. Muste, Grace Paley, John Hyde Preston, Jules Rabin, Susan Sontag, Harvey Swados, Dr. Albert Szent-Gyorgyi, Stanley VanDerBeek." [11]

Stevenson did not know that he was going to be asked to resign, although he might have guessed it, and this declaration must have come as a body blow, for it hit him where he was most vulnerable: his humanity and his compassion. But he did not lose his composure then, or later. He looked up and said quietly that they should get any idea of his resigning out of their minds immediately. "That's not the way the game is played." A number of times the conversation, sometimes sharp but never rude, came back to this point. When asked if he had even considered resigning, Stevenson smiled and said, "No, I will not resign. I would never take advantage of my political position to resign for political reasons. That's not the way we play the game."

Goodman pressed him on this. "But don't you feel you have a greater obligation to the people of the United States and of the world than to the Administration?"

"I think I meet that by representing my country at the UN. No, I wouldn't think of resigning."

The conversation jumped back and forth with Macdonald, Goodman, and McReynolds carrying the burden. Later, there was general agreement that McReynolds was the best prepared and the most effective, no doubt because he was the only full-time peace worker in the group. Goodman, although a gentle and peaceful man, frequently used the rough language for which he is known in his circle, and at one point Kay Boyle asked him to be quiet, thinking that the use of such tactics was not the best way to get a response from Stevenson.

Stevenson tried to defend Administration policy, reciting the Administration story that Americans had been in danger in the Dominican Republic, but he was interrupted by McReynolds, whose brother had covered the intervention for United Press International. When McReynolds said that his brother had told him there was no danger to Americans until the Marines landed, Stevenson dropped that line and never resumed it. After his various arguments on the Dominican Republic had been demolished, he conceded, "Perhaps it did represent stretching the Monroe Doctrine a little." Asked about the Communists that he had told the Security Council were taking over the revolution, Stevenson said, "I don't know about Communists in the Dominican Republic. It's all very speculative."

Stevenson also attempted to defend Johnson's policy in Vietnam, marshaling the customary arguments, but in this as on the Dominican Republic, the others felt that he was halfhearted. And he never did argue against what was implicit in the statements of his guests—that he had been lying to the world. McReynolds has said of the meeting:

> "His attitude was not defensive, particularly on Vietnam. The only time when he seemed to be defensive was [on] the Dominican situation, where he admitted he was not fully in agreement with the policy—although I cannot recall his exact statement. If he was not defensive, it is also true that he was not very willing to defend his position, and on two or three occasions when he would start to give the standard line, one of us would interrupt by saying that this simply was not the case and could we discuss the substance of the matter. He usually did not discuss the substance of the matter but shifted to something else, but in no case argued against what was the implicit statement that he was lying and that we were aware of this. *Lying* is a strong word to use, but there is no question that he was well informed on a number of the situations and perfectly aware that the statements that he was presenting to us were not accurate or factual. I have had other confrontations with the State Department and found them more inclined to waste a couple of hours defending statements that were perfectly absurd. Mr. Stevenson was not prepared to do that...." [12]

At one point in the discussion, Kay Boyle "suddenly felt very desperate." [13] One of the members of the group had just told Stevenson that he had let pass two moments in history when he should have resigned in protest: at the time of the Bay of Pigs and when the Marines landed in the Dominican Republic. Now, with

Vietnam being annihilated, the third opportunity had arrived. Miss Boyle leaped in, declaring with passion that the group badly needed a leader, that they were not Communists, that Stevenson had the required integrity and that the group was appealing to him to resign and provide the nontotalitarian and democratic leadership that was needed. "It was a very emotional moment. Afterward Dwight Macdonald said to me that he thought Stevenson was going to cry, and I said I thought I was not going to be able to keep from crying. Stevenson looked into my eyes, visibly moved, but the diplomat triumphed, and he said, 'I am going to act for you, here in my capacity as Ambassador to the United Nations.' "

That was not the only emotional moment. When the group entered, Stevenson greeted former Congressman Meyer with affection, putting his arm around his shoulders. During most of the time, Meyer sat quietly on a sofa. But toward the middle of the meeting, he said, "Adlai, I fought for you through three campaigns. I believed in you. I would have given anything I owned to see you win. But now you've let us down."

Stevenson looked brightly at Meyer and asked, "What do you mean by that, Bill, by 'I let you down'?"

Meyer sat impassively on the sofa, looking straight ahead. "I'm a farmer. I'm a plain-speaking man. You know what I mean by 'let us down,' Adlai. You betrayed us."

Stevenson said he didn't know what Meyer meant by the word *betray*.

"Yes, you do. You know what betrayal is." He spoke very quietly, without emotion. "You know exactly what betrayal is." [14]

Although Stevenson did defend Administration foreign policy, albeit halfheartedly, he did let slip some remarks that caused the others to think he had the deepest reservations about that policy. At one point, after saying that we should never have gotten into Vietnam in the first place, he spread his arms and asked angrily, "But how the hell are we going to get out of there?" And about the Dominican Republic he did say, "There is no way to condone it." Goodman thinks Stevenson was at his wit's end, because those weren't the kinds of remarks a man in his position should have made before such an audience.

Goodman also sensed that Stevenson "felt he was being estranged from the people he esteemed." McReynolds said Stevenson "struck all of us as being rather lonely and rather grateful for the chance to meet with intellectuals. This may be terribly arrogant, but I think this is the feeling that virtually all of us had. That what was involved was more than courtesy—although certainly he was courteous—he seemed to us thirsty for the kind of contact we were providing, even though it was in the context of the demand that he resign." [15] And McReynolds, who had never been an admirer of Stevenson, found he liked him more after this encounter than he ever had before. "What impressed me was his courtesy. We all felt the guy was finished, trapped, in a certain sense had sold out without knowing it. He couldn't change anymore." [16]

Swados said the meeting left him with an awareness that Stevenson "was a pathetic but hardly a tragic figure . . . although he did leave me with the impression that he had little respect for such fellow members of the team as Rusk. I should add that based on this meeting, I place no credence in the stories that he was in fact planning to resign at the time of his death. I am convinced rather that he liked the remnants of power, that he had persuaded himself of the rightness of his conduct (if not of all his unhappy apologetics), and that he was determined to play the string out to the end." [17] Goodman's opinion on this was much the same. He felt Stevenson had to be in the swim, that he was forfeiting his manliness in order to hang around.

Hentoff, too, was impressed by Stevenson's courtesy. "He received us . . . with grace. That rare, unforced, unfeigned grace. . . ." [18] Writing that at first Stevenson tried to defend the Administration, Hentoff said that "finally—though only intermittently— there were echoes of the Stevenson of the 1952 campaign. I am not saying he was explicitly in opposition to LBJ with us. We were strangers. But his concern with what he had compelled himself to do broke through at times.

"At the end, he said—and I did not feel it to be rhetoric—'You honor me by coming. I do not have the chance often these days to have this kind of dialogue.' Leaving, I was depressed. I had the sense of his impotence—and the sense of his knowing and caring deeply, hopelessly, about the impotence. He could not resign. That was not the way he played the game. And because he could not—would not—change the rules, he had been trapped by them."

Stevenson's grace certainly was unfeigned, for he was that rarity among American politicians, a gentleman both by training and by instinct. Many of us develop acceptable manners, but often they are merely an obeisance to social convention. With Stevenson, however, the courtesy was deep and instinctive. Even though these visitors had come to exert the most embarrassing private and public pressure on him to resign, and though he could have listened politely for a few minutes and then dismissed them, pleading justifiably that he was terribly busy, he heard them out for nearly an hour and a half. As the seven were leaving, he shook hands with each of them, said that he had enjoyed the talk and that they should come to see him again. Macdonald suggested, "What about the same time, same place tomorrow?" Although Stevenson looked a bit panic-stricken at the prospect, he laughed. When the group left the U.S. Mission, even though they regarded his decision to stay on the job as indefensible, even immoral, they talked for a while and were all depressed that so gracious, so decent a man had trapped himself.

It is easy to understand, with even this brief account, how so sensitive a man as Adlai Stevenson was profoundly affected by this encounter, for although not all of the group had been Stevenson supporters, they certainly represented not only the people who had been the heart of his political support but the ideas—the ideals even—that had been the basis of that support.

But that meeting was not the end of it. Paul Goodman went home and within a couple of days wrote a letter to Stevenson:

> "On Monday when a group of us urged you to resign, you explained that you could not use your position, or quitting it, to make a political point . . . 'that's not the way we play the game.'
>
> "This is commendable team-loyalty, but an odd conception of democratic government. You are our public servant and have a prior responsibility to the welfare of the country, as you see it. As a man, you have a prior responsibility to ethical principles. It must have been clear to you that we were sufficiently disturbed by the present policy to be appealing to you on both higher levels.

You will, of course, draw the line in some decent place. But my fear is that over the past twenty years we have been step by step participating in the preparation of a fantastic catastrophe. Will we then say, 'But none of us intended *that?*'

"Above all, Governor—I speak as a writer—you must not condone lies. When you are put in the position of repeating them, we are deeply ashamed. Please, go down and nail them and get yourself fired.

"I have the impression that your government is entirely out of touch with the immense and desperate need of the youth of our country for authenticity." [19]

It was this letter, written in what Goodman calls self-mockingly his "high moral tone," that caused Stevenson to draft the letter that was among his papers at the time of his death just three weeks later, a letter that, as we saw, would never have been sent in its draft form.

The Stevenson draft was printed in the New York *Times* of December 15, 1965. That same day Goodman answered it. Although the *Times* thought it necessary to print the Stevenson draft verbatim, it did not think it necessary to print Goodman's reply. Here is what he wrote:

"May I comment on Adlai Stevenson's letter to me, published in your issue of December 15, in which he argues for containment as a basis for peaceful reconstruction of the world?

"Making a comparison with the Chinese, the Ambassador says, 'I remind you that the French Revolution led to a prolonged war before the limits of France's power to control its neighbors were established.' I think his history was here faulty. The expansionism of the French followed, it did not precede, the foreign invasion by the Austrians, Germans, etc. When let be, revolutionary peoples want independence, peace, and land; they do not want expanding power until they are forced into military dictatorships in self-defense. Our own revolution during its first generations is an example. Franklin Roosevelt adopted a generous attitude toward

Mexico, and things went well enough. If we had adopted a generous, or at least forbearing attitude toward Cuba, I doubt that we would have come to the missile crisis. Certainly in Vietnam it was we who broke the Geneva accords, which represented world opinion on the peaceful reconstruction of Southeast Asia; thereby we drove the Vietnamese to heavy reliance on Russia and now China.

"At the meeting with some of us that your story refers to, the Ambassador said in exasperation that we should never have gone into Vietnam but 'what in hell would you do now?' (Present were Dwight Macdonald, Harvey Swados, David McReynolds, and a few others.) I will answer this question. I would agree to withdraw and pay an enormous indemnity for the damage we have caused, which would still come to less than the estimated cost of next year's war, seven to twelve billion dollars. I think this would be an acceptable basis for a Common Market in the region, the development of the Mekong River, and other measures to fill the power vacuum that is so feared. It is the part of a great power like ours to be magnanimous, as the Ambassador himself was." [20]

Stevenson's preoccupation with this confrontation with the intellectuals was revealed also by his sending to Kay Boyle copies of three recent speeches, including one before the annual commencement meeting of the Harvard Alumni Association on June 17, four days before he met Miss Boyle, Goodman and the others. Here he sounded more like the old Stevenson, less like the defense attorney for the cold warriors. He defended the Administration, to be sure, but he also said:

"But equally we must not . . . put too much faith in power. We have among us advocates of much stronger action. For them it is the idealism of America that is at fault. Get the allies back into line. Confront Russia over Berlin and East Germany. Bomb China's nuclear capacity before it increases. Back any anti-Communist Government anywhere. Teach everyone they can't push us around.

"But this won't work either. What power do we have to coerce our friends in Europe? What assurance have we that direct action against either Communist giant will not unleash the nuclear war from which we would suffer as much as they? How can we be sure that unlimited support of any authoritarian anti-Communist Government may not merely hasten the day when their citizens become Communists as the only means to change?

"If total isolation is no answer, total interventionism is no answer either. In fact the clear, quick, definable, measurable paths are all ruled out. In this new twilight of power there is no quick path to a convenient light switch." [21]

In this speech Stevenson seemed clearly to be flirting with heresy. If he hadn't tucked that passage in among others making the ritual defense of the Administration, it could easily be interpreted as what it no doubt was, an eloquent and effective criticism of the implacable cold warriors in the White House and State Department who were committed to "unlimited support of any authoritarian anti-Communist Government" like those in South Vietnam and the Dominican Republic. And it might well have been directed at the "nuke'm (nuclear bomb them) back to the Stone Age boys" in the Pentagon who indeed wanted, and no doubt still want, to "bomb China's nuclear capacity before it increases." Stevenson simply would not have said such things were he not deeply disturbed by the course of American foreign policy under Johnson. Nor, would he have also said at Harvard:

"But if you should ask me whether the task of defending and upholding this right [of self-determination] should be the responsibility of any one power, particularly of a large white western power whose past behavior in its own hemisphere has not, shall we say, been wholly without 'imperialist' overtones, then I say emphatically 'No.'

"In short, what I believe we should seek in this new age of more limited power but still unlimited challenge is not so much new policies, but a new emphasis, a new tone. We should be readier to listen than to instruct—with that curiosity which is the beginning of wisdom. It will take a greater effort of imagination for us to see the world through others' eyes, to judge our policies as they impinge on others' interests."

This was the Stevenson the intellectuals went to see at the U.S. Mission and this was the Stevenson who occasionally, but only occasionally, showed through the careful facade of the attorney for the defense. For these were the words of a man who questioned profoundly the policies it was his lot to defend before a disbelieving world.

It was to this Stevenson, the old Stevenson, that Kay Boyle responded:

"Thank you for sending me copies of three of your 1965 addresses. I am heartened by much of what you have said in these particular talks. The one of June 17th, given at Harvard, seems to me the most explicit of the three. This I value, for the lack of that quality is one of the many troubling aspects of our present political scene.

"I am happy that in at least two of the addresses you commend the responsible involvement of university students as expressed in campus demonstrations. I am impressed that you have spoken so movingly of the gap between wealth and poverty in our contemporary world. I value the wisdom of your comments, such as 'Most wars break out on the confused and disputed boundaries of changing power systems'; and: 'We have the tools of plenty, and we use them mainly for arms'; and that what 'we should seek in this new age of more limited power but still unlimited challenge is not so much new policies, but a new emphasis, a new tone. We should be readier to listen than to instruct—with that curiosity which is the beginning of wisdom.'

"There are other words of yours which I value, some spoken as far back as 1959 in Constitution Hall, when you quoted Dr. A. Powell Davies as saying: 'The world is now too dangerous for anything but the truth, too small for anything but brotherhood'; and again, on that same occasion, your own words: 'The urgent thing is to feel the need for re-thinking and to set to work the ultimate energies of a free society —which cannot be done by the fist of government but only

by the troubled conscience of responsible men and women';
or again: 'In a free society, there is no other alternative but
to tap the vigor, the faith, the imagination of the people
themselves.' " [22]

These words were no doubt welcome to Stevenson, but those
that followed must have cut deeply into so sensitive and troubled
a man, especially coming from so decent a human being as Kay
Boyle:

"But I deeply deplore that you have expressed yourself as
unable to act politically for us, and for yourself, in this tragic
moment in our country's history. It is a desperate moment,
when the foreign policy of the present Administration is
blackening our nation's name throughout the world.

"At the present time, I am finishing the writing of a history
of Germany. It is to be called *The Noblest Witnesses*. This
history is written through and around the lives of responsible
men and women (such as you have spoken of) whose con-
sciences were troubled in their times and by their times. That
you yourself have been here in America, and for so long, a
noble witness is the reason we turn to you now. Last Monday
I said to you that we had come to you in true desperation,
and I want to repeat this now. You bear a grave responsibility, for there is no one else who wishes to hear us, no one
else in a position of authority who can speak for us, no one
else to whom we can turn.

"Although I say 'we,' I write you this letter not as a member of a group, as I was last week when we called on you,
but as an individual. Our century needs you, our country
needs you in its present tragic crisis. I feel with all my heart
and mind that you cannot refuse to recognize and accept the
noble and historical role that concerned men and women
throughout the world now look to you to play."

Stevenson, the humane, compassionate, troubled man, could
not have been anything less than deeply moved by this *cri de
coeur*. Perhaps he had made his decision to stand by the Administration, perhaps he would not have changed it, but he could not

have gone unaffected. Certainly Eric Sevareid was not overstating when he said Stevenson, in their midnight conversation just two weeks after the Kay Boyle letter and two days before his death, "revealed a profound frustration, a certain resentment that stopped just short of bitterness." [23]

A few days after his confrontation with the intellectuals, Stevenson was out in San Francisco for the observance of the United Nations' twentieth birthday. What a difference those twenty years had made. When Stevenson had been in that beautiful city to help establish the UN, it had been the period of postwar hope—even belief—that the UN would help banish war. Now, in 1965, the United States was engaged in an ugly war in Vietnam and, although most of its members didn't like the situation one bit, there was nothing the UN could do about it. Indeed, the UN was powerless even to carry on its own routine business because of the deadlock over Article 19. Although, as we saw, Stevenson believed in the principle of collective responsibility which is, after all, the very heart of the UN, he knew the Russians were not going to back down. And whether the United States liked it or not, there was no way to enforce Article 19 and deprive Russia of its vote in the General Assembly without crippling the UN, perhaps fatally.

Thus Stevenson hoped, and had been led to believe, that when President Johnson made the address that was to highlight the birthday celebration, he would tell the delegates from the world over that the United States would not stand in the way of a compromise arrangement whereby the UN could resume its work. But because Assistant Secretary of State Harlan Cleveland had leaked the story to New York *Times* columnist James Reston, Johnson changed signals and offered the expectant audience only platitudes and a defense of the American position on Vietnam.

The celebration, already tepid, sank even deeper into a round of empty parties, a situation that was hardly improved when, the next day, June 26, Russian Ambassador Nikolai T. Federenko bitterly attacked American actions in Vietnam. Stevenson, who had hoped to speak in language appropriate to the occasion, had to launch a counterattack. Thus, what was meant to be a celebration of man's joining man "to save succeeding generations from the scourge of war" [24] ended up as one more acid cold war exchange. And outside the San Francisco Opera House, birthplace of the UN, pickets by the hundreds chanted against the Vietnam War. If there were any two cities in America that were Stevenson cities, they were San Francisco and New York. Yet they were picketing Stevenson in San Francisco and, when he returned to New York, they were picketing him there, for his intellectual visitors, having received the expected rejection of their appeal, arranged a demonstration outside the U.S. Mission. On July 1, scores of artists, writers and assorted intellectuals circled quietly in front of Stevenson's office, having been recruited by this message:

"On Monday June 21st, seven of us, acting as a delegation from the larger committee listed below, met with Ambassador Stevenson, United States Ambassador to the United Nations. We presented him with a copy of the enclosed declaration, and for well over an hour we pressed upon him the urgent need that he resign his post in protest over the Johnson Administration's policies in Vietnam and the Dominican Republic.

"Ambassador Stevenson at one time enjoyed the sympathy and trust of many in America's intellectual community, and to the general public he remains a symbol of the finer, more idealistic trends in U.S. politics. Stevenson's support is therefore very valuable to the Administration, and that is why we must put every conceivable pressure on him to join us in speaking out against the frightening course of our foreign policy.

"From the beginning of our discussion, which was courteous and spirited on both sides, Ambassador Stevenson said that he would not consider resigning, that to do so at this time because of disagreement with Johnson's foreign policy would be to take unfair advantage of his position and would be in violation of his obligations as a member of the Johnson team. It would be against the rules of the game.

"But it is precisely this putting of rules above principles which is leading us into the abyss. We think that for Stevenson to remain at his post constitutes a violation of a much deeper obligation than any he may have to Johnson: it violates his obligations to the American nation.

"We appreciated the gracious spirit in which Ambassador Stevenson received us and heard us out, but it is now our unanimous opinion that in addition to personal appeals to Stevenson to resign—from old friends and admirers like Murray Kempton, William Gibson and others, as well as from ourselves—it is now necessary to make public the enclosed declaration." [25]

Depressed by the impasse over Article 19 and the refusal of President Johnson to allow a way out, troubled by the escalating course of the war in Vietnam, worn out by the long weeks of telling the UN Security Council what he knew not to be true about the Dominican Republic, affected profoundly by the appeals that he resign from this academic-intellectual community of which he regarded himself a member—this was the Adlai Stevenson who left America early that July, never to return alive.

The main reason for his European trip was the summer meeting of the UN's Economic and Social Council in Geneva. Although the exhausted Stevenson did not want to go, he had made it a custom to address ECOSOC annually at its summer meeting. He believed that the UN's economic, social and humanitarian activities were usually overlooked by the people and the press since they, by the seemingly immutable laws of journalism, did not provide the "good stories" afforded by the dramatic clashes in the UN Security Council and the General Assembly. Stevenson had great belief in the UN's quiet but useful work in the nonpolitical fields, thought that it was recording substantial, if often overlooked successes, and believed it was his responsibility to help bring this work to the attention of the press and people of the world, particularly of the United States. So he rallied his flagging energies and battered spirit and flew off to Geneva. On July 9, he made his last formal speech on UN business. Evidently drafted by his good friend Barbara Ward, the economist-journalist, this final speech was one of which he was very proud. In it he said that we could never again be a "squabbling band" of nations before the awful majesty of outer space:

"We travel together, passengers on a little space ship, dependent on its vulnerable reserves of air and soil: all committed for our safety to its security and peace; preserved from annihilation only by the care, the work and I will say the love we give our fragile craft. We cannot maintain it half fortunate, half miserable, half confident, half despairing, half slave—to the ancient enemies of man—half free in a liberation of resources undreamed of until this day. No craft, no crew can travel safely with such vast contradictions. On their resolution depends the survival of us all."

From Geneva he flew to London for a few days, combining business with pleasure. He stayed at the embassy residence of Ambassador and Mrs. David Bruce. Every day he tried to arrange a tennis match with his hosts or other houseguests, but everyone else but Stevenson was too tired. The day after his Geneva speech, he and old friend William Benton, the former Connecticut Senator who had held a number of high State Department posts, went out to Chequers, the country home of British Prime Ministers made so famous by Winston Churchill. They spent the afternoon with Prime Minister Harold Wilson, an old friend of Stevenson. Although here were two of the most articulate men in the English-speaking world, communications broke down. Wilson thought Stevenson wanted to see every room in the house, and Stevenson thought Wilson wanted to show him every room, so they trotted interminably from room to room. Each was later to complain in jest about the other, Stevenson saying something to the effect that "Wilson showed me every damn john in the place."

The following day, Sunday, he and Benton had lunch with Lady Spears, Stevenson's former wife's aunt. Sunday night, Stevenson, a fellow of Worcester College, went to Oxford to dine with Lord Franks, the provost of Worcester. Among the guests was a lively octogenarian, Sir John Masterman, to whom Stevenson took an immediate liking. Given Sir John's card, he had scribbled on it, *"Bits and Pieces* by J. C. Masterman, Hodder and Stoughton." The next day, Monday, he gave the card to Ambassador Marietta Tree, an old friend and member of his staff, and asked her to get the book and send it to Sir John for his inscription. This was typical of Stevenson; he was always asking Mrs. Tree and other ladies on his staff or in his circle to do little personal errands for him.

Mrs. Tree treasures this card as the last thing Stevenson gave her and, as of this writing, still carries it in her purse, rather dog-eared now.

On Monday night, Stevenson was interviewed on BBC television by Robin Day, a broadcaster with a reputation as a tough inquisitor. But Day took it easy. Clearly his personal regard for Stevenson overcame his journalistic instincts. Day was not alone in this. For years Stevenson and newsmen had had a rapport unequaled perhaps since the time of Franklin D. Roosevelt. They liked and respected him so much that they were kind to him, particularly in the last months, when they sensed, or knew, that he was out of sympathy with the policies for which he was the foremost public defender. No doubt many of them felt sorry for him and did not want to make his burden any heavier. Whatever the reason, Day was discreet, and Stevenson got through the interview using much of the same language that was in the draft of his letter to Paul Goodman, although he did say that "this isn't a war that can be resolved by military means, nor can we find a solution there except by political means." [26]

After the TV show, he was the guest at an off-the-record dinner given by British and foreign newsmen. Those there reported that he acquitted himself well in the frank exchange but seemed halfhearted in his defense of American policies. He was told that he was admired by newsmen more than any other American political figure. As the dinner was breaking up, Stevenson approached Eric Sevareid, then in London for CBS News, and said he wanted to speak to him alone. It was a bit embarrassing for Sevareid because Elie Abel, his chief competitor as the London correspondent for NBC, was standing next to him.* As we saw earlier, it was during the long and intense conversation with Sevareid that followed that Stevenson said he was on the verge of resigning and revealed how the Administration had turned down U Thant's proposal for Vietnam peace talks.

Tuesday passed uneventfully, and on Tuesday night Stevenson went to a splendid party given by Lady Pamela Berry, wife of the London publisher. Sometime after midnight, Stevenson remarked that it was Bastille Day, and someone suggested laughingly, "Let's

---

* Abel was later to scoop Sevareid on Stevenson's death, for he happened to be in the American Embassy when the word was received from the hospital.

charter a plane to Paris to celebrate." "Wonderful," said Stevenson, who seemed in the best of spirits.

Wednesday, July 15, 1965, was his last day. At midday Stevenson and Robert Hutchins, former president of the University of Chicago, were guests of honor at a luncheon at Claridge's Hotel given them as directors of the *Encylopaedia Britannica* by William Benton, head of *Britannica,* and Mrs. Benton. At four o'clock he returned to the American Embassy on Grosvenor Square, where he held a small press conference. Then, with a couple of free hours before his evening engagements, he asked Mrs. Tree if she'd like to go for a walk. A tall, handsome woman who loves to walk, she readily agreed, and they set off.

"First, I want to show you where I lived during the war." He led her to a mews, or little street, off Grosvenor Square, 2 Mount Row, where he had lived in the final days of World War II and during the time he had headed the U.S. Delegation to the UN Preparatory Commission in the latter half of 1945. Those had been happy, hopeful days with his wife Ellen and his first two sons, Adlai III and Borden. But when they got there, Stevenson was crestfallen. The pleasant little house had been torn down and replaced by an ugly, dreary apartment house. "It makes me feel so old," he said sadly.[27]

They turned and retraced their steps through the square. Along the way they met a Jamaican diplomat with whom they chatted for a minute. Then they resumed their progress, striding along Grosvenor Street toward the park. "You're going much too fast for me," Stevenson called. Mrs. Tree was a very fast walker, which terribly irritated her friends. When Stevenson was with her and she went too fast, he often played tricks, like ducking into a doorway. She'd look back to speak to him, and he wouldn't be there.

So they slowed down and talked of this and that. Stevenson said that if there were no crisis, he'd retire after the next General Assembly, that is to say, at the end of 1965. He was thinking about joining a law firm, had probably decided to live in New York. He had received offers of a number of high-paying jobs, one in Hollywood to head a motion picture organization (the job later taken by Jack Valenti, President Johnson's close aide). He had also been offered many lucrative university posts, some as president, others to hold lectureships that would provide him with time and a staff so that he could write. Stevenson told Mrs. Tree as they strolled along on that pleasant London late afternoon that if he didn't retire then, he wouldn't be able to start a new life. "I have ten more years of working life."

As they approached an iron picket fence, Stevenson stopped and said, "I feel terribly faint."

"He looked ghastly," Mrs. Tree said. "I spotted a crate or something in a doorway, and I rushed to get it for him to sit down on. As I moved toward it, I felt his hand hit hard against me as he went down hard. I thought that he had merely fainted but that he might have cracked his skull.

"I ran into what I thought was a hotel but turned out to be a club. I shouted for someone to call a doctor. People brought blankets. His eyes were open, but he was unconscious. It never occurred to me that he was mortally ill. A man came along, said he was a doctor and began chest massage. He asked someone to give mouth-to-mouth resuscitation, and I volunteered. He instructed me and then said I was going too fast. After a few minutes, Adlai began to breathe in long, shuddering gasps. Along came the doctor that had been called. He gave injections after having trouble finding the great vein inside the elbow.

"I sent someone to the embassy to get David Bruce. For some reason, I didn't say who it was who was ill. I thought I shouldn't. The man came back and said Bruce was in Paris. I knew that wasn't so. I sent the man back to the embassy to ask for Philip Kaiser, the minister."

Stevenson was still breathing when he was lifted into the ambulance that had arrived promptly. In seconds, doctors were huddled over him and an oxygen mask covered his face. Mrs. Tree was about to climb into the ambulance when she took one last look around. Stevenson was always leaving stuff behind. She saw a manila envelope with classified documents scattered all over. She hastily gathered them up, jumped into the ambulance, and they sped to a nearby hospital, St. George's.

A few minutes after they arrived, a doctor came out and gently told Mrs. Tree that Stevenson was dead. "I asked to see him. They said, 'No, you'd rather remember him as he was in life.' It wasn't only that I wanted to see him. I was concerned about any classified documents. I was brought up to be terribly careful about security.

Also I wanted the nurse to take personal things, like his grandfather's watch.

"I tried from the hospital to reach his sister and son. I failed but got them a while later from the embassy."

Before long the word flashed around the world. In this connection, one point must be made. At the time of Stevenson's death, since it then seemed so unexpected, there were rumors that his death was not a natural one. This, in view of Kennedy's assassination, was probably inevitable, and the rumors cropped up again some months later, when the Warren Commission Report left so many questions unanswered. Although this writer occasionally encountered these rumors during months of research, there was never the slightest evidence to give them credibility. While my purpose was not to determine the circumstances of Stevenson's death, I have absolutely no reason to suspect that Stevenson's death was caused by anything but a heart attack. Just after one o'clock New York time, Pauline Frederick, the able UN correspondent for NBC News, began to spread the word. She was palpably distraught, for she was a friend and a great admirer of Stevenson, one of the many newsmen saddened by the melancholy situation he had been in in recent months. She probably got the word from her New York office, which had been informed by Elie Abel, who had been at the American Embassy when it received the news of Stevenson's death. Almost simultaneously, confirmation came in from the wire services, and word spread spontaneously through the press section and the delegates' lounges and upstairs through the forty-one-story Secretariat building. Someone rushed the news to Secretary General U Thant, who not only admired Stevenson deeply but felt close to him personally. It is a routine journalistic cliché to write that shock is felt at the UN whenever a leading public personality dies, but this time it was true. Stevenson was not only the biggest political figure ever to serve at the UN as an ambassador but, to many, he personified all that was good about America. One ambassador, the young, lively and able Achkar Marof of Guinea, said, "When I heard he died, my feelings were exactly as if World War III had broken out. He was so identified with peace. I thought, who's going to succeed him? Who's going to exercise a moderating influence?" [28] These thoughts were clearly shared by the many at the UN who had become deeply alarmed by America's interventionist policy in South Vietnam and in the Dominican Republic.

But in the press section there was no time for more than a moment's sad reflection. A job had to be done. Like the other correspondents, the author had work to do. Within minutes, I had written an inadequate obituary, drawing on scanty files and rich memories. When I went on the air, trying to tell the world over the "Voice of America" something of this unique man who had died, I struggled to keep the emotion out of my voice. I am not sure I succeeded, for, as I was to write the next day, Adlai Stevenson was my first—and last—political hero.

The news of Stevenson's death was received in Washington at the same time it was received at the United Nations. President Johnson was just going in to lunch at the White House with a group of Japanese Cabinet ministers. He told them that his immediate reaction had been to cancel the luncheon, but then he, some of his Cabinet to whom he had spoken, and some of Stevenson's friends realized that "works of peace and works of progress and, most important, the works of understanding, which have prevailed and predominated throughout this meeting, must go on." And he told the Japanese Cabinet ministers, "We realize that America lost its foremost advocate and its most eloquent spirit and one of its finest voices for peace in the world. The world of freedom has lost, I think, perhaps its most dedicated champion." [29]

A few minutes after lunch, Johnson appeared on television to tell the nation that he was sending a delegation headed by Vice-President Humphrey to London to bring Stevenson's body back to America on the Presidential plane:

> "His great hero, Abraham Lincoln, said at the beginning of his political career that 'I have no other ambition so great as that of being truly esteemed of my fellow men, by rendering myself worthy of their esteem.'
>
> "And although his disappointments were many, in this, like Lincoln, he was vindicated. . . .
>
> "Like Lincoln, he will be remembered more for what he stood for than for the offices he held, more for the ideals he embodied than the positions in which he served, for history honors men more for what they were than who they were. . . .

"One by one he sounded the great themes of our times—peace and justice and the well-being of humanity. And many men will labor many years toward the vision and high purpose which was the generous outpouring of this man's heart and skills.

"He was an American. And he served his country well. But what he saw, and what he spoke, and what he worked for is the shared desire of humanity. He believed in us, perhaps more than we deserved. And so we came to believe in ourselves, more than we had. And if we persevere, then on the foundation of that faith we can build the wondrous works of peace and of justice among the nations." [30]

His words were, doubtless, sincere, but who can escape the irony of a call to "build the wondrous works of peace and of justice among the nations" from America's Commander in Chief in Vietnam and the Dominican Republic? Nor is there any intention to question the President's sincerity in ordering the national tributes to Adlai Stevenson, for Stevenson merited them and Johnson is a sentimental man. But it is also true that Johnson embraced Stevenson more in death than he ever had as a Presidential candidate or as his Ambassador to the United Nations.

There is no doubt that many in America grieved, many who had voted for him and many who had not, for there was an uncommon common decency about this man who, although he sought great power, seemed genuinely to want it not for itself, as do most politicians, but mainly as an instrument to achieve the American aspirations for which he was so eloquent a spokesman. And Stevenson would have been amused to see the great princes of the press, who had done their considerable best to keep him out of the White House, compete to sing his praises now that he was dead.

So the Presidential plane flew to London to be his in death. Aboard were Stevenson's three sons—Adlai III, Borden and John Fell—and his nephew, Timothy Ives, along with the wives of Adlai III and John. Hubert Humphrey, the devoted follower of Stevenson, who as Vice-President was unable to help the President's Ambassador get through to the President, led the official delegation of Republicans and Democrats from the Senate and

House. Another old friend, Labor Secretary Willard Wirtz, was aboard, as were UN Under Secretary Ralph Bunche and Mayor Richard Daley, the Democratic boss of Chicago. In London, his sister, Elizabeth Stevenson Ives, and her husband joined the mourners. Marietta Tree, Mrs. Marshall Field, an old Chicago friend, Lady Spears and William Benton also boarded the Presidential plane, and the body of Adlai Stevenson of Illinois, in a plain white mahogany coffin, was placed aboard for the flight home to America.

When Air Force One rolled to a stop at Andrews Air Base just outside Washington, President Johnson was waiting, along with members of his Cabinet and Sir Patrick Dean, now British Ambassador to the United States but earlier Stevenson's close and trusted colleague when he was Her Majesty's Representative at the UN. After a military ceremonial, the body was taken to the National Cathedral, where just six months before, Stevenson had bade America's farewell to Winston Churchill, a fitting turnabout, for as Churchill was America's favorite Briton, so was Stevenson Britain's favorite American.

Thousands came to the Bethlehem Chapel that Thursday night and Friday morning, some of them, as Mary McGrory wrote in the Washington *Star,* like "a transplanted Chicagoan [who] looked at the long line of people ahead of him and the longer line behind him at the Washington Cathedral. 'Ah,' he said, 'if it could have been this way at the polling places. It's a good turnout—very good. I knew they'd be here.'

"He was the true Stevensonian, protective of his hero, and apprehensive that Adlai E. Stevenson, in death, as in life, might be deprived of the full measure of honor and recognition that was due him." [31]

Washington turned out all right, for although publicly it worships political power, in its heart it yearns for humanity. Stevenson had had a measure of the first, but there were many gods and demigods in that pagan city with more. But of humanity there were none.

On Friday the national funeral was held in that magnificent unfinished cathedral. The President was there and the Vice-President and their wives, the Supreme Court, Senators and Representatives, diplomats by the score and, of course, the immediate family. The task of eulogizing this most eloquent of men was given to an old and dear friend, Judge Carl McGowan of the U.S. Circuit Court of Appeals, who was one of the first of many to be drawn by Stevenson out of the comfort of private life into the turmoil and satisfaction and disappointments of public life. Judge McGowan's words were well-chosen:

"That voice is still now. But its echoes are likely to be sounding down the corridors of history for a long time. For it is the essence of faith to believe that the world in its advancing age will set no less store than have we upon reason, upon intelligence, upon gaiety, upon charity and compassion and grace—all these things and more of and with which this voice has spoken to us so often and so clearly in the past." [32]

Yet although the words were eloquent, some present thought that McGowan spoke coldly, without emotion, as if he were afraid to let loose the reins of his grief. Among the mourners, yet at work, was again Mary McGrory, that lovely person and true friend. She too grieved, not only for his death but for what had happened to him in his last months, the apostle of peace become the advocate of force. But despite her grief she had work to do, and this is what she wrote of the ceremony for the Washington *Star* of the next day:

"The ceremony, itself, was curiously irrelevant for a man whose failure to fit the mold was his problem and his glory. When John Kennedy died his violent and untimely death, ritual had a soothing grandeur. But, however abbreviated, pomp did not befit Stevenson, whose fate had been to be patronized by lesser men. The deafening grandiose organ chords were jarring—he was a man for chamber music or a waltz."

True, ceremonies did not seem quite right for Adlai Stevenson, for he was a man, not the monument of state they (whoever they were) were trying to make him. Yet the eulogies continued. After the service in the National Cathedral, the body was flown, again in the Presidential plane, to Springfield, Illinois, where the memory of Abraham Lincoln was consciously evoked. His simple coffin was placed on the same walnut table on which Lincoln's had been placed when his body had been brought back to Illinois a century before. And on the way into Springfield from the airport, the hearse and the three cars bearing the immediate family detoured to pass Lincoln's tomb in Oak Ridge Cemetery. Again the body lay in state, this time in the gloomy rotunda of the State Capitol. Again people filed by, this time not the cosmopolites of a national capital but plainer people dressed in simple summer clothes because of the hot prairie sun. And then again, another ceremony, this time in Stevenson's beloved hometown of Bloomington. Thousands crowded the streets as the cortege drove into town after crossing the rich green cornfields between the capital and the county seat. Again people filed by, now in the Jesse Fell Assembly Room of the small Unitarian Church.

The final ceremony on Monday morning was meant to be a small private one, but that was changed when President Johnson decided to attend the last rites. Mrs. Johnson came, too, and Vice-President and Mrs. Humphrey and Chief Justice Earl Warren and Mr. and Mrs. John Steinbeck, who had been guests at the White House, and Justice Arthur Goldberg, who was to be Johnson's surprise but splendid choice as Stevenson's successor. Again thousands lined the streets, but whether to pay tribute to their former governor or to see Johnson one cannot say, perhaps both.

This final ceremony was the most moving, perhaps because it was on a human scale in the tiny church sanctuary which seated only 150 people. After the church service there was one final cortege to Evergreen Cemetery, where Adlai Ewing Stevenson II was laid to rest not far from the grave of Adlai I. His journey was over, and whether it would gradually be forgotten, whether he will be merely a footnote to history as just another defeated candidate, only time will tell.

This concern with Stevenson's place in history was also felt at the United Nations, where his old friend and deputy at the U.S. Mission, Francis T. P. Plimpton, presided over a memorial service in the great-domed chamber of the General Assembly. As he closed the brief memorial attended by more than 2,000 people from all over the world, he said simply, "The memory and influence of Adlai Stevenson have not ended." That was, of course, a speculation fitting to the occasion. What was more appropriate, and more certain, was what was said about the man as he had lived.

One of the four speakers was Dean Rusk, who had never appeared in the General Assembly as head of the American delegation while Stevenson was permanent representative. It was his right to do so, a right invariably exercised by other visiting foreign ministers, but whenever Rusk visited the General Assembly, as he did each year, he met other foreign ministers outside the UN grounds as a gesture of deference to Stevenson, who was, after all, his subordinate. And although Rusk certainly did not share all Stevenson's views, he, unlike many of the other hawks around Kennedy and Johnson, genuinely admired Stevenson. So, despite their real differences, it was not as surprising as it seemed to some when Rusk spoke movingly of Stevenson. Stevenson, he said, was "a universal man. But not merely because he was informed, well-travelled, urbane, sophisticated, eloquent and gifted; he was all of these. But his universality did not rest upon his being a prince among plain men, but upon his being a plain man among princes. His was the simplicity of fundamental human values—with what is permanent in the midst of change: the love of peace; the instinct of tolerance; the feeling of compassion; the devotion to human rights; the urge to act for human welfare." And with simple eloquence, Rusk said: "Three Presidents of the United States sent Adlai Stevenson to the United Nations. They sent you our best." [33]

No one could have expected Rusk to refer to Stevenson's growing unhappiness with Administration foreign policy, nor would it have been appropriate for the other speakers to do so on such an occasion. But if they did not make direct reference, it did not take much perception to recognize the indirect references in the tributes by Secretary General U Thant and poet Archibald Mac-Leish, an old friend.

Thant, who understood Stevenson's deep and growing doubts, told the hushed audience: "It has often been said that in war the first casualty is truth. The cold war is also capable of inflicting the same casualty. The weapons designed and utilized to crush and mutilate the human mind are as potent as any of the weapons designed for physical destruction.

"The weapons of the cold war contaminate our moral fiber, warp our thinking processes and afflict us with pathological obsessions. These are the invisible but, nevertheless, the most devastating effects of the cold war on humanity. I believe Adlai Stevenson, in his innermost thoughts, realized these truths."

These words could hardly have been comforting to that implacable cold warrior, Dean Rusk, seated only a few feet from the Secretary General, for you will remember that it was Thant himself who had said only months before that "in war the first casualty is truth," meaning that the Administration, Rusk's Administration, was not telling the truth about the Vietnam War to the American people. Nor could Thant's words have been comforting to those admirers of Adlai Stevenson who knew what he was going through in recent months. Nor could much comfort be derived from the words of Archibald MacLeish. MacLeish was, of course, the most eloquent. He expressed the appropriate regrets: "What we have lost, as he said of his friend, Eleanor Roosevelt, is not his life. He lived that out, if not to the full, at least more fully than almost any other man. What we have lost is himself. And who can name the warmth and richness of it?" But then MacLeish put Stevenson's life into the context of the world at his death, saying Stevenson was a man "whose life had a particular singleness, an unusual wholeness, its own law.

"And it is here in this room, I think, that that wholeness best appears. For the United Nations, though it knows and suffers from our contemporary trust in power, is dedicated to another end: the subordination of power to the hope for peace—which is to say the hope for humanity."

True, Stevenson was such a man, but in the last days of his life he was not able to stand up to power, look it in the face, and demand that it subordinate itself "to the hope for peace—which is to say the hope for humanity." In the final analysis, Stevenson the political philosopher surrendered to Stevenson the political realist. It might not have been so a month later or a year, but we will never know. We cannot know what Adlai Stevenson might have done, only what he did.

# ✦ VI ✦

## *Stevenson: Attorney for the Defense*

ALTHOUGH we saw in the last chapter many of the extraordinary pressures on Adlai Stevenson in his final months,
before we can attempt a conclusion as to whether or not he was
on the verge of resigning and what the terms of such a resignation
might have been, we must take an even closer look at him in his
role as Ambassador to the UN. But first, we must view the United
Nations in its relationship to the United States. Absolutely basic
to any understanding of the UN is the fact that it is dominated by
the United States, has been since the first day, and will be for the
foreseeable future. The reasons for this are simple. The UN is an
American creation by Roosevelt out of Wilson. The Charter was
substantially written by Americans, and the bills are paid by Americans, about 32 percent of the regular budget of some $140 million
and higher percentages of various special budgets, a total amount
absolutely crucial to the operation of the UN but petty cash in
terms of the American budget.

One of the ludicrous fictions that the right wing in this country
has tried to promote is that the Soviet Union runs the UN. This is
easily refuted. At this writing, the Russians have cast the veto in
the Security Council 104 times. That means that 104 times the
Soviet Union has felt it had to block the UN from doing something
it did not want it to do. The United States has never cast the veto,
which means that the UN has never done anything embarrassing
enough to the United States to cause it to exercise its right of veto.

It is true, of course, that in the last decade American domination has been modified somewhat as the UN grew from a Western club to a worldwide organization, but this modification has been more apparent than real. The nonaligned nations of Africa and Asia do have the necessary votes in the General Assembly to pass resolutions that the United States sometimes regards as silly, unproductive, inconvenient, unrealistic and, occasionally, even embarrassing. But the assembly's resolutions, although they do carry some moral weight, are mere recommendations; they are not mandatory. Only the Security Council has mandatory powers—although it has hardly ever used them—and there the U.S. position is secure, for the time being at least.

Since the UN's first day, there has been no nation that has professed its passion for the world body more often than the United States. Every major foreign policy statement or speech has a ritual reference to America's devotion to the UN, but the fact remains that in recent years the White House and the State Department have regarded the world organization as a nuisance, except, of course, when the United States wanted to use it. Talk privately to anyone high in the State Department and you will hear about nothing but the artificial world at the UN, about the fact that the "wild men" of the African and Asian countries are running roughshod over accepted UN precedents.

These arguments merit brief examination, although the relationship between the UN and the United States requires a book yet to be written. True, the UN is an artificial world, indeed something of a club. A visit to the enormous and handsome North Delegates Lounge—possibly the largest bar in the world—is enough to demonstrate this. There you see little knots of delegates, most often Africans and Asians, engaged in intense conversations, or consultations, as they are called in UN jargon, or strolling arm in arm along the boulevard-wide main corridor. Often the subject under discussion is a draft resolution that the Western nations—that means the United States, Canada, Western Europe, Australia, New Zealand and, curiously but not infrequently, Japan—don't like. In this club Chad and the Central African Republic and Togo and Malaysia, even the Maldive Islands, have a vote in the General Assembly equal to those of the United States, Britain, France and the Soviet Union. This seems to disturb the State Department, even though it was the United States that proposed one-nation, one-vote when the UN was founded. But for some reason this really distresses the United States, perhaps because the newer nations forget their place and sometimes say things that the United States doesn't like to have said publicly. Perhaps the United States doesn't like these nonwhite countries to pass resolutions on colonial and racial matters that the United States regards as unrealistic.

Unrealistic, according to the United States and a few other major industrial nations, are resolutions that ask these countries to take actions matching their words. The United States and a few others are eloquent in speeches proclaiming their devotion to national freedom and racial equality, but when the smaller nations ask them to demonstrate their support by taking action against the racist governments in South Africa or Rhodesia or against Portuguese imperialism, the resolutions are invariably described as unrealistic. Unrealistic they are indeed, primarily because the United States, Britain, France and a few others are the only nations who can make them effective, and there is not a chance in the world of their sacrificing their own economic or military interests even to a modest degree to support the Afro-Asian position although, even by their own definition, it is the just and honorable one.

Thus, since the General Assembly has no real power, it is hard to understand why it bothers Washington so. Possibly it's nostalgia for the good old days when the UN was a Western club populated almost entirely by gentlemen who knew the rules and always played the game. But most probably the United States would like the UN to be silent as well as powerless, a rather vain hope since no power on earth could achieve that. What it seems to come down to is that Washington not only doesn't want to be opposed; it doesn't even want to be questioned.

Washington, of course, would never admit this. Rather, it would base its objections to certain UN actions (however impotent) on a belief that the UN doesn't have an accurate picture of the real world, implying that Washington's view is the only valid one. This would be amusing, were it not for the fact that Washington really believes that it, and only it, has a true appreciation of the world situation. And if the rest of the world does not share that view—as increasingly, with the exception of a few client states, it does not—then the rest of the world is crazy. It is easy to see how such a belief has led to the American disasters in Cuba, the Dominican Republic and Vietnam. The United States has become an isolated interventionist, all the while believing it is working toward peace and the general good.

All this is not to say that the small states at the UN do not have an inflated view of their own importance—indeed it is only at the UN that these small, weak states have any importance at all—nor that they aren't sometimes carried away by emotionalism nor that they don't occasionally pass meaningless resolutions out of frustration. And it is true that they continue to overestimate the UN's influence, particularly in regard to the great powers, although they should have learned by now from their own frustrations how pitiful that influence really is. Perhaps they continue to confuse hope with reality. Yet with all its flaws, the UN does represent whatever morality exists in international politics.

This background is necessary to an understanding of how the American Ambassador to the UN functions. And when the American is a real UN man, as Stevenson was, the White House and the State Department tend to discount severely (in the financial sense of deducting a percentage of the face value) his recommendations as representing his constituency. This extends to the entire Bureau of International Organization Affairs. In other words, if the people at State concerned with UN matters make a recommendation, it is discounted because of the fact that they have made it. This is reasonable to a degree, for any ambassador is likely to overemphasize the concerns of his embassy, but even in view of Washington's deep-seated bias against the UN—except, of course, when it serves American interests, as it often does—the discount is usually much too high. This was true during Stevenson's UN years under both Kennedy and Johnson, although Kennedy did seem to have more appreciation of the UN and Stevenson's role there.

George Ball, the former Under Secretary of State, reported one incident that would tend to confirm this. Once during the Congo crisis, Stevenson called Kennedy at the White House. Ball, who was conferring with the President, took the call because Kennedy was on the massage table. Stevenson was proposing a course of action that would strengthen UN intervention in the Congo, a course opposed by Britain and France. Ball, although not sympathetic to the suggestion—he was, and is, a NATO man—told me that Stevenson had to make such a proposal in view of the circumstances at the UN. Kennedy said, "George, tell Adlai to go ahead and do what he has to because he has a hell of a time in New York. He lives in an artificial world and has to accommodate to it." And later, according to Ball, Kennedy said, "The UN is not like the real world; it's very special and separate. I feel very sympathetic with Stevenson." [1]

Also necessary to an evaluation of Stevenson is an understanding of his relationships with Kennedy, Johnson and Rusk. In his *A Thousand Days,* Arthur Schlesinger has written well of relations between Kennedy and Stevenson. They were certainly correct, possibly even cordial but always a little strained and never really warm. Curiously, Jacqueline Kennedy felt greater warmth toward Stevenson, and he often squired her when she came to New York both before and after her husband's death. The reasons for the strain were perfectly obvious. Kennedy was in the White House and Stevenson wasn't. Stevenson felt, and one can hardly argue with the feeling, that Kennedy was too ambitious and had rudely shoved him aside. He felt, too, that things had been too easy for Kennedy. And he was disappointed that Kennedy didn't ask his advice on matters outside the UN. After all, for eight years Stevenson had been the spokesman for the Democratic party on all matters foreign and domestic and, indeed, had staked out the positions on which Kennedy now stood. There was also Kennedy's easy arrogance. "That young man in the White House, he never says please and he never says thank you."

On the other hand, Kennedy had a curious jealousy of Stevenson, even though it was he who had been elected and not Stevenson. He felt that the liberal heart of the Democratic party—not the popular masses, for they were clearly his—still belonged to Adlai. He envied Stevenson's eloquence and wit, his standing abroad and in the universities. And he was often impatient with what he regarded as Stevenson's fussiness. It is true that in Kennedy's presence, Stevenson was not his normal, gay, witty self. And when Kennedy asked his opinion, he would give the pros and cons at considerable length, indicating that while he felt this was so, he might be wrong. This was completely alien to Kennedy, who wanted succinct, lapidary statements. But there was no way Stevenson could change. He liked to examine a question and then re-examine it, to "cast up the accounts," as he used to say at his UN staff meetings. Here it was Kennedy who was wrong. Brevity is much to be admired, but oversimplification is more dangerous to a President than fussiness, and perhaps if Kennedy had examined the circumstances more carefully, he would not have permitted the political, military and moral catastrophe of the Bay of Pigs or allowed the United States to be sucked into the quicksands of Vietnam.

An added handicap to the Kennedy-Stevenson relationship was the hostility to Stevenson of most of the men around Kennedy. Partly they thought Stevenson was too soft, but mostly it seemed to be vengeful dislike for the man who had threatened, even so slightly as he had, Kennedy's progress toward the White House. They seemed to feel, even more than Kennedy himself, that it was his sacred right to sit in the White House and that anyone else who had an eye on it was not only presumptuous but sacrilegious. After the Bay of Pigs disaster, Kennedy assigned Schlesinger of his White House staff to keep in touch with Stevenson, and this certainly helped. However, Schlesinger was not really in the inner circle—Bundy, Rostow, Rusk and McNamara—that had the most influence on Kennedy. And in any case, these hard-nosed realists were hardly receptive to Stevenson's views.

Stevenson's relationship with Johnson was at the outset much warmer than with Kennedy. But gradually at first, and then more rapidly, it fell off until at the end it was much less close. Johnson naturally felt that his first job after taking office was to consolidate the government, and no one in the government had as much polit-ical strength as Stevenson, who also represented the liberal wing of the party that had long been hostile to Johnson. Stevenson also had the knowledge and experience in foreign affairs that, as events would prove, Johnson so tragically lacked. Further, Johnson did feel real gratitude toward Stevenson for keeping his promise before the 1960 convention not to back any candidate. Johnson, of course, knew the incredible pressure put on Stevenson to throw his decisive weight behind Kennedy, and he knew that this had cost Stevenson the job of Secretary of State he wanted so badly. Also, although it is a cliché, Johnson often does act in a Texas, outsize sort of way. Whatever the reason, the first meeting of the two men after Kennedy's death was an extraordinary occasion, one that left Stevenson almost stunned.

From various accounts, one gathers that Johnson turned on Stevenson the full force of his powerful personality. He told him, in effect, that if Stevenson hadn't kept his word before the 1960 convention, he, Stevenson, would be sitting in the White House and not Johnson. This evidently meant that Stevenson would have gotten the Vice-Presidential nomination if he had backed Kennedy. However, there is no evidence that Stevenson had the slightest interest in being Vice-President or that Kennedy for a moment considered him as such. This was not, however, a moment for logic. Johnson evidently recalled their old comradeship (quite a trick, since neither had ever had much use for the other) and convinced Stevenson that he regarded him not only as indispensable, but destined to play a decisive role in foreign policy. It was at this meeting that Stevenson urged Johnson to speak at the UN before the General Assembly adjourned before Christmas, an appearance that was a great success, since Johnson promised to carry on Kennedy's foreign policy and pledged continued American support for the UN. Both men were evidently carried away by the occasion, and soon afterward Stevenson was known to have said wonderingly, "I think if I had said 'Fire Dean Rusk,' he would have."

Remarkable though the meeting was, there were good reasons for it. First and foremost, both men were still under the very real shock of Kennedy's assassination. Also, they were the two great Democratic leaders, albeit of different wings, who had been pushed aside by the younger man. And beyond their own ambitions, they had been genuinely disturbed by Kennedy's ruthless rush to the White House. They were members of the same generation, passed by, it had seemed, but now, by an accident of history, back in the saddle. Johnson did need Stevenson at first, both politically and practically, and Stevenson both wanted to serve the new President, so cruelly thrust into office, and hoped to play a larger role than he had previously. So, however incredible the encounter may appear, it was not unusual that under the circumstances the two men sentimentalized their relationship. But the honeymoon, however real, was not destined to last.

At first, to the continued amazement of Stevenson, Johnson was always on the phone, asking his advice about all sorts of things, not just about UN matters. Schlesinger stayed on a while at the White House, maintaining Stevenson's entrée. But little by little the phone calls diminished in number and importance. As Johnson increasingly came to rely on the cold warriors (Rusk, McNamara, Bundy and Rostow), he turned less often to Stevenson. Then, as the schism among Democrats began to develop over Vietnam and the Dominican Republic, Stevenson found himself separated from the White House by a steadily widening chasm. Toward the end, the special relationship had all but vanished, and Stevenson plaintively had to ask Vice-President Humphrey how to get through to the President. Poor Humphrey, a loyal friend who was soon to destroy himself as a liberal by his enthusiastic cheerleading for Johnson's Vietnam policy, didn't have an answer. Thus, Stevenson found himself increasingly isolated from the President, only to be embraced after death with a fervor surpassing any Johnson had demonstrated in life except for that one extraordinary meeting.

Stevenson's personal relationship with Rusk is more difficult to define. Although Rusk is open to the most severe criticism for his unrelenting pursuit of the cold war and even for the way he functioned in his job, he always bent over backward in order not to make Stevenson any more uncomfortable than was inherent in the organizational relationship. Although he did not share Stevenson's views on the cold war, he did appear to be a genuine admirer. This is proved, I believe, not by his words at the UN memorial service, for they could have been spoken ritually even by one who despised Stevenson, but by his behavior over the years. First, and Rusk made this clear to Kennedy before he was appointed Secretary of State, he had preferred Stevenson in 1960. Indeed, in 1960 Rusk sent a cable to Averell Harriman saying, in effect, "Don't lose your mind, back Stevenson." [2]

All through Stevenson's years at the UN, Rusk was solicitous on a personal level. If he had any resentment that his subordinate was much better known, he never let it show but treated Stevenson with unvarying courtesy and respect. He welcomed Stevenson's views even when, as was often the case, he did not share them. He considered Stevenson useful in identifying the problems that lay behind the immediate obstacles. He thought Stevenson provided "a useful yeast and ferment and looked at things other people took for granted." [3] He appreciated the fact that Stevenson's interests were worldwide, not centered almost exclusively on Europe and NATO, as were those of Dean Acheson, George Ball and John McCloy, other important advisers under Kennedy and Johnson. Rusk valued Stevenson's dedication to seeking a solution by negotiation and to building bridges to the Communist world. Yet if Rusk shared this interest intellectually, he seemed to have some visceral block to such action.

Rusk also had the highest possible regard for Stevenson's performance at the United Nations and he knew a great deal about the UN, having served as Assistant Secretary for UN matters under Truman. But it is clear that he believed Stevenson's greatest contribution to the Kennedy and Johnson Administrations was not his counsel—there were others who offered similar advice—but his performance as advocate or, perhaps, salesman. Rusk's view—and it is widely shared in Washington—is that by far the most important job of the American Representative to the UN is to advocate the American position to the member nations and the vast world public beyond that is watching it. And, to use a football analogy, he must be a two-way player. He must advance the American position when the United States is on the offensive and, perhaps even more important, must defend it when the country is on the defensive. He must be persuasive, he must have debating skill, but most of all he must have personal prestige and stature. Rusk believed that Stevenson was the best UN Ambassador the United States has ever had simply because he was Adlai Stevenson, the American most respected—and trusted—the world over. Stevenson, of course, recognized that this was why he was chosen, and this very fact—that his personal honor was an instrument of the Administration—was at the heart of his dilemma, both when he considered the job in the first place and when he considered leaving it at the last.

What was the view of the Stevenson-Rusk relationship from Stevenson's side? He clearly approved of the Rusk appointment or he would not have taken the UN job. Stevenson, of course, wanted to be Secretary of State, but he did not sulk over his disappointment. And he knew that Rusk had not sought the job. In any case, resignation was very much a part of Stevenson's character, and having accepted the lesser post, he no doubt genuinely wanted Rusk to succeed. If there were any tension between them because of Stevenson's frustrated ambition, it was in no way conscious.

But as time went on, and it did not take much time, only the few months prior to the Bay of Pigs disaster, Stevenson began to have doubts about Rusk, based not so much on policy differences —which had just begun to emerge—as on the way Rusk went about his job. He often described Rusk as "wooden," referring to his curious passivity in the job. Although he has always been characterized as hard compared to the soft Stevenson, Rusk, as we saw during the Bay of Pigs and the Cuban missile crisis, had a way of sitting silently at policy meetings as though he were just a spectator rather than Secretary of State. Stevenson thought this a strange way for the President's principal adviser on foreign policy to act. He thought an adviser should advise. For all Stevenson's careful, some would say fussy, examination of a problem, he always reached a timely conclusion and was not hesitant to express it. Nor is it certain that Stevenson understood to what lengths Rusk had gone so as not to offend his sensibilities.

Although the policy differences between Stevenson and Rusk were not many, they were grave. They centered on differing views of the cold war. Both had developed their foreign policy ideas during and after the Second World War. Both were believers in the containment policy, but Stevenson, although he did make the ritual statements about Communist determination to rule the world, did not seem to be a believer in the "devil theory." He had a great distaste for Communism and was in no way soft on it, as Senator Joseph McCarthy and Vice-President Richard M. Nixon had charged. However, he realized that the Russians for their part had reasons for the deepest suspicions of the United States, and he was convinced that Russia did not want war, if only for the simple reason that it had suffered so grievously in the last one. Also, he had a profound human sympathy for the Russian people, indeed all people. Thus, he believed not only that it was America's duty to try to end the cold war—a great danger and an enormous waste of precious resources—but that Russia, too, wanted it ended, although not necessarily on the same terms. Above all, he believed in negotiated political settlements, not military confrontations— confrontations that not only were unable to solve political problems but presented awesome dangers. This was not new. As long before as 1952, Stevenson had said in a campaign speech in Hamtramck, Michigan, "I tell you now I will never fear to negotiate in good faith with the Soviet Union." This was more than a decade before Kennedy, in his famous American University speech of June 1963, seemed to be opening the door to a Russian-American *detente,* a door that would be slammed shut by the escalation in Vietnam that began soon after Kennedy's death in November.

Clearly Stevenson thought the cold war had at last run its course, and he definitely did not share what has come to be an obsession with Rusk: the belief that an accommodation with the North in Vietnam would be an Asian Munich. As the escalation in Vietnam grew, so did Stevenson's doubts about the Johnson-Rusk foreign policy, and with America's precipitate intervention in the Dominican Republic, in open violation of international law and the UN Charter, Stevenson found himself as the foremost public defender of a dangerous course with which he could not agree.

Having discussed, however briefly, Stevenson's relations with Kennedy, Johnson and Rusk, we can now consider a question important not only to an evaluation of Stevenson but to the structure by which the United States conducts its foreign policy. The question is: Should the United States Ambassador to the United Nations have Cabinet rank and thus direct access to the President, as he did under Eisenhower, Kennedy and Johnson, or should he be an ordinary ambassador operating solely under the Secretary of State, as was the case under Truman? There are powerful arguments on either side. Let's take the negative arguments first. Obviously there is the matter of administrative untidiness. Almost any administrator would argue that an organization can operate efficiently only if there is a clear line of command. With the UN Ambassador a Cabinet member, he is at the same time subordinate to the Secretary of State and his equal, an impossible situation, many would contend. A bureaucracy as sprawling as the State Department is difficult enough to administer under ordinary circumstances, but this anomalous situation can undermine the authority of the Secretary of State, who is both the President's chief adviser on and chief executor of foreign policy. At the top level it could lead to dangerous, or at least harmful, polarization in the

Cabinet. And at a working level it could lead to the development of a "little State Department" at the U.S. Mission to the UN.

Both of these objections are valid, at least in theory. However, Stevenson was scrupulous about keeping Rusk fully informed whenever he got in direct touch with the President, which was only when he thought it essential. And Rusk, however he may have felt about such direct access by Stevenson, accepted it and did not permit it to affect their relations. Of course, with two other men the results could be diametrically different, with each seeking to undermine the other. And even if the two were not the kind to undercut one another, the President could introduce tensions by undue reliance on the advice of the UN Ambassador. This could not long be kept from the Secretary of State and would inevitably introduce harmful tensions.

This question goes far beyond the institutional relationships. If the UN man is one of prestige and of Cabinet rank, he has access not only to the President but to the top levels of the entire government establishment and to the press and public. This, under the right circumstances, could lead to the formation of two foreign policy camps and, although diversity of opinion is essential so that the President can have a wide spectrum of alternatives from which to choose, two warring camps could only cause trouble.

Dean Rusk has strong views on this. He does not see the relationship as three-cornered: President, Secretary and Ambassador. The President is, he maintains, in charge of foreign policy, and his instructions are issued through the Secretary of State. Although the UN Ambassador has the right to be heard by the President either before or after a policy decision, the Secretary of State is still the principal foreign policy officer. But he says there is very seldom a problem, because the Ambassador's right of access is not used too often and that, in any case, there is usually a consensus on foreign policy—indeed, more of a consensus than one would suppose. However, he considers it essential that the man at the UN know the Secretary is the boss. And he asserts the government could not run its foreign affairs if the officer with the constitutional responsibilities, that is, the Secretary, were not free to act.[4] This view is no doubt valid but will prevail only if shared by all three men, as it was during Stevenson's tenure at the UN.

As to the development of a "little State Department" at the

U.S. Mission, this is probably inevitable. Over the years the U.S. Mission, no matter who its chief, has developed an identity stronger than that of the ordinary embassy. Perhaps it is because lower, middle and upper-middle-rank members tend to serve there much longer than at an overseas post. Then, too, the U.S. Mission is involved with the day-to-day operations of the jurisdiction to which it is accredited far more than any other embassy is concerned with the operations of the host government. Indeed, the U.S. Mission is the single most important influence on the UN itself and on its members collectively. There is a constant coming and going between the UN on one side of United Nations Plaza and the U.S. Mission across the street. This involves not only the Secretariat but other nations wanting to take this or that action at the UN, for U.S. support is usually crucial to any action, whether proposed by the Secretary General or by member states. This naturally helps develop a particular identity. Then there is the presence at the U.S. Mission of the national figure who is its head. Human nature makes it inevitable that the members of the mission develop a sense of loyalty to the famous man at hand rather than to the more distant Secretary of State.

Furthermore, over the years the U.S. Mission has come to believe, not always but often, that its view of the world is clearer than Washington's. Even should this be true, and it often is, it does strengthen Washington's tendency to discount in advance any proposals by its UN people.

However, all this is often exaggerated in the press. The people at the U.S. Mission are loyal to American interests even though they sometimes have a different concept of what America's interests are and think they are best served by policies moderately or greatly different from those determined in Washington. But at all levels, the Mission people are constantly on the phone with their counterparts in Washington. They also read all, or just about all, the cables that Washington receives from overseas posts. Thus the difference, although real, is not harmful—is, indeed, beneficial because it sometimes provides Washington with a binocular rather than monocular view. Moreover, if Washington chooses to close its international eye in favor of its nationalist eye, there is little its UN people can do about it.

There is still another problem, one seldom considered but, in

the view of George Ball, important.[5] Ball, who believes it is nonsense to have the UN Ambassador a member of the Cabinet, says
it gives the country a false impression of his influence on policy.
Further, he believes it is unfair to the Ambassador himself. A
normal diplomat is considered by his colleagues merely to be
carrying out policy which he had no real hand in formulating and
thus is not subject to personal criticism. However, if during a difficult time the Ambassador is assumed, as it must be assumed of
a Cabinet member, to have had a hand in deciding policy, it puts
him in an unnecessarily difficult position. This, too, may be true
in theory, but it did not seem so in practice during the Stevenson
years. In fact, whenever the United States, as it increasingly did,
took a posture unwelcome to most UN members, it was assumed,
with some justice, that Stevenson had done all he could to prevent
the adoption of such a position. Consequently, Stevenson himself
was seldom the object of personal attacks by friendly or nonaligned nations, even if they leveled the deepest possible criticism
at U.S. policy. However, hostile nations used such policy decisions
as the occasion for the most bitter personal acrimony toward
Stevenson, acrimony that affected him profoundly, not only because it was a violent departure from the diplomatic usage by
which he set such store but because it was American policy that
triggered such attacks on him. It was one thing to be the lightning
rod for policies with which one agreed—after all, that was part
of the job—but quite another when he believed the policies un-
wise or even dangerous.

The above considerations are all important, but most crucial
of all is the degree to which the UN Ambassador can influence
American policy. Both Kennedy and Johnson gave Stevenson
solemn assurances that he would play a major role in the formula-
tion of foreign policy. Both Presidents presumably made the
promise in good faith, but it did not work out that way, nor could
it have. No matter how able the UN Ambassador, no matter how
skilled in foreign affairs, no matter how great his personal stature,
he cannot do two things at once. American foreign policy is made
in Washington, and it is not made in formal meetings of the
Cabinet or the National Security Council attended by the UN
Ambassador. It is made in hastily summoned little conferences in
the State Department, the Pentagon or, most of all, the White

House or in telephone conversations among those accustomed to working together. All the crucial decisions are made this way, and to be in on them, it is necessary to be within a few minutes' limousine ride of the White House. Occasionally a problem develops in such a way that there is time to summon the UN man, as Stevenson was called for the Cuban missile crisis talks, but almost always the vital decisions are made by the Rusks, the McNamaras, the Bundys, the Rostows and, of course, the Kennedys and Johnsons. These are men in constant touch who have their hands closest to the throttles of power. This may seem a strange and haphazard way for the most powerful nation in the world to arrive at a foreign policy, but in an era of instant communication, and thus instant crisis, foreign policy seldom is the result of a careful, thoughtful process. It seems, at the time at least, to be a series of unforeseen accidents requiring immediate response. Perhaps in later years, historians can impose some order, discern some trends to which all these accidents conform. But while they are actually occurring, they seem an unending series of crises, each trying to shoulder aside the one before.

Friends of Adlai Stevenson were always telling him that he should spend more time in Washington so he could participate more fully in decision making. Stevenson tried and was one of the best customers of the Eastern Airlines New York-Washington shuttle. And he was forever on the phone to Washington. But if the UN Ambassador is to do his job, he must be in New York to see the endless stream of delegates who insist on talking to the top man and to make crisis appearances in the Security Council and General Assembly. When Arthur Goldberg took the job, he was determined that he would not be left out the way Stevenson was, and he visited Washington still more often. But even the much more aggressive Goldberg discovered, to his deep disappointment, that the UN man would have to be in Washington full-time in order to be really effective. And even if he were, the White House and State Department people would try to keep him out of things unless there were a specific UN connection. In any case, Goldberg discovered, as had Stevenson before him, that the UN job demands constant attention and that any more than occasional trips to Washington can mean a sacrifice in New York.

In short, no matter what the President says and no matter how determined the UN Ambassador, he simply is unable to play a decisive role in foreign policy. Like it or not, he must face the fact that his job is not determining foreign policy but executing it.

Is there any justification, then, in view of all these considerations, for making the UN Ambassador a member of the Cabinet? My answer, despite these many and often valid objections, is a flat yes. As one of Stevenson's closest colleagues put it, "If the United States is really to make as much of the UN as we claim, it is better to use the irregular system." He is right, of course, for even if the UN Ambassador were given the high, but non-Cabinet, rank of Under Secretary, he would be submerged in the bureaucracy. This may not make much administrative sense, but it is vital to demonstrate to the world at large and, no less important, to the people of the United States by the appointment to Cabinet rank of a man of stature that this country is committed to the principles and purposes of the United Nations, of which it is by far the most powerful member. However, the appointment of such a figure is alone not enough. As Stevenson's final months proved, such a symbolic appointment is hollow if the symbol becomes a shield behind which the United States carries on a policy in violation of the UN Charter of which it was so largely the author.

Having established the context of Stevenson's job, we can now take a closer look at him at work. Since so much has been devoted to the administrative relationship with his superiors, perhaps a good place to start would be his administration of the U.S. Mission. Stevenson had no passion for administration, but he did have a genius for recruitment, as he proved by staffing Kennedy's New Frontier with his own supporters. Although the level was not quite so high, he was just as careful in putting together his own organization at the UN. Harlan Cleveland, former publisher of *The Reporter* magazine and dean of the Maxwell School at Syracuse University, was brought to Washington to be Assistant Secretary of State for International Organization Affairs, in effect Stevenson's high-level representative in the State Department bureaucracy, although Cleveland often demonstrated that he had a mind of his own and a taste for publicity. At the Mission itself, Stevenson's two top aides were Francis T. P. Plimpton, a Harvard Law School roommate and leading New York lawyer, and Charles W. Yost, a career Foreign Service officer. Although he tended to be a bit lawyerish, Plimpton was hard-working, dedicated and, in the restrained way of the Yankee aristocrat he was, stylish. Yost was an absolutely superb professional, with all of the virtues and few of the failings implied therein. Although he was a career ambassador, his independence of thought had survived unscathed and, unlike many Foreign Service officers, he was completely devoted to the UN. Indeed, he, like Stevenson, had been a member of the American delegation to the San Francisco conference which founded the organization.

Serving as Stevenson's confidential aide was an old friend, Clayton Fritchey, a lively and plain-spoken former newspaper editor who had been director of public information under George C. Marshall at the Defense Department, a special assistant to President Truman, a ranking member of Stevenson's campaign staffs and, as deputy chairman of the Democratic National Committee, editor of the short-lived but bright and provocative *Democratic Digest.* He handled many of Stevenson's press and confidential political matters.

Other top posts were filled by Jonathan Bingham, by Marietta Tree, who has appeared earlier in these pages, and by Richard Pedersen, a Foreign Service officer who had spent almost his entire career at the U.S. Mission and had an extraordinary knowledge of the workings of the UN. The day-to-day press relations were handled by Francis W. Carpenter, who kept the confidence of the UN press corps, because his instinct, unlike that of the ordinary government press officer, was to tell and not withhold. He had an extraordinary skill at telling—from the State Department point of view—almost too much so, but he never stumbled across the line and acted always with courtesy, wit and patience. He served Stevenson well, as he had Henry Cabot Lodge before him.

Incidentally, their treatment of Carpenter perhaps illustrates something about Stevenson and his successor, Arthur Goldberg. As he did with all his trusted aides, Stevenson gave Carpenter great latitude in doing his job. However, Goldberg after some months became dissatisfied with the press he was getting and decided that Carpenter was responsible. He tried to force Carpenter's retirement, but Dean Rusk, who knew and respected Carpenter, would have none of that and found Carpenter a good job with State in Washington. This whole incident perplexed the

UN press corps, a fairly sophisticated and widely-traveled group that generally regarded Carpenter as the best press officer at the UN and perhaps the best anywhere. The press corps agreed that if Goldberg were having trouble getting the kind of press treatment he so obviously wanted, it was his fault and not Carpenter's. Carpenter, for instance, could not save Goldberg from his own gaucheries, such as calling a press conference very late in the afternoon at an hour when correspondents were normally going home or finishing up their day's work to announce the engagement of his son.

Stevenson looked for intelligent, energetic, public-spirited people, and when he found them, he gave them their head. Without exception his top subordinates were grateful for this freedom, and if any of them every let him down, it was seldom indeed. This is not to imply that Stevenson didn't know what they were up to. He held two or three senior staff meetings each week just to make sure that the mission was well coordinated, albeit in his nonbureaucratic way. After all, it must be remembered that although his mind did not run along administrative lines, he had been the governor of one of the most important and populous states in the Union, an administrative job of the first magnitude.

His relationship with the entire U.S. Mission was good, from his senior aides down through the lower level clerks and building personnel. It would be silly to say that he had a personal relationship with those at the lower levels, but he always had a cheerful word when he encountered them in the halls or elevators. The entire Mission took pride in serving under such a man, and morale was good from top to bottom.

Stevenson took a real interest in those with whom he worked and would always take time to hear their personal concerns, often going to considerable trouble to help them. For instance, in 1962 Jonathan Bingham, then one of Stevenson's top aides, considered running in the Democratic primary against Bronx boss Congressman Charles Buckley. Since Buckley had been one of Kennedy's first and most important backers for the 1960 nomination, Bingham did not want to embarrass the President by asking for his support, even though Bingham, an articulate, youngish liberal, was much closer in style to Kennedy than the old-time political boss. But he felt Kennedy should be notified that Bingham was contemplating a challenge to the iron-handed rule of the narrow-minded old despot. Kennedy sent back a very strong recommendation—meant, of course, to be an order—that Bingham stay out of the primary. At first Bingham did not accept the recommendation, believing Kennedy did not realize that Buckley was going to be challenged whether or not Bingham ran. Bingham believes that Kenneth O'Donnell, a special assistant to Kennedy who handled many of his political matters, twisted Bingham's position, causing Kennedy to get very angry. In the face of such determined opposition from the President, Bingham did not run. Instead, David Levy opposed Buckley and lost. Bingham told Stevenson of his disfavor at the White House, and Stevenson did his best to smooth it over, keeping Bingham on the job and raising him from minister to ambassador. Bingham stayed at the UN until 1964, when he successfully ran against Buckley in the salty old politician's "last hurrah" and went on to win a seat in the House of Representatives that he has filled with distinction.

Stevenson was patient on professional matters as well and would hear others out, although he sometimes seemed to have difficulty in concentrating on the matter at hand if it did not interest him. Then he might act preoccupied and scribble notes to himself about something else. His mind was always active, and he lacked Kennedy's fortunate quality of shutting all else out of his mind other than the immediate concern. Often, too, when under pressure he would appear slightly harassed and then act aloof and distant.

He was a master of the little note, sometimes sending ten or twelve of them a day to various staff members, perhaps asking Marietta Tree to find out if his loyal secretary, Roxane Eberline, were really happy, or to someone else to take a look at a proposed luncheon list, or to thank a staff member for a speech he had written or to congratulate someone for something he had done. These were frequently amusing, informal notes, often treasured by their recipients.

His relations with the other delegates were good, even though they did occasionally grumble that he didn't attend their parties. However, his warmth and attentiveness, his world fame and the fact that he represented the United States made for good relations with his foreign colleagues. Not only did they appreciate his personal qualities, but despite their sophistication, they were no more immune to fame and power than lesser mortals. Stevenson was the star at the UN, and everybody likes the star.

Stevenson's relations with the press were excellent. This was important, not only because he, like any political leader, wanted a favorable press, but because his effectiveness as spokesman for the United States depended to a significant degree on his relations with the UN press corps, which had correspondents from all over the world. He was greatly aided in this on a day-to-day basis by Francis Carpenter and on a quieter editor-columnist level by Clayton Fritchey. Indeed, several mornings a week Fritchey would arrange private breakfast meetings at the Waldorf with editors, columnists, magazine writers and important correspondents. These were unusually frank sessions. Stevenson thought it demeaning to a reputable professional to ask him to keep things off the record. He spoke candidly, trusting to the discretion of the newsman not to print anything that would violate his confidence. And although he took more chances this way than any other politician, his trust was almost always justified. Some around Stevenson, particularly those in the Administration angered by the disclosures, have said that if he had lived, Eric Sevareid and David Schoenbrun would never have made their storm-arousing broadcasts that Stevenson was on the verge of resigning. That's very probably true, but both are newsmen of reputation, and each came to the independent conclusion that it was in the public interest that Stevenson's distress over American foreign policy be made known. They were right.

Stevenson's frankness with journalists carried over into his private conversations. At dinner and cocktail parties he was forever making, and not always amusingly, unflattering comments about this or that aspect of Administration policy, trusting to the discretion of his listeners not to pass the story on. But here his trust was often misplaced and, particularly in Washington, which seems to live on inside government gossip, the stories would sometimes reach the White House or State Department, with predictable results. To use the words of one of Stevenson's colleagues, this occasionally caused Kennedy "to blow his stack." This "teatime chitchat," as he called it, was Rusk's only criticism of Stevenson. Some have suggested that occasionally there was a Machiavellian intent to these leaks, but more likely it was just his disdain for the somebody-is-watching-us aspect of twentieth-century life, a disdain demonstrated also by his habit, horrifying to the watchdogs that abound in our society, of carrying classified documents with him instead of leaving them safe—and unread—in locked files.

But to get back to the press. Although Stevenson was very good about seeing members of the press in individual, private sessions, the UN press corps as a whole sometimes grumbled that he wasn't as accessible as other ambassadors. What they meant by this was that he didn't wander around the corridors at the UN or frequently drop into the Delegates' Lounge for a drink. For this the press had only itself to blame. Whenever Stevenson did tarry at the UN, he was immediately besieged by correspondents who bombarded him with questions. Invariably he would find himself in the midst of the shoving contest that the gentlemen of the press seem to find an appropriate way to conduct their important business. Even when he explained that he really didn't have anything to say, they would harass him until he finally decided to stay away. Thus, for most of the time at the UN, he would leave the building immediately after doing whatever had brought him there, and the press deprived itself of useful informal contact with the most important man there.

This didn't mean, however, that he would try to avoid the press whenever he was involved in an important news story. For instance, during the weeks after the Cuban missile crisis when he was meeting with Secretary General Thant virtually every day, he always stopped in the lobby of the Secretariat Building to answer questions or, if not to answer them, to respond with the stock diplomatic phrases: "We had a fruitful discussion." "It was a productive meeting." He appreciated the meaninglessness of such phrases and always uttered them with a big grin and departed with a cheery wave of the hand, as if to say, "Boys, I know you have to ask questions you know damn well I can't answer, and I know my answers are silly." As the tension over the missile crisis began to diminish with the passage of time, these routine encounters became quite jolly affairs. I was a regular participant in these scrimmages—usually on the outer edges because I was not so skilled or so determined a fullback as some of my colleagues—and I remember one notable evening, it must have been in November 1962, when Stevenson's path crossed that of Anastas Mikoyan, Soviet

First Deputy Premier, who had been sent to New York by Premier Khrushchev. With big smiles on their faces, they engaged in good-natured raillery, and I remember Mikoyan saying something, in effect, that all this would never have happened if Stevenson had been President. He was right.

Yet if Stevenson was perfectly willing to meet with the press when there was an important story developing, he was no longer willing to be badgered in the corridors. He simply did not have the time. The heads of smaller delegations spent a good deal of time in informal press consultation, but the heads of the big delegations, and Stevenson's was by far the biggest, simply had too much work, too many appointments, to spend much time at the UN other than that taken up by important meetings. However, this is not to say that the time spent there by other delegates was a waste. A good deal of fruitful give-and-take was done in the corridors and lounges, and useful personal relationships were developed. Further, the small delegations did not have large enough staffs (sometimes there was only the Ambassador and often only another one or two diplomats) to send all over midtown Manhattan for discussions at other missions. The Ambassadors had to do most of it themselves right at the UN. There were, of course, other reasons as well. Many of the delegates from these smaller African and Asian countries did not have enough to do—government papers and reports to read, cables to read and reply to, staff to administer; their bureaucracies had not yet swollen enough to become all-consuming—to keep them at their small offices. Too, and this was probably most important, they did not feel confident enough in the vastness of New York City to take full advantage of it. There was some justification for this. Many colored delegates —and, of course, most of the nations are nonwhite—suffered housing and other forms of discrimination that deeply distressed Stevenson, and consequently they huddled together at the UN for mutual comfort and entertainment. It became their club, the one place where they felt at home and were always welcome.

Although Stevenson's official job was that of U.S. Representative to the United Nations, he had an unofficial job almost as important: UN representative to the United States. This job he filled superbly. There is no doubt that the mere fact that he was appointed to the UN, furthered by his performance there, greatly increased the UN's standing in the eyes of the American people. He was most conscious of this role and devoted a great deal of time and thought to it, journeying all over the country to speak about the UN and to encourage American support for it. However, he was aware of one very real danger: American advocates of the UN tended to oversell it, to make it seem the answer to all international problems. Such a belief, and it was widely accepted, would inevitably lead to disillusionment when the UN was unable to make good on what its supporters promised. While on the one hand he praised the UN's very real accomplishments, particularly in the often overlooked economic and social areas, he cautioned against expecting too much. He pointed out that problems arrived at the UN only when they couldn't be solved elsewhere. And often the reason they couldn't be solved elsewhere was that they were simply insoluble anywhere, given the intractable attitudes of the nations involved. But he often said that if the UN was unable to solve these problems, it was at least able to keep them from exploding and spreading until the passage of time itself could have its healing effect. However, if he was realistic in not expecting the UN to perform miracles, he also had great faith in it, often terming it "the last hope of mankind." And he devoted many speeches to a call for strengthening the UN's peace-keeping machinery. Here, like many UN supporters, he was less than realistic, for as Secretary General Thant and others have pointed out, it is not the UN's machinery that is behind its failures, but the refusal of its members to use that machinery. Perhaps in this Stevenson was merely being American, for we are a pragmatic and optimistic people who believe that if a machine doesn't work now, it will if we tinker with it long and determinedly enough. Stevenson, however, so much wanted to believe in man that he preferred to think that it was mechanics at fault and not man himself. Yet there is no doubt that after Stevenson's four and a half years at the UN, it stood much higher in the estimation of the American people than it had before.

And one can suspect that Stevenson also regarded himself as the UN's ambassador to the U.S. government. Doubtless the UN was considered more often—although far from often enough— simply because Stevenson was there. This may have been largely because the UN was hard to miss with Stevenson so often on the front page of the New York *Times,* that document so indispensable to the Washington Establishment. Perhaps, too, the Administration wanted to accommodate him insofar as it did not disturb their plans, for both Kennedy and Johnson were well aware that Stevenson still had a considerable political following and could be a major source of trouble if he walked out. And, of course, there is the real possibility that the Administration, or some of its members, wanted to be decent to a man who had twice led the party and suffered grievous personal disappointments.

We have discussed Stevenson's accomplishments on the job, but there were real shortcomings as well. Even some of those closest to him concede that he did not devote as much time to the job as he might have. This is not to say he did not spend long and crowded hours at it. He did. But such a job demands a single-mindedness that precludes virtually all other activity. Stevenson as a public figure and as a man was not capable of that. As well as being ambassador, he was also a political leader second in stature only to the President. This demanded time. He was also the leading public speaker in the country. This demanded time. And he was active in the philanthropic work of the Eleanor Roosevelt and Field Foundations. This, too, demanded time. These demands his colleagues did not question, for they were implicit in a man of his stature. But what did concern them was the time he devoted to what seemed to some an essentially trivial social life. They did not for a moment question his need for relaxation and release. These were essential to a man under such constant and terrible pressures. But they felt he spent too much time in meaningless social rounds. He simply did not do all his homework because he was not at home. Furthermore, he kept late hours that sapped his strength. Such criticism was fairly widespread: from his own staff, from other delegations, from the Secretariat and from Washington. Time after time, I was told he did not have nearly the grasp of detail possessed by Arthur Goldberg. This particularly irritated some senior Administration officials in Washington whose waking hours were spent reading cables and memoranda.

Stevenson was also scored for lacking great skill as a negotiator. Often he was termed "unrealistic" or "too idealistic." Lord Caradon (the former Sir Hugh Foot), an old and dear friend and the only one at the UN who approached Stevenson as a speaker, said he "was too fastidious for the ugly world we live in. He didn't enjoy the fierceness and dirtiness of international negotiations." [6]

These criticisms were valid and serious, yet too much should not be made of them. One of the reasons Stevenson did not have a complete grasp of detail was that details bored him. This was never understood by the "realists" in Washington who thought that an overwhelming command of facts necessarily constituted wisdom. They were, to our country's great and tragic loss, classic examples of those who could not see the forest for the trees. They thought that if they devoured enough cables, enough briefings, enough memoranda, they were bound to come up with the right answers. Well, they devoured them and came up with the Bay of Pigs and Vietnam and the Dominican Republic. They simply could not understand that all the facts in the world could never substitute for intuition and understanding and a sound sense of perspective on what was important. All this is not to say that Stevenson was not well-informed; he was, even if he did not submerge himself in detail, and he had a skilled and reliable staff to take care of details for him, even though he should have done much more homework than he did. The actual amount of detail was staggering. Each year the agenda of the General Assembly had about one hundred items, on each of which the United States had to take a position. And on any given day during the assembly session, there could be ten or twelve meetings of its main committees. Also the Security Council met, usually in a crisis situation, about one hundred times a year. Each of these meetings required careful preparation and often an important statement by Stevenson. There were also meetings of the Economic and Social Council, the Trusteeship Council and hundreds of meetings on trade and development, industrial development, human rights, refugees, international law, colonialism and even more specialized topics, such as commodity agreements and the transit and transportation problems of landlocked countries carried out in scores of committees, commissions and working groups. Stevenson, of course, attended only a tiny fraction of these meetings, but he had the ultimate responsibility for them all.

However, as Chief S. O. Adebo, Nigeria's capable and well-respected delegate, observed, "Stevenson's proper role was not to be engrossed with detail but to be an effective spokesman. International politics are different from negotiations around a table." [7] Chief Adebo was right. Despite the valid criticism, Stevenson was the best UN Ambassador the United States has ever had or is ever likely to have just because he was Adlai Stevenson. As Secretary General U Thant said to me, "He was the symbol of everything good in the American community." [8] As an American uniquely respected abroad and at home, he was America's spokesman as no other man could be. And added to his symbolic value were his unequaled gifts at articulating the aspirations not only of his own people but of all the world's.

Stevenson as symbol and spokesman could be equaled by no other American. This was his unique gift and his unique tragedy, for in the final months he saw this gift being used not to promote steps, however faltering, toward peace but in defense of a policy that anywhere but in Washington could be seen as interventionist and militaristic. To put it in blunt but accurate terms, his honor was being used to shield America's dishonor, and he felt powerless to do anything about it. He was trapped, just as he had recognized from the beginning he might one day be trapped. However, it is hard to believe that he ever conceived it might be as bad as it became when he said in 1960 to Harry Ashmore, former Pulitzer Prize editor and later chairman of the executive board of the Fund for the Republic: "The point is that Jack Kennedy is going to make his own foreign policy, as he should, and there simply isn't enough in his record to indicate how much of it I agree with. And yet if I accept this appointment, I am committed to support him this side of treason or madness. There is no way for a man as prominent as I am to quietly step down. If I were to resign, no matter the excuse, it would signal a major break over United States policy." [9] It was this dilemma that so profoundly disturbed him at the end; how could he quit without causing a political storm?

Thus, we must reexamine the question discussed at the beginning of this book; should Stevenson have taken the job? It was probably inevitable that he accept. He was a man who believed deeply in public service, and since he had persuaded so many of his friends and supporters to give up their private lives, he could hardly refuse to do the same. Also he had a surpassing interest in foreign affairs and hoped, although he recognized the limitations of the job, to influence the Administration in its quest for peace. And, of course, he believed deeply in the United Nations. Further, and this is sometimes overlooked, he was, despite his reputation as an egghead, not a man who preferred quiet reflection. He was a man of action who had grown restive during eight years of being an outsider, albeit an immensely influential one. He did, of course, devote more time to thought (and more intelligence) than most politicians, and this, combined with his unique eloquence, his idealism and his cultivation, made him a rare bird indeed among politicians. They can hardly be blamed for thinking him an intellectual, a term in political circles not always implying praise. And true intellectuals were so surprised, so delighted to find a politician who appreciated them both as individuals and for what they had to offer, that they were eager to welcome him. Yet, as was demonstrated by his service in the Navy Department, in the early days of the UN and as Governor of Illinois, he was, despite his intellectual and philosophic side, primarily an activist. The job wasn't what he wanted, he recognized its limitations and its dangers, but it was a good job and, more to the point, the only one available that interested him, so he took it.

However inevitable it might have been that Stevenson take the job, one can still argue that this was not, as it turned out, in his best interest or in the nation's. Although I believe the UN ambassadorship is one that should always be filled by a big man, Stevenson was too big. An interesting observation about this was made by Ambassador Achkar Marof, the delegate from Guinea. He said that Stevenson's "first obligation was to refuse the appointment. If not, he should later have said, 'This is not the kind of job for me.' " [10] Achkar went on to say that "a less big man can adjust his will to that of the government. Stevenson was beyond that," and consequently the job became "fantastically frustrating." He suggested that Stevenson could, from time to time, have been appointed as a special envoy to make use of his talents, but only on assignments that were in keeping with his convictions.

Stevenson, of course, hoped to have a significant, even if limited, influence on the Administration. It did not matter so much when the Administration followed a course with which he generally agreed, but in the last months his influence, never decisive, shrank even further, and many of those around him believed that Stevenson felt his usefulness was over. But he had locked himself in. His greatest gifts—his independence of thought, his ability to articulate basic goals, his need to speak the truth—were all lost to him. This was a personal tragedy to be sure, but even more it was a terrible loss to the American people. He had sacrificed a real, perhaps crucial capacity to influence the Administration from outside for what turned out to be an utter incapacity to influence it from inside. Thus, however difficult it would have been for him politically or privately, he should have preserved his independence by not taking the job. But perhaps that choice was not really open to him. If so, then disaster was set in train as inevitably as in a Greek tragedy.

Before we attempt a final conclusion as to whether or not Stevenson was going to resign, we should find out how he liked his job. He was forever grumbling about it, telling all who would listen of its frustrations. Something that particularly bothered him was the knowledge that Washington was always looking over his shoulder, second-guessing him. Whenever he was speaking, he could be watched if the session were on television or listened to by means of a special hookup if it were not. Sometimes even in the course of a meeting he would get instructions from Washington. This used to infuriate him, for he thought he knew more about foreign relations in general and about the UN in particular than those who chipped in with suggestions as to how he should meet a tactical situation. This problem was inevitable with the UN so close to Washington. Whereas other delegations were some distance from their capitals and thus were not under constant scrutiny, there were dozens of people in Washington who were always listening to every word said in the United Nations and many more if the situation were serious. Not only were such interventions from Washington unsettling, but it meant that policy was being made extemporaneously, not necessarily the best way to reach sound decisions.

Stevenson's griping was an essential release. His close colleagues agree on this. As one of them said, "If he held it in, he would have exploded." But he would often conclude his grumbling by saying, "Well, I guess we're accomplishing something." It was this feeling that kept him at it. But all this was prior to the regular bombing of North Vietnam and before the Dominican Republic. Before these two events that were to disturb him so profoundly, Stevenson discussed his job with writer Martin Mayer.

"This job has been a terrible drill. In my own life I've been accustomed to making policy. I've sometimes been a little restless in this role of executing and articulating the policies of others. There is a disadvantage in being anywhere other than the seat of power. And every issue that comes to the UN has its antecedents before it gets here. The State Department has been involved in the negotiations, and now the situation has become insoluble, so it gets dumped onto us. . . .

"Besides, I can't help but believe that you wear out on a job like this. You become such an old and familiar face. You take on the coloration of your country, your country's face, and you become predictable. You lose some of the rosy glow you brought with you. Apart from my taste for more creative aspects, the time comes when you should bring in a fresh face and outlook." [11]

Although Stevenson enjoyed the sense of participation, the prestige that went with his job, these were clearly the words of a man who was considering resigning. And it should be remembered that he spoke them even before he was so shaken by events in Vietnam and the Dominican Republic. There is other ample evidence he was considering that course. We saw how he talked of his future with Marietta Tree just before he collapsed. And he was discussing it with many others as well. Francis Plimpton was constantly pressing Stevenson for a decision because he, too, wanted to leave after helping out Stevenson's successor for a while. Others close to him also suggested that the time had come to resign.

But if he were to resign, what would he do? Despite his reputation as a thinker, he was much too gregarious to go back to Libertyville to think and write. Illinois, although his affection for it was real, simply did not offer the companionship and stimulation he found in New York. Chances are, according to his friends, that he would have spent most of his time in New York or Washington. Some suggested that he could do a great service by writing and speaking, but others point out that he had done that after 1952 and 1956 and found it less than completely satisfying. These colleagues, and old friend George Ball is among them, believe that if Stevenson had lived, he would have stayed on the job simply because nothing else appealed to him.

One close aide suggested that Stevenson write a newspaper column. He felt sure that seventy-five to a hundred newspapers would have bought it overnight, making Stevenson the new Walter Lippmann, able to enunciate his own foreign policy and be cultivated by leaders all over the world. Although Stevenson did not say how he felt about this, he had often expressed an interest in journalism. However, he had done little writing for years, and it might have been too demanding at his age to write for a constant deadline.

Stevenson could, of course, have had his pick of any number of jobs. Law firms—and many of the top New York lawyers were personal friends—would have offered him staggering salaries. But he had enough money, although he was always worried about it, and was reluctant to spend his final years involved in cases that didn't really interest him. Then there were possible jobs as university president, but this, too, didn't appeal to him because he did not want to become a fund-raiser. A more likely possibility was a well-paying chair at a university where he would have had staff and facilities to help in his writing. In this he might have made his greatest contribution. Even if, for reasons of party loyalty, he had refrained from criticism of the Administration, he could have written about American politics and society and perhaps have produced, as Eric Sevareid suggested to me, "a couple of volumes about political philosophy that would have been compulsory reading for a hundred years." [12] Certainly whatever he wrote would have greatly enriched America's political literature.

Was he, then, going to resign? Many of those working closest with him thought he was, and William Benton, who was a constant companion during his last few days in London, wrote flatly that at Benton's home in Southport, Connecticut, the next weekend, "We were to talk about his future after his anticipated resignation as U.S. Ambassador to the United Nations at the end of 1965." [13] However, even some of those who were convinced that Stevenson was going to resign in the immediate future question whether he was as deeply distressed as Sevareid said in that last interview that "revealed a profound frustration, a certain resentment that stopped just short of bitterness." Many of Stevenson's friends say this was just his characteristic griping, that although he was indeed thinking of resigning and was disturbed by the course of American foreign policy, he was not on the brink of despair. But Sevareid says he was fully aware of Stevenson's habit of grumbling and had often been exposed to it in the past. "I wouldn't have written it if I thought it was just another bellyache. He just poured it out. I didn't print everything, some stuff about personalities. I'm absolutely certain he had decided in his guts to resign. Believe me. The body was telling him something. He was exhausted. Either you take my word for it or you don't. He said, 'I'm desperate. I've got to do it in the next week.' " [14] According to Sevareid, what bothered Stevenson most was the reaction to his staying on the job of the intellectuals, those represented by the seven who had asked him face-to-face to resign toward the end of June. Clearly Stevenson put great stock in the opinions of the academic-intellectual community, which had so long sustained him in his quest for political victory and after the defeats that followed. He was disturbed enough by Johnson's foreign policy and the unhappy role he had to play in defending it, but it was a bitter wound that the intellectuals, as he often complained in the last few weeks, did not understand how difficult it would be for him to quit during a crisis. And it hurt to have them accuse him of betraying his commitment to peace and justice.

What seemed to Sevareid to be the immediate problem was how Stevenson, having made the decision, could carry it out. Obviously it would not have been easy to make Johnson accept the resignation when it was clearly in Johnson's interest for Stevenson to stay at the UN. Not only was Stevenson an unequaled advocate but his departure, however amicable, would be taken to mean a major break with the Administration, causing the worst possible trouble for Johnson. And if Johnson were to ask Stevenson who he suggested to take his place, there would be no easy answer since Stevenson realized full well there was no other Stevenson in America.

But there were ways out. Stevenson hated scenes, but he could have legitimately pleaded physical exhaustion. And he could have minimized the possibility of his resignation's being interpreted as a break over policy by resigning with an effective date some time in the future, say, in December 1965 after the adjournment of the UN General Assembly. He could also have made, if he chose, a flat declaration of support of Johnson and/or a repudiation of Administration critics. As to his successor, well, there was no one who could completely take his place, but Johnson had no difficulty in finding an eminently suitable replacement following Stevenson's death.

After a careful examination of the evidence, my conclusion is that Stevenson would have resigned, probably by the end of 1965. Yet, despite the gravest reservations over Johnson's foreign policy, there is no indication that he would have given that as his reason. The chances are great that his would have been a gentlemanly resignation with professions of admiration and respect exchanged between the two men. He would, I believe, have gone on playing the game. This, of course, is speculation, for no matter what a man says he will do, one cannot be certain until he does it, for often there is that great difference between a man's intentions and his actions. Thus, no one can say for sure. If he had lived, Stevenson might have stayed on the job, continuing to find rationalizations for his decision. Or he might, as the pressure on him increased —for even his great friends John Kenneth Galbraith and Arthur Schlesinger were reluctant critics at first—have made a public break. But this is speculation no different from that which says Kennedy would not have escalated the conflict in Vietnam. We do not know what he might have done. We know only what he did— or did not do.

What, then, can finally be said about this man, Adlai Ewing Stevenson? If he is evaluated in the narrowest sense—how did he do his job at the UN?—well, then the answer is easy, and perhaps Lord Caradon's words put it best. "He was a racehorse doing the work of a carthorse and doing it well." [15] But Adlai Stevenson was more than just an ambassador, if the Ambassador to the United Nations can be so described. He did represent, for a generation at least, the ideal of what a political leader could be. It is against his own standard that he must be judged, and if this be cruel, there can be no other.

Here we must again speculate for a moment, for the question

about Stevenson must inevitably be, what kind of President would he have made? Again, no one can know for sure, but I think now as I first thought in 1952, when he stirred me, and many others, as we have never been stirred before and will doubtless never be again, that this man could have been a great President. Many have said that his indecisiveness would have been a fatal handicap. I prefer to think that what has been termed indecisiveness was rather an agonizing over the difficult choices, an agonizing that prevented him from acting before the fullest possible examination of available alternatives. This, I believe, rather than indecision was a demonstration of his profound humanity, of a concern for the consequences of his actions that should be the first requisite of a leader. There was no doubt of the decisiveness of Kennedy, and we got the Bay of Pigs and Vietnam, or of Johnson, and we got Vietnam and the Dominican Republic. But in any case, as he proved as governor, Stevenson could make decisions. He simply wanted to be as sure as man could be—which, as he recognized, was not very sure at all—that they were the right ones. It is not frivolous, the comparison that has often been made between him and his hero, Lincoln. Both brooded, both agonized and both possessed deep wellsprings of humor. But Lincoln had the chance to make great decisions, and Stevenson did not.

We will never know, of course, but I am convinced that if Stevenson had been elected President, the cold war, which he regarded as an obscenely wasteful anachronism, would have been much nearer an end on both its European and Asian fronts, enhancing the prospects of lasting world peace and releasing resources to be used to set our own crumbling house in order.

But he was not President, nor was he even Secretary of State. This, too, was our loss, for had Kennedy possessed the wisdom and the confidence to put Stevenson in charge of the State Department, there would have been no Bay of Pigs and thus no Cuban missile crisis; there would have been no plunging heedlessly into the quicksands of Southeast Asia, and there would have been no Dominican Republic disaster. This, too, can be dismissed as speculation, although I am sure others must share my conviction that this would have been so.

But we must judge him for what he was: a man who twice had sought the Presidency and twice lost, and the American Representative to the United Nations. What were his accomplishments? He did achieve one notable goal in his decade and a half as a public figure. Again Lord Caradon's words: "He was constantly trying to set standards and communicate ideas to raise the level of public life and, by Jove, he did so." And he further enriched public life by the caliber of men he attracted to it. It would be nice to say that these were permanent contributions to the American heritage, but that is doubtful. They might have been, were it not for that accident of fate in Dallas on November 22, 1963, for Kennedy might have made permanent, or at least lasting, what Stevenson started. But under Johnson the standards degenerated, and good men were reluctant to serve. So even that was denied Stevenson. All that remains of those marvelous candidate years are rich memories. But that is not inconsiderable, and if circumstances change before not too many years, perhaps these memories will rekindle his spirit and perhaps some of those who were young when Stevenson first captured their imaginations will return to public life and help end the dark ages. For just as Stevenson himself was resilient, so too might be some of those he inspired.

What, then, is left? Of actual service in high office there is only those four and a half years at the United Nations. If Stevenson had died, say, in mid-1964, the judgment would have been simple. He could have been described as a great American who in his final years devoted himself to peace as the spokesman not only of the American government and people but of the voiceless millions all over the world. But he did not die in mid-1964. He lived for another year and saw his reputation and his eloquence become the first line of defense for policies in Vietnam and the Dominican Republic that could only have grieved him deeply. This was the man who said, on being nominated in 1952, "Let's talk sense to the American people. Let's tell them the truth. . . ." But he was not talking sense; he was not telling the truth. This was the man of rectitude who had always believed in doing his duty no matter how painful. Yet this man could not bring himself to do it now. He who had instructed the American people for a decade and a half was unable to distinguish between his duty to a man who was President and to the nation and ideals that man was supposed to represent. He could no longer speak the truth; he could only play the game. He was pained, perhaps even tormented, but he could not bring himself to put his loyalty to the nation he had served so well above his loyalty to Lyndon Baines Johnson as a member of the team. Twice the American people in what passes for its wisdom had deprived itself of his great service. But in this final opportunity for great service—and there was no other American who might have been able to halt the Administration's rush toward disaster—it was he who deprived the nation of his service. Nor could he even tell Johnson that if he would not attack him, neither could he any longer serve him. Adlai Stevenson, whatever the reason, was not up to this final test. Maybe we were asking too much. Maybe he was too old, too tired, too much the gentleman. Maybe he had been defeated too often.

There were those who were bitter that he would not fight this last fight. There were those who mocked him then and after his death and called him a coward. But perhaps they should have tried to understand. Perhaps they should have recognized that this gallant old man (and it is still hard to think of that gay spirit as old) simply no longer had it in him. He could not bear to make a scene. He could not bear to be disloyal to his President, even though the man who was President had forfeited all right to loyalty. Perhaps John Kennedy was right when he "once remarked that one could not fairly judge what kind of man Stevenson might have become, for no experience could have been more destructive of self-confidence than to have been twice defeated for President; victory would have changed him in another direction." [16]

Whatever the reason, Stevenson would not, could not make the fight. And many of us who had admired, even in a way loved him, were not so much angered as saddened to see what had become of him. For it was sad indeed to see this once-valiant warrior die not in defiance but in torment, saying right up until his death, and ironically on tape over the BBC, even after his death, words in which he could not have believed.

So death came to Adlai Stevenson and he was widely mourned, by some for what he was and by others for what he had been. And President Johnson was to tell the American people on nationwide television: "His great hero, Abraham Lincoln, said at the beginning of his political career that 'I have no other ambition so great as that of being truly esteemed by my fellow men, by rendering myself worthy of their esteem.'

"And although his disappointments were many, in this, like Lincoln, he was vindicated."

But did Adlai Stevenson die in the esteem of his fellow men? He did indeed to those old friends who rightfully put that friendship above all else. And he did to those middle-class, middle-aged and older members of the Establishment who also believed in playing the game. To some others he died not in esteem—that was no longer possible—but in affection. But to others still, many of the intellectuals and the young and the idealistic, for whom he once had such enormous and unique appeal, he died not in esteem but in disgrace. And for this we were sad, for we recognized that there was truth in what Barbara Garson wrote:

> Oh, nation that has lost thy breed of men!
> When could we say but now of this great land
> That her far shores encompassed but one man?
> Ye Gods, there was an Egg of Head here once
> That would have dared the devil . . . and yet now . . .[17]

# Bibliography

Brown, Stuart Gerry, *Conscience in Politics: Adlai E. Stevenson in the 1950's.* Syracuse, Syracuse University Press, 1961.
————, *Adlai E. Stevenson.* Woodbury, New York, Barron's (softbound), 1965.
Busch, Noel F., *Adlai E. Stevenson of Illinois.* New York, Farrar, Straus and Young, 1952.
Davis, Kenneth S., *The Politics of Honor: A Biography of Adlai E. Stevenson.* New York, G. P. Putnam's Sons, 1967.
Doyle, Edward P., ed., *As We Knew Adlai.* New York, Harper & Row, 1966.
Evans, Rowland, and Novak, Robert, *Lyndon B. Johnson: The Exercise of Power.* New York, New American Library, 1966.
Garson, Barbara, *MacBird!* New York, Grove Press, 1967.
Geylin, Philip, *Lyndon B. Johnson and the World.* New York, Praeger, 1966.
Ives, Elizabeth Stevenson, and Dolson, Hildegarde, *My Brother Adlai.* New York, Morrow, 1956.
Martin, John Bartlow, *Adlai Stevenson.* New York, Harper, 1952.
Muller, Herbert J., *Adlai E. Stevenson: A Study in Values.* New York, Harper & Row, 1967.
Ross, Lillian, *Adlai Stevenson.* Philadelphia, Lippincott, 1966.
Schlesinger, Arthur M., Jr., *A Thousand Days: John F. Kennedy in the White House.* Boston, Houghton Mifflin, 1965.
Sorensen, Theodore C., *Kennedy.* New York, Harper & Row, 1965.
Steiner, Paul, *The Stevenson Wit and Wisdom.* New York, Pyramid (softbound), 1965.

Stevenson, Adlai E., *Major Campaign Speeches of 1952*. New York, Random House, 1953.

————, *Call to Greatness*. New York, Harper, 1954.

————, *What I Think*. New York, Harper, 1956.

————, *Friends and Enemies*. New York, Harper, 1959.

————, *Putting First Things First*. New York, Random House, 1960.

————, *Looking Outward: Years of Crisis at the United Nations*, edited with commentary by Robert L. and Selma Schiffer, with a Preface by President John F. Kennedy. New York, Harper & Row, 1963.

United Nations, *Everyman's United Nations*. New York, 1964.

————, *The United Nations and Disarmament*. New York, 1967.

Whitman, Alden, *Portrait—Adlai E. Stevenson: Politician, Diplomat, Friend*. New York, Harper & Row, 1965.

# *Notes*

The Beginning:

1 Barbara Garson, *MacBird!* (New York, Grove Press, 1966), p. 41.

2 Murray Kempton, New York *Post,* November 2, 1960.

3 Arthur Schlesinger, *A Thousand Days* (Boston, Houghton Mifflin, 1965), p. 157.

4 Schlesinger, p. 138.

5 Schlesinger, p. 139.

6 Interview with George Ball, September 13, 1967, in New York.

7 Kenneth S. Davis, *The Politics of Honor: A Biography of Adlai E. Stevenson* (New York, G. P. Putnam's Sons, 1967), p. 170.

8 UN Document S/4378, July 11, 1960.

9 UN Document S/4605, December 31, 1960.

10 Schlesinger, p. 271.

11 Davis, p. 455.

12 Interview with Francis T. P. Plimpton, June 12, 1967, in New York.

13 Davis, p. 458.

14 Schlesinger, p. 297.

15 Theodore C. Sorensen, *Kennedy* (New York, Harper & Row, 1965), p. 684.

16 Schlesinger, p. 808.

17 Schlesinger, p. 821.

18 Schlesinger, p. 836.

19 Interview with Secretary of State Dean Rusk, August 18, 1967, in Washington.

20 Sorensen, p. 695.

21 Schlesinger, p. 837.

The Congo:

1 UN Document S/4707, February 14, 1961.

2 Adlai E. Stevenson, *Looking Outward: Years of Crisis at the United Nations* (New York, Harper & Row, 1963), p. 12.

3 Interview with Daniel Watts, October 26, 1967, in New York.

4 UN Document S/4940, Add. 4, September 17, 1961.

5 UN Document ICJ/187, July 20, 1962.

[6] UN Document SG/1307, August 25, 1962.

[7] UN Document CO/262, December 10, 1962.

[8] UN Document CO/264, December 18, 1962.

[9] State Department Press Release 109, January 29, 1963.

[10] U.S. Mission to the UN, Press Release, November 13, 1964.

[11] UN Document S/6055, November 21, 1964.

[12] UN Documents S/6062,3, November 24, 1964.

[13] UN Document S/6066, November 25, 1964.

[14] Plimpton interview.

[15] Interview with Chief S. O. Adebo, Nigerian Ambassador to the UN, August 7, 1968, in New York.

Disarmament and Other Matters:

[1] Schlesinger, p. 468.

[2] Schlesinger, p. 478.

[3] Schlesinger, p. 479.

[4] Interview with David Guyer, July 6, 1967, in New York.

Vietnam:

[1] John F. Kennedy, *The Strategy of Peace* (New York, Harper & Row, 1960), p. 60.

[2] Schlesinger, p. 997.

[3] Department of State Bulletin, September 30, 1963, pp. 488, 499.

[4] New York *Times,* January 1, and 2, 1964.

[5] Further Documents Relating to the Discussion of Indo-China at the Geneva Conference, June 16–July 21, 1954. Miscellaneous No. 20 (1954), Command Paper 9239 (London, Her Majesty's Stationery Office, 1954).

[6] U.S. Mission Press Release No. 4424, August 5, 1964.

[7] New York *Times,* August 5, 1964.

[8] U.S. Mission Press Release Nos. 4424–26, 4428–29, August 5 and 7, 1964.

[9] Eric Sevareid, "Why Our Foreign Policy Is Failing," *Look* (May 3, 1966), pp. 25–26.

[10] Stuart Gerry Brown, *Conscience in Politics: Adlai E. Stevenson in the 1950's* (Syracuse, Syracuse University Press, 1961), p. 138.

[11] New York *Times,* November 25, 1967.

[12] UN Office of Public Information Note 2725.

[13] Mario Rossi, "U Thant and Vietnam: The Untold Story," *New York Review of Books* (November 17, 1966). This account, confirmed with me by Ramses Nassif, U Thant's official spokesman, was easily the best available at the time of this writing.

[14] UN OPI Note No. 3075, February 24, 1965.

[15] New York *Times,* April 8, 1965.

[16] UN OPI Note No. 3092, April 8, 1965.

[17] Adlai E. Stevenson, *Putting First Things First* (New York, Random House, 1960), p. 19.

[18] The author was present.

[19] Davis, p. 501.

[20] *Ibid.*

[21] Interview with Arthur Schlesinger, Jr., October 26, 1967, in New York.

[22] Ball interview.

[23] New York *Times,* July 14, 1965.

Stevenson's Last Months:

[1] U.S. Mission Press Release No. 4492, January 26, 1965.

[2] U.S. Mission Press Release No. 4495, January 28, 1965.

[3] UN Document S/6174, February 7, 1965.

[4] U.S. Mission Press Release No. 4543, May 5, 1965.

[5] Schlesinger interview.

[6] Interview with David McReynolds, August 11, 1967, in New York.

[7] Letter from Harvey Swados, dated November 2, 1967, Cagnes, France.

[8] Interview with Paul Goodman, September 20, 1967, in New York.

[9] Letter from Dwight Macdonald, August 14, 1967, in which he enclosed a transcript of notes taken by him at the meeting with Stevenson.

[10] Letter from Kay Boyle, September 25, 1967, San Francisco.

[11] Declaration provided by Dwight Macdonald.

[12] Letter from David McReynolds, August 11, 1967, that was still in his office when I arrived for our interview.

[13] Above letter from Miss Boyle.

[14] Above letter.

[15] Above letter from McReynolds.

[16] McReynolds interview.

[17] Above letter from Swados.

[18] *Village Voice,* July 22, 1965.

[19] Taken from a letter from Paul Goodman to Adlai Stevenson, June 23, 1965.

[20] Letter from Paul Goodman to the New York *Times,* December 15, 1965.

[21] U.S. Mission Press Release No. 4588, June 16, 1965.

[22] Letter from Miss Boyle to Adlai Stevenson, June 28, 1965.

[23] Stevenson interview with Eric Sevareid, *Look* (November 30, 1965).

[24] From the Preamble of the Charter of the United Nations.

[25] From a letter sent widely by *Artists & Writers Dissent,* 224 Fourth Street, New York.

[26] "BBC Television Panorama." Recorded from transmission 2025, July 12, 1965.

[27] The account of Stevenson's final minutes was given by Mrs. Marietta Tree on September 12, 1967, in Albany, New York.

[28] Interview with Achkar Marof, Ambassador from Guinea to the UN, May 23, 1967, at the UN.

[29] New York *Times,* July 15, 1965.

[30] New York *Times,* July 15, 1965.

[31] Washington *Star,* July 16, 1965.

[32] New York *Times,* July 17, 1965.

[33] These and other quotations from the UN Memorial Service are taken from UN Documents SG/SM 338 and Notes Nos. 3166–68, July 19, 1965.

Attorney for the Defense:

[1] Ball interview.

[2] Rusk interview.

[3] Rusk interview.

[4] Rusk interview.

[5] Ball interview.

[6] Interview with Lord Caradon, October 26, 1967.

[7] Adebo interview.

[8] Interview with Secretary General U Thant, May 13, 1967, at the UN.

[9] Harry Ashmore, contributor to *As We Knew Adlai* (New York, Harper & Row, 1966), p. 231.

[10] Achkar interview.

[11] Martin Mayer, New York *Times* Magazine, February 7, 1965.

[12] Interview with Eric Severeid, October 12, 1967, in Washington, D.C.

[13] William Benton in *As We Knew Adlai,* p. 209.

[14] Sevareid interview.

[15] Caradon interview.

[16] Schlesinger, p. 463.

[17] Garson, p. 44.

*Index*

# Index

## DATE DUE

| DEC 3 '69 | | | |
|-----------|---|---|---|
| FEB 25 70 | | | |
| | | | |
| | | | |
| | | | |
| | | | |
| | | | |
| | | | |
| | | | |
| | | | |
| | | | |
| | | | |
| | | | |
| | | | |
| | | | |
| | | | |
| | | | |
| | | | |
| GAYLORD | | | PRINTED IN U.S.A. |